Studies in Christianity
and Judaism / Etudes sur le
christianisme et le judaïsme : 2

Studies in Christianity and Judaism /
Etudes sur le christianisme et le judaïsme

Studies in Christianity and Judaism / Etudes sur le christianisme
et le judaïsme presents publications that study Judaism and Christianity together in an effort to reach an understanding of how the
two religions have related and relate to each other as well as
studies that offer original insight into some central aspect of the
two religions or of one of them. Three groups of studies are
envisaged: studies of doctrine, historical studies, and textual
studies. Whereas there exist similar publications produced in
Canada in a theological context, this Series reflects the specific
nature and orientation of the departments of religious studies in
Canadian centres of learning. In these departments Christianity
and Judaism are studied from the perspective of the history of
religions. Such a perspective is not necessarily aligned with one
of the two traditions. It tries to transcend traditional antagonisms
as well as confessional limitations. After several decades of work
from such a perspective, Canadian scholars are now in a position
to offer studies that put forward less conventional views of the
two religions.

STUDIES IN CHRISTIANITY
AND JUDAISM

Number 2

ANTI-JUDAISM IN EARLY CHRISTIANITY

Volume 2
SEPARATION AND POLEMIC

edited by
Stephen G. Wilson

Published for the Canadian Corporation for Studies in
Religion/Corporation Canadienne des Sciences Religieuses
by Wilfrid Laurier University Press

1986

Canadian Cataloguing in Publication Data

Main entry under title:
Anti-Judaism in early Christianity
(Studies in Christianity and Judaism = Etudes sur
le christianisme et le judaïsme, ISSN 0711-5903 ; 2-3)
Includes bibliographical references and indexes.
Partial contents: v. 1. Paul and the gospels /
edited by Peter Richardson with David Granskou —
v. 2. Separation and polemic / edited by Stephen G.
Wilson.
ISBN 0-88920-167-6 (v. 1). — ISBN 0-88920-196-X (v. 2).

1. Christianity and other religions — Judaism.
2. Judaism — Relations — Christianity.   3. Christianity — Early church, ca. 30-600.   4. Paul,
the Apostle, Saint — Attitude towards Judaism.
I. Richardson, Peter, 1935-   . II. Granskou,
David M.   III. Wilson, Stephen G.   IV. Series:
Studies in Christianity and Judaism ; 2-3.

BM535.A57 1986   261.2′6   C86-093124-2

Order from:

Wilfrid Laurier University Press
Wilfrid Laurier University
Waterloo, Ontario, Canada   N2L 3C5

Printed in Canada

Contents

Notes on Contributors

LLOYD GASTON is Professor of New Testament in the Vancouver School of Theology, Vancouver, British Columbia. His main interest currently is Paul's view of Judaism. He is the author of *No Stone Upon Another* (Leiden: Brill, 1970), *Horae Synopticae Electronicae* (Missoula: Scholars Press, 1973), and numerous articles.

WILLIAM KLASSEN is currently Academic Dean at the Interfaith Peace Academy in Jerusalem. His main interest is the relation between the Stoics and Cynics and the New Testament, an interest that he has explored in a number of articles. His most recent book is *Love of Enemies: The Way of Peace* (Philadelphia: Fortress Press, 1984).

JACK LIGHTSTONE is Professor of Religion at Concordia University, Montreal, Quebec. His current interests are in the interaction of Judaism and Christianity with each other and with the Graeco-Roman world. He is the author of *Yose the Galilean: Traditions in Mishna and Tosefta* (Leiden: Brill, 1979) and *The Commerce of the Sacred: Mediation of the Divine among Jews in the Graeco-Roman Diaspora* (Chico: Scholars Press, 1984).

HAROLD REMUS is Professor of Religious Studies at Wilfrid Laurier University, Waterloo, Ontario. He was for a number of years Director of Wilfrid Laurier University Press. He is the author of *Pagan-Christian Conflict over Miracle in the Second Century* (Cambridge, Mass.: Philadelphia Patristic Foundation, 1983).

PETER RICHARDSON is Principal of University College and Professor of Religious Studies in the University of Toronto, Toronto, Ontario. He is the author of *Israel in the Apostolic Church* (Cambridge: Cambridge

University Press, 1969), *Paul's Ethic of Freedom* (Philadelphia: Westminster Press, 1979), and the editor of the companion (vol. 1) to this volume.

ALAN F. SEGAL is Professor in the Department of Religion, Barnard College, New York. His book *Two Papers in Heaven* (Leiden: Brill, 1977) explores the relationship between Judaism, Gnosticism, and Christianity.

MARTIN B. SHUKSTER is a graduate student at the Centre for Religious Studies in the University of Toronto, Toronto, Ontario, where he is writing a dissertation on "The Church of God" in Paul.

STEPHEN G. WILSON is Professor of Religion at Carleton University, Ottawa, Ontario. He is the author of *The Gentiles and the Gentile Mission in Luke-Acts* (Cambridge: Cambridge University Press, 1973), *Luke and the Pastoral Epistles* (London: SPCK, 1979), and *Luke and the Law* (Cambridge: Cambridge University Press, 1983). His current research is on Jewish-Christian relations 70-170 C.E.

Introduction

The essays in this volume represent the final two years of a five-year seminar held at the annual meeting of the Canadian Society of Biblical Studies (Halifax, Nova Scotia in 1981; Ottawa, Ontario in 1982). They extend into the late first and second centuries the work begun in earlier years of the seminar, a selection of which appears in the companion volume edited by Peter Richardson (*Anti-Judaism in Early Christianity, Volume 1: Paul and the Gospels*).

Most of the papers in this volume were completed by 1982, though some were revised in 1983. Some significant work has appeared since, which, unfortunately, could not be referred to. It has, on the whole, however, supported and extended some of the suggestions made here: for example, R.J. Hoffman in *Marcion: On the Restitution of Christianity* (Chico: Scholars Press, 1984) has a not dissimilar assessment of Marcion's view of Judaism, even though he emphasizes different causal factors; and J. Gager's *The Origins of Anti-Semitism* (Oxford: Oxford University Press, 1984) expands L. Gaston's thesis about the significance of Gentile judaizers into a major causal factor of Christian anti-Judaism in the early centuries.

As with the first volume, not all of the papers presented to the seminar could be included. There are, moreover, topics which could have been considered but for the constraints of time and personnel. Many of these papers do, however, take a fresh look at issues central to Jewish-Christian relations in the obscure and somewhat neglected period between 70 and 200 C.E. Viewed as a whole, they point to at least three important conclusions. The first is that no simple hypothesis is adequate to explain the complex and varied evidence of this period. To argue, for example, as does R.R. Ruether in *Faith and Fratricide* (New York: Paulist, 1974), that christology is at the root of Christian anti-Judaism—its so called "left-hand"—would be to fly in the face of much of the evidence considered in these essays. It *is* an important element,

for example, in the Epistle of Barnabas and in Melito's *Peri Pascha*. Yet
to single it out would be to ignore, in the case of Barnabas, the importance of the threat from a rejuvenated Judaism anticipating the rebuilding of the Temple, and to belittle, in the case of Melito, a host of
other contributory factors, not least the presence of a prominent and
influential Jewish community in Sardis and the possibility of a Gentile
judaizing movement there and elsewhere in Asia Minor. There is a
further sense in which the Christian evidence of this period cannot
simply be lumped together. For while many Christian writers harp on
the same themes they do so with a considerable range of tone and
emotion. There is a noticeable difference, for example, between Barnabas and Melito on the one hand and Hebrews and Justin on the
other. And it should not be overlooked that Justin, for all his trium-
phalism, does at least place a recognizably Jewish side to the debate on
the lips of Trypho.

Second, any adequate picture of Jewish-Christian relations in this
period must attempt to see things from the Jewish side too. It is a
natural temptation to concentrate on the Christian evidence since a
great deal more of it is extant and immediately usable. Jewish evidence
has to be disentangled from rabbinic literature or reconstructed from
disparate archeological and papyrological finds, all of which present
daunting problems. The essays by A. Segal and J. Lightstone, however,
make significant head-way in these directions.

Third, the arguments presented in these essays clearly pose as
many problems as they purport to answer. This occurs not only because
of the ambiguous nature of much of the evidence, but also because the
solution to one problem often leads to the exposure of several others.
L. Gaston's concluding reflections show this so well that I need not
labour the point. In the long run the importance of this volume may be
as much in the agenda it sets for other scholars to pursue as in the
solutions proposed to discrete problems.

Recent events in Canada—where the courts have twice been required to consider whether denial of the Holocaust is an indictable
offence—have brought home the relevance of the issues at stake in
these volumes. While in one case the issue was, strictly speaking, the
historicity of the destruction of Jewry under Hitler's regime, in the
other it was the open propagation of anti-Semitism in a school class-
room. The issue of Christianity's contribution to modern anti-Semitism
is, as an increasing number of Christian scholars are willing to recognize, intimately tied to the anti-Jewish strain which arose in the early
Christian centuries. We thus work in the conviction that the com-
plexities of early Jewish-Christian relations not only pose a fascinating
range of historical problems, but also raise profound theological and
existential questions for our own time.

The genesis of the seminar in which these essays were read is
described by Peter Richardson in his Introduction to volume 1. By

virtue of its broad scope the seminar eventually attracted the enthusiasm and interest of a large number of Jewish and Christian scholars with diverse research interests. For one section of the Society it led to a distinct improvement in the focus and quality of papers presented at the annual meetings, and it has been considered one of the most successful ventures undertaken in recent years. It is only the second time that a collection of papers emanating from the annual meetings has been published in this form. The participants are only too aware that they owe a great deal to Peter Richardson, the prime mover and subsequent coordinator of the seminar.

The editing of this volume has been made considerably easier than it might have been, since I have been able to follow the precedents established by P. Richardson and Wilfrid Laurier University Press for volume 1, to use the same typists who had prepared that volume for press, and to benefit from the professional assistance of my wife in editing and proofreading. The indices have been prepared by a graduate student at Carleton University, Ms. Sandra Little. Part of the costs of typing and proofreading was covered by a grant from the Dean of Arts, Carleton University, and the Edgar and Dorothy Davidson Fund administered by the Department of Religion, Carleton University. This book has been published with the help of a grant from the Canadian Federation for the Humanities, using funds provided by the Social Sciences and Humanities Research Council of Canada.

Stephen G. Wilson

1

To the Hebrews or
Against the Hebrews?
Anti-Judaism and the
Epistle to the Hebrews

William Klassen

Introduction

The writing of the New Testament commonly known as the epistle to
the Hebrews has engaged the attention of New Testament scholars to
an inordinate degree. The long and detailed article by Erich Grässer,
describing the research on Hebrews from 1938 to 1963 and running for
almost 100 pages, demonstrates the breadth of interest this book has
aroused.[1] Nor is there any evidence that the interest has abated since
Grässer's article was published.

The reasons for this are complex and need not detain us here.
Undoubtedly, however, the fact both that certain themes in the book
have been seen as coming from gnostic circles and that theses have been
proposed which relate the book closely to Qumran means that it has
received a lot of attention by virtue of new discoveries and analysis of
new data in those two areas. It can also be suggested that scholars are
drawn to the mysterious, for there is agreement that, like Melchizedek,
whose origin and destination are known to none, the epistle has no
certain point of origin and no clear destination.

---

1 E. Grässer, "Der Hebräerbrief 1938-1963," *Th.Rundschau* 30 (1964), 138-236. I have
 summarized his essay at a number of points as noted.

The Addressees

The earliest manuscript to carry the superscription, "to the Hebrews," is p[46], which dates from about the year 200 C.E. The superscription was known already by Pantaenus and Clement of Alexandria as well.

Whether the superscription goes back to any apostolic tradition or was deduced from the contents of the writing can no longer be determined. In any case it is clear that more recently the superscription has brought more confusion than clarity because it has provoked scholars to enquire who these "Hebrews" could be. Attempts have thus been made to relate the book to the priests of the Essene community, the Qumran sect, Jewish Christians, or even more mainstream Jewish communities.

Even if we were to accept the genuineness of the title, addressing Hebrews, we would still have to determine its significance with respect to the content of the epistle. As early as 1905 Schiele argued that the word "Hebrews" here refers to the homeless who move across the earth seeking a heavenly home.[2] This interpretation caught the attention of Bertram and was also considered by Käsemann.[3] It has to be rejected, however, because there is simply no evidence that such an etymology of the word "Hebrews" was known to the early Christians.[4]

In this connection it is noteworthy that "Hebrews" are contrasted with "Christians" in the Gospel of Philip 2:52: "when we were Hebrews we were orphans and had only our mother, but when we became Christians we had both father and mother." At another point the apostles and apostolic men are called Hebrews (2.55) and in another saying it is claimed that "He who has not received the Lord is still a Hebrew" (2.62).[5]

On the basis of the content of the writing, M. Röth in 1836 established the alternative "Jewish Christians or Gentile Christians." This alternative has been picked up by the scholarly interpreters. Those who assume that it was addressed to Jewish Christians presuppose that the letter wants to warn its readers not to retreat into Judaism and does this by means of an anti-Jewish polemic. Accordingly the letter reflects a crisis within the development of Jewish Christianity of the earliest times. Scholars who take this position are William Manson, Howard, Kosmala, Benoit, Spicq, Snell, and Hewitt.[6] Others would argue that it

---

2 F.M. Schiele, "Harnack's 'probabilia' concerning the Address of the Author of the Epistle to the Hebrews," *AJT* 9 (1905), 290-308.
3 G.W. Bertram, *TDNT* 5:852 n. 64; E. Käsemann, *Das wandernde Gottesvolk. Eine Untersuchung zum Hebräerbrief* (Göttingen: Vandenhoeck und Ruprecht, 1959).
4 Grässer, "Hebräerbrief," 149.
5 Wesley W. Isenberg, trans., in James M. Robinson (ed.), *The Nag Hammadi Library* (New York: Harper & Row, 1977), 131-51.
6 Grässer, "Hebräerbrief," 148.

is addressed to Gentile Christians and deals with the danger of general weakness of faith and other problems typical of the second Christian generation.

Riggenbach argues that considering the letter as addressed to Jewish Christians should not be dismissed as an ancient error, but rather as "a newly recognized truth to which one must return if one wishes to attain a historical understanding of the letter."[7] Käsemann, with his usual vigour, welcomes rejection of the anti-Jewish character of the Hebrews because through it "so much exegetical confusion has been established that its final burial would be equivalent to being freed of a pernicious ghost."[8]

Literary Format

There is an emerging consensus that the writing combines two dimensions, thesis and paraenesis. It has been suggested that in the paraenesis there is no differentiation or separation from Judaism; the differentiation from Judaism comes rather in the thesis. That is, in the paraenesis no warnings are given against the Jews nor against being like the Jews, but in the thesis the differences between Jews and Christians are clearly spelled out.

Certainly we would agree with Grässer that

the detailed comparison of the old and the new covenant is not an indication of the polemical anti-Jewish character of the letter to the Hebrews, because for him this represents simply a part of the hermeneutical method by means of which he seeks to make clear to them the irrevocable guarantee of the promise which has been subjected to questioning.[9]

All hypotheses about the epistle being directed towards a sectarian group in Judaism, for example Qumran, have likewise been proven untenable. Insofar as they consciously or unconsciously start from the premise that Hebrews carries on any form of anti-Jewish propaganda, they fall under the verdict of F.J. Schierse: "Once the main building of the old Jerusalem hypothesis has been destroyed through criticism, every compromise solution is like dwelling in a house of building ruins. One has to either go back the whole way or look around for new enduring foundations."[10]

If it is true that the literary riddle of the book has been solved then to a large extent Otto Michel deserves the credit for this.[11] If not the

---

7 E. Riggenbach, *Der Brief an die Hebräer* (Leipzig: Deichert, 1922), xxv-xxvi.
8 Grässer, "Hebräerbrief," 148.
9 Grässer, "Hebräerbrief," 149.
10 Quoted in Grässer, "Hebräerbrief," 150-51.
11 So Grässer, "Hebräerbrief," 160. Th. Häring, "Gedankengang und Grundgedanken des Hebräerbriefes," *ZNW* 18 (1917), 145-64, deserves the credit along with Michel

first, he at least most energetically stressed the view that in Hebrews paraenesis took precedence over thesis, or that all of the assertions made by the writer point in the direction of paraenesis.[12] Secondly, the recognition that proclamation in the primitive church is the key to the understanding of the literary character of Hebrews has also carried the day. The stress on the word *logos* and the absence of words like *graphē* or *epistolē* indicate that we have here a sermon. Most scholars therefore accept it as what Grässer calls "a sermon sent from one place to another."[13]

There is also a consensus that the structure of the book moves clearly from hearing to believing to confessing. The principle of organization is a theological one, and the author proves to be a theologian of first rank as well as of eclectic tastes: "the elevated speech, the dignity of the style, the choice of expressions, and the introduction of hymnic pieces at particularly prominent places, all underline his peculiar cultic and liturgical connections."[14]

Here we can only touch on the important question about the extent of Hellenization in this writing. Snell argues that the Philonic dimensions of Hebrews are merely verbal or conceptual and not theological. He certainly overstates it when he says that "his theology and forms of religious thinking were in accord with a thoroughly Hebraic and Old Testament outlook."[15] How, one could ask, can the language itself be so thoroughly Hellenized and the thought itself remain so thoroughly Hebraic?

Even more extreme is the conclusion to which Burch comes when he accuses all commentators of Hellenizing the letter. He sees it as a letter of comfort from one Jew to others which is thoroughly "Hebrew in ideas." One can agree with Grässer that such a thesis is quite absurd.[16] Conversely, E.F. Scott exaggerates when he says that Hebrews is "the least Hebrew book in the New Testament."[17]

Our main concern is as follows: What is the central thrust of the epistle and what view does it have of Judaism, its history, its divine function, its current status, and its future? Above all, how does the author see the relationship between the salvation which he proclaims and that which Judaism offers?

---

for he dealt with the objections raised to the position that the style of Hebrews is patterned after Greek rhetorical writings.

12 "Die Spitze des theologischen Gedankens liegt in den paränetischen Teilen . . ." in Otto Michel, *Der Brief an die Hebräer* (Göttingen: Vandenhoeck und Ruprecht, 1960), 5.

13 "zugesandte Predigt," 160.

14 Michel, *Hebräer*, 372; Grässer, "Hebräerbrief," 167.

15 Antony Snell, *New and Living Way: An Explanation of the Epistle to the Hebrews* (London: The Faith Press, 1959), 40. See also Grässer, "Hebräerbrief," 169-70.

16 Grässer, "Hebräerbrief," 170.

17 E.F. Scott, *The Varieties of New Testament Religion* (London: Scribners, 1943), 222 (cited in Grässer, "Hebräerbrief," 170).

The Theme of Hebrews

With respect to the central theme of the writing we would agree with Oepke—it is the concept of the people of God which is found throughout the Old Testament. That concept of peoplehood is deeply rooted in the Hebrew conviction of election and in their sense of mission. Can this be harmonized with Käsemann's emphasis upon the motif of the pilgriming people of God? No one can deny that this motif is to be found but one may wonder whether Käsemann has not exaggerated its importance.

The manner in which this Old Testament idea of the people of God is harnessed for the diastasis of earthly and heavenly is unique. The promise to enter into the holy of holies is fulfilled. That is where the church now stands. In order to see it thus, we admit that to understand the way in which the author looks heuristically at Jewish traditions we must bring Hellenism into play. When we do so we can no longer make a sharp dichotomy between Hebraism and Hellenism in this epistle. Here we have a Jewish-Christian in a Hellenistic-Jewish context.

While it is generally recognized that we are dealing here with a writing addressed to second generation concerns or, as Goodspeed put it, a time when "Christianity was coming to be an old story," there is still vigorous debate as to whether the major problem was the delay of the parousia (so Martin Werner, Sandmel, Carl Immer, and to some extent Vos) or a general slackening of enthusiasm.

Whatever the causes, one of the symptoms of the weakening of the strength of Christianity was the faltering of hope.[18]

Hebrews as an Exercise in Comparative Religions

How does the author view the relationship between Christianity and Judaism? Clearly he is concerned to compare them. A glance at the concordance under *kreissōn, keittō* indicates how fundamental this category is for this writer in contrast to other writers of the New Testament. It appears twelve times in Hebrews, three times in Paul, and once each in 1 and 2 Peter.

The idea appears in such places as Matt. 12:6, in connection with the statement that something greater than the temple is here (only in Matthew), and in the Johannine writings in the form of rhetorical questions. In John 4:12 the Samaritan woman asks, "surely you are not

---

18 In this connection Heinrich Zimmermann, in his monograph, *Das Bekenntnis der Hoffnung* (Koln: Peter Hanstein, 1977), has used the correct category in order to analyze tradition and redaction in the writing.

greater than our father Jacob?" and in 8:53 the Jews say, "surely you are not greater than our father Abraham?" The answer on both occasions is implicit.

In Hebrews the word "superior" is used in several different contexts. The sense "to be superior" or "to be better than," the comparative form of the adjective, appears only in the epistle to the Hebrews with reference to the relation between Christianity and Judaism. It appears indirectly when it is stated that Jesus, or at least the title he has inherited, is superior to that of the angels (1:4), but this is a peripheral comparison. It may be that there were people who heard the epistle read who worshipped angels or had lofty ideas about them, but it certainly cannot be said that for Judaism as a whole the angels were seen as higher than the Messiah.[19]

More to the point are references to a "better" hope (7:19) or comments about "how far superior must the covenant also be of which Jesus is guarantor!" (7:22). Along similar lines, 8:6 affirms: "In fact service which has fallen to Jesus is as far superior to theirs as are the covenant he mediates and the promises upon which it is legally secured. Had that first covenant been faultless (*amemptos*) there would have been no need to seek for a second one in its place." The author quotes Jeremiah 31:31-34 to prove that God himself found fault (*memphomenos*) with them.

In his long eleventh chapter illustrating the nature of faith, he argues that although the ancient worthies all died in faith, they did not yet possess the promises but saw them from a distance and confessed themselves no more than strangers or passing travellers on the earth. "If their hearts had been in the mother country they had left, they could have found opportunity to return. Instead, we find them longing for something better—I mean the heavenly one" (15-16). The author is saying that something better was needed, and that God was pleased to prepare a city for them.

In 11:35 reference is made to a better resurrection. The meaning is certainly obscure since there is no indication with what resurrection it is being compared. And at the conclusion of that great catalogue of faith he says that while all of them are commemorated for their faith yet they did not enter into the promised inheritance "because, with us in mind, God had something better, that only in company with us should they be made whole" (v. 40).

---

19   C.P. Anderson has proposed that Hebrews was associated with Paul and entered the Pauline corpus through association with Colossians. It is the writing referred to in Colossians 4:16. Colossians 2:18 directs itself against those who go in for angel-worship and could easily support Hebrews' position on angels. See Anderson's articles "Hebrews Among the Letters of Paul," *SR* 5 (1975), 258-66, and "Who Wrote the Epistle From Laodicea?" *JBL* 85 (1966), 436-40.

Finally, attention may be called to that section of the epistle which is too often neglected in this whole discussion, namely Heb. 12:18-29, which represents the high point of the author's argument. The term "better" appears here only in connection with the blood of Abel. Nevertheless the whole sentence indicates that the covenants are being compared, for he says at the end of a list of things he is enumerating, "you stand before Jesus, the mediator of a new covenant, whose sprinkled blood has better things to tell than the blood of Abel" (v. 24).

The whole argument in this section hinges on the question of contrast between the old and the new; the allusions and quotations come from the patriarchal period, the period of the Exodus, the period of Davidic kingship, as well as the time of Haggai and the later prophets. There is no doubt that the author is here bringing to its highest pitch the element of contrast and comparison.

The writer does use the term "greater than" once, in a comparative sense, when he describes the priesthood of Christ and says that "the tent of his priesthood is a greater and more perfect one, not made by man's hands, that is, not belonging to this created world" (9:11). The formula *posō mallon* or *poly mallon* (9:14) appears once more in 12:25, but the comparison there is not with the old covenant in principle but is rather a comparison between what happened to those who did not listen to God when he spoke from Sinai and the hurt that will come to those who do not listen to him now. What is striking in 9:11 is the reference to something more perfect. Generally in the English language that cannot be a comparative. It is a *hapax legomenon*.

It is already clear that the comparisons that he draws have to do not with peripheral matters but with things at the centre: covenant, hope, promises, law, approach to God.

The author, however, does not confine himself to lauding the new. He moves beyond that to say depreciatory and directly negative things about the old. Even the use of new and old, derived as it is from the book of Jeremiah, cannot be seen as being totally non-judgmental. In some societies, of course, the old is always better than the new, in others the reverse is true. A more neutral way of describing the two covenants would have been to talk about the first covenant and the second one. It seems that in early Christian tradition Paul is the first to refer to "the new covenant" in connection with the institution of the Lord's Supper (1 Cor. 11:25), which may go back to earliest traditions in the Jerusalem church (Luke 22:20; variant readings Matt. 26:28 and Mark 14:24). Overall however, although Paul speaks of covenants (Rom. 9:4; Gal. 4:24; Eph. 2:12?) he never speaks of "first" and "second", but only of "old" and the "new", covenants (2 Cor. 3:6, 14). The writer of Hebrews does use the term "the first covenant" (Heb. 8:7, 13), and talks as well about the first tent (9:2, 6, 8). In 9:15, however, where it would have been most logical to compare first and second, he does not say second but prefers "new": "and therefore he is the mediator of a new covenant, under which, now that there has been a death to bring deliverance from sins committed under the first covenant, those whom God has called may receive the promise of the eternal inheritance." He also uses the term "first covenant" in 9:18.

Only at one point does he use enumerative terminology when, in Heb. 10:10, he says, "he annulled the first in order to establish the second." The impact of the sentence immediately makes it clear how the second is to be viewed. It totally displaces the first.

As indicated, the terminology "old" and "new" is heavily weighted in this author's usage. When we look, for example, at what he says in a pejorative way about the old, we have the following statements:

The earlier rules are cancelled as impotent and useless, since the law brought nothing to perfection; and a better hope is introduced through which we draw near to God (7:18).

Had the first covenant been faultless, there would have been no need to look for a second in its place (8:7).

By this the Holy Spirit signifies that so long as the earlier tent still stands, the way into the sanctuary remains unrevealed. [All this is symbolic, pointing to the present time.] The offerings and sacrifices there prescribed cannot give the worshipper inward perfection. It is only a matter of food and drink and various rites of cleansing—outward ordinances in force until the time of reformation (9:8-10).

For the law contains but a shadow and no mere image of the good things which were to come; it provides for these same sacrifices year after year, and with these it can never bring the worshippers to perfection for all time (10:1, 2).

To top it all off he says, in 10:9, that the former has been annulled (*aneireō*) which means that it is no longer operative, it has been rendered invalid, while the second has been firmly established.

Context of the Comparison

We must now look at the meaning of all of this and try to place it into its sociological context. The question that is asked more than any other with respect to the epistle of Hebrews is, when was it written? Clearly if it was written before the destruction of the Temple in 70 C.E. we have one problem; if it was written after that date we have quite a different problem. A good case can be made that the writer, if he had been writing after the destruction of Jerusalem, could have clinched his argument by a reference to that destruction. While this has some force it is not altogether persuasive. In any case what we must remember is that the argument revolves not around the Temple as such but rather around the institution of the tent of the tabernacles. The focus is not so much on the high priest as it is on Melchizedek.

Since it is not our task to go into all of those problems, we will focus instead on the question of the manners or etiquette of the writer in his clear and obvious attempt to show that the religious commitment system which has come into being in Jesus, and over which he rules as Lord, is better than that which preceded it.

It is important to notice that there is a progression in the terms that he uses for comparisons. For example, the terms "first and second" and "new and old" are comparisons which are relatively neutral. For the antique dealer that which is old is much more valuable, while the person desiring the latest news prefers the most recent newspaper. Overall we live in a society which assumes that value is related in some way to the question of how recent something is. It is doubtful that our author shares that point of view. For him the category of newness is taken from Jeremiah and its meaning must be derived from that author. It may still be the case that although he derives it from Jeremiah he has not been consistent in his use of the category.[20]

Apart from the quotation from Jeremiah in 8:8 and a comment thereon in 8:13 the word *kainos* appears in 9:15, where reference is made to a "new covenant." He refers also to a new (*neas*) covenant in 12:24. In addition he uses the verb *egkaivizō*, "renew" or "inaugurate," with respect to the first covenant (9:18) and with respect to the way in which Jesus has inaugurated the second (10:20). This latter reference comes in the midst of a long and involved sentence which extends through verses 19-25. The best translation would surely be "inaugurate" rather than "renew."

It is clear that for our author the categories "new" and "old" are fundamental to the way in which he describes the relationship between Israel and the people of Jesus. This contrast is born in the prophets of Israel, Isaiah, and Jeremiah, and not from Greek thought, and may very well have received its peculiar stamp from Jesus himself.

How are we to describe it? Two key texts from the prophets illuminate it: Isaiah 43:16-19a; and Jeremiah 31:31-34. The latter is quoted at length in this writing and only here in the New Testament.

What seems clear is that the New Testament writers saw the prophets as looking forward to a time when God would establish a "new" covenant, a new way of dealing with his people. Contrary to the

---

20 C. Wolff, *Jeremia im Frühjudentum und Urchristentum*, TU 118 (Berlin: Akademie-Verlag, 1976), has shown that Jeremiah's statement on the New Covenant is ignored by Jewish sources until after the year 70 and the destruction of the Temple, even those sources which speak of a New Covenant, as e.g., the Qumran group. Does this suggest that Jewish sources began to use it in response to the way it emerges in Hebrews? Or does it suggest that Hebrews itself was not written before the fall of Jerusalem?

dreary pessimism of the writer of Ecclesiastes (1:9) who believed that
there was nothing "new" under the sun, the writer of Deutero-Isaiah
proclaims:

> No need to recall the past,
> no need to think about what was done before.
> See, I am doing a new deed,
> even now it comes to light; can you not see it?
> Yes, I am making a road in the wilderness,
> paths in the wilds. (43:18-19)

It seems clear that Isaiah sees the actions of Yahweh to liberate his
people in two phases: the first, the exodus from Egypt and the second
from Babylon. He sees that these are not only parallel, but also that in
some ways the second is greater. It is clear that in so doing Second
Isaiah challenges the original creed of Israel and he tries to persuade
his contemporaries to redirect their eyes from the first exodus to that
which God is about to perform for them. Clearly he sees two phases, the
former and the new, the former having been brought to an end by the
destruction of Jerusalem and the new to be inaugurated at any time.[21]

It is important for Isaiah that all of this was prophesied ahead of
time for it provides continuity to the actions of Yahweh. As von Rad
puts it: "With the 'New' he means the saving acts announcing themselves after a long pause to the prophet, as saving events in the movement of history." The words cited above from 43:18 are stated so
crudely that, especially for the devout, they must have seemed somewhat blasphemous.[22]

For Deutero-Isaiah this meant the end of one aspect of history.
The first had passed away and the new was about to come. The first
retains its validity as a type of the new. No one had up till that time so
frankly designated the breaking in of the Eschaton and bracketed it off
from the previous authority Yahweh had exercised over history.[23]

The element of "newness" in the kerygma of the early Christians
has been studied and the results published in a book too often neglected.[24] Harrisville has shown that the concept of newness is an
eschatological part of the early Christian kerygma. While Harnack
could designate eschatological features of the kerygma as an "evil

---

21   For example, he refers to the "earlier times" (43:18), "the beginning time" (41:22;
     42:9; 43:9, 18; 46:9; 48:3), the "new" (Isa. 42:9; 43:19; 48:6), that which is to follow
     (Isa. 41:23). See G. von Rad, *Theologie des AT* (Munich: Kaiser, 1960), 2:258-64. Also
     in particular, C.R. North, "The 'Former Things' and the 'New Things' in Deutero-
     Isaiah," in H.H. Rowley (ed.), *Studies in OT Prophecy* (Edinburgh: T & T Clark, 1950),
     111ff.
22   Von Rad, *Theologie*, 2:261.
23   Von Rad, *Theologie*, 2:262.
24   Roy A. Harrisville, *The Concept of Newness in the New Testament* (Minneapolis: Augs-
     burg, 1960), 28.

inheritance from the Jews" we cannot follow that path. Nor can we read them out of the kerygma as legendary and mythological features.[25] Harrisville affirms that wherever the concept of newness appears in the New Testament it is in an eschatological frame of reference and includes four aspects: continuity, contrast, finality, and dynamism.

Harrisville finds the most specific and outstanding feature of the new to be its dynamic aspect. "The intrinsic energy or dynamic of the new is first of all revealed in the fact that the new asserts itself over against the old and actually crowds it out of existence. It is also revealed in the power of the new to perpetuate itself in contrast to the old which is transitory."[26]

The matter becomes much more complicated, however, when we look at such categories as obsolete or useless. We are dealing here with a distinct value judgment. That which is ancient has inherent value for the antiquities dealer and even though it may be obsolete from a functional standpoint it retains value. The author of Hebrews does not seem to think in those terms at all. He rather takes the position that the new has made the old obsolete and that indeed it has superseded that which went before.

It may be of help to list the depreciatory references in the writing so that we can get an overview of them:

The earlier rules (*entolēs*) are cancelled (*athetēsis*) as impotent (*asthenes*) and useless (*anōpheles*) since the law brought nothing to perfection (*teleioō*); a better hope was introduced, through which we draw nigh to God. (7:18-19)

How far superior must the covenant also be of which Jesus is the guarantor! (7:22)

For the law installed frail men as high priests, but the word of oath which came after the law (installed) a perfected son, for ever [my own translation; the *NEB*'s "supersedes the law" is incorrect; the *JB*, while translating the last part correctly, renders *ho logos* as "promise" and that seems incorrect as well]. (7:28)

But in fact the ministry which had fallen to Jesus is as far superior to theirs as are the covenant he mediates and the promises upon which it is legally secured. Had that first covenant been faultless, there would have been no need to look for a second in its place. But God, finding fault with them, says, "The days are coming..." [quoting Jeremiah 31:31-34]. (Heb. 8:6-13)

By speaking of a new covenant, he has pronounced the first one old; and anything that is growing old and aging will shortly disappear. (8:13)

We can conclude that the author goes beyond the contrast between first and second or new and old to declare:

---

25   Harrisville, *Concept* 30, citing Harnack, *Entstehung des kirchlichen Dogmas* (4th ed.; Tübingen: J.C.B. Mohr, 1909), 1:87-90, 98-99, 102-3; this quotation from 113-15.
26   Harrisville, *Concept*, 19-20.

(1) The old covenant, with its law and commandments and sacrificial system has been annulled, set aside and indeed cancelled (7:18; 10:9). The words that are used here, *atheteō* and *anaireō*, allow no other interpretation than that. In particular, the word *atheteō* is well documented in the papyri as meaning abolition and appears as such in Hebrews itself (7:18; 9:26; 10:28). The word *anaireō*, meaning fundamentally to wipe out through murder, here means "to abolish" and stands in 10:9 as the opposite of "to establish" (*histēmi*).

(2) The reason why this has been done is that God in his sovereignty decided to do so, because of certain defects in the law and the first covenant. This follows from such statements as: "The earlier rule's cancellation *dia to autēs asthenēs kai anōpheles*" (7:18), or "Had that first covenant been faultless (*amemptos*), a second would not have had to come to take its place" (8:7). *Amemptos* is not attributed to the first *diathēkē* and yet, when the author continues, he cannot bring himself to say that God calls the first covenant faulty. Rather the fault is now attributed to "them." "God finding fault with them says . . ." (Jeremiah 31). What is the antecedent to "them"? It has to be understood as the disobedient Israelites. Nevertheless it should not be used to soften this writer's perception.[27] He has already implied that the first covenant has to be faulted but it is God himself who does the faulting for it remains his covenant.

(3) The old is growing old and obsolete and will shortly disappear (8:13). For the writer it is not the force of history that brings about obsolescence. It is only God, the subject of history, the one who initiates all and terminates everything who makes the first obsolete by what he has done in the second: *en tō legein kainēn pepalaiōken tēn prōtēn to de palaioumenon kai gēraskon eggys aphanismou* (8:13). In that respect the author argues that whoever clings to the old denies that God has indeed acted in the new.

Thus the author with apparent sharpness delineates the difference between the old and the new. If Marcion in later days was to accentuate the difference between the old and the new in ways unacceptable to the church, later attempts to wipe out the differences between the old and the new have not been successful either. For the modern interpreter it is especially disturbing that those who argued for a union of the two covenants were among the most anti-semitic thinkers of their times.[28] For what they did was to reclaim the Old Testament as a

---

27   As does Grundmann (*TDNT* 4:572); he also makes the astounding statement that for Paul "zeal for the Law and the fulfilment of Halacha became sin and thus righteousness through the Law impossible, not because he could not fulfill the Law but because fulfilling the Law became sin."

28   One thinks in particular here of men like Martin Bucer and John Calvin. See H.H. Wolf, *Die Einheit des Bundes; Das Verhältnis von Alten und Neuen Testament bei Calvin*

Christian document and to see Christ at work already there, rather than to respect the uniqueness of the old covenant.

For our author the issue is more complex. For he sees, like Jeremiah and Isaiah, the relation between old and new covenants in dialectical terms.[29] As Käsemann puts it: "The relation between the old and new covenants is not simply polemical, with respect to the ceremonial law. Rather it is dialectical since the old *diathēkē* is both surpassed and invalidated. Consequently it receives recognition as shadow and example."[30]

It would seem clear that the author does not hesitate to explicate the differences that exist between him and the religion, Judaism, to which he himself and certainly many of his readers belonged. He even warns his people to "go outside the camp" and there is every reason to believe that he means thereby that they are to break their ties with Judaism.[31] There is a sharp edge to this, but it is not fed by hatred. Rather it emerges out of an enthusiasm for something new that has occurred, a total commitment to that new way, and a firm belief that it has a continuity with the old; in fact, the continuity is so great that the new obviously must not be separated from the old.

The high point of the epistle is 12:18-19, and it may be worth our while to take a look at this as an example in which the author draws together the two systems, particularly at the point where the people gather for worship. In all, it seems clear that while the same God welcomes the approach of his people, a new system can in no way expect that treatment by this God will be more lenient or that an encounter with this God under the new covenant will be any less a call to commitment or a demand for faithful exercise of responsibility.

By reference to virtually every major era in the history of Israel, the author skillfully weaves his allusions and citations to the point where he comes to the present situation. It can, of course, be argued that he highlights the frightful and palpable dimensions of the old covenant, evidence for which could also be found in other parts of the epistle. He obviously emphasizes in the old that which will put the new into a better light. Again, however, it would be wrong to cite this as evidence of malice or even of lack of respect for that which has gone before. He fully sees God as having been at work in the old covenant;

(Neukirchen: K. Moehrs, 1958), 69ff., and also J. Mueller, *Martin Bucers Hermeneutik* (Gütersloh: Gerd Mohn, 1965), 203-04, on anti-Semitism see 154-56.

29 The thesis by Rudolf Schreiber, "Der Neue Bund im Spätjudentum und Urchristentum" (Dissertation, Tübingen, 1954), kindly supplied to me by Klaus Mueller, speaks of the dominant role which the quotation from Jeremiah plays in the theological structure of the writing (116).

30 As cited in Schreiber, "Neue Bund," 121.

31 See Floyd V. Filson, *'Yesterday' A Study of Hebrews in the Light of Chapter 13* (London: SCM, 1967), 62-65.

the word that he has spoken has been fully God's word, but it has been partial.

Remember Where You Stand

Sinai	*Mount Zion*
NOT	BUT
1. *pselaphomeno*—something toucha-ble or graspable-palpable-tangible, 1 John 1:1, Acts 17:27, sermon on Mars Hill; Luke 24:40	1. *Mount Zion*
	2. *City of the living God*
2. *blazing fire*	3. *Heavenly Jerusalem*—in Jewish thought this is the 4th heaven
3. *darkness*	4. *Myriads of angels*—5th heaven. *Festival-gathering*
4. *gloom*	5. *Assembly of First-born enrolled in heaven*—Mal. 3:16: book of remembrance was written before him of those who feared the Lord and thought on his name
5. *whirlwind*	
6. *trumpet-blast*	
7. *oracular voice* (parenthesis—) CONCLUSION: Frightful Sight (*phoberon* used only in Hebrews, 3 times)	6. *The Judge: God of all*
	7. *Spirits of good men made perfect*
8. EVEN Moses: I shudder with fear—literally: I am afraid and I tremble	8. *Jesus, mediator of a new Covenant,* whose sprinkled blood speaks

The antithetical parallelism is as fully developed here as anywhere in the New Testament. The focus is on the church at worship and its definition of itself as a community under the new covenant and its mediator. He indicates that they have a much greater opportunity; that the possibility of their living through a greater shaking than any that has ever come upon mankind is real and that they are therefore not to reject the one who now speaks to them. As at the beginning of the sermon, so here at the end, he stresses the "Word" and their response to it. Unshakeable is the kingdom alone which we are in the process of receiving (v. 28). The community finds itself in *latreia* acceptable to God; and God retains his character as of old, a burning fire.

What is the continuity with the old people of God? We have the same God, the same opportunity; we, like they, face a tremendous shaking for the foundations of the world are not secure. But the better speech which his blood delivers is not defined. Presumably Abel's blood cried out for vengeance whereas the blood of Christ brings atonement.

In assessing this position we cannot merely criticize what the author has done, but must suggest a better alternative. The alternative that has been proposed most consistently in the history of the Christian church is to say that there are really not two covenants but one. It has been an attempt to rub out historical lines of differentiation. Those who have criticized this position have, correctly, indicated that the incarnation then makes little sense and Jesus becomes simply one more misguided prophet in the line of many who had delusions of grandeur.[32]

It would seem clear that the writer of Hebrews cannot be accused of ignoring historical reality. He takes seriously what has happened within his lifetime, he sees it within the context of the history of God's dealings with Israel, and he devoutly believes that something decisive took place in Jesus which is incomparable. At the same time he sees a very deep continuity between the people who lived in the wilderness and received the ten commandments and the tabernacle with the people of his own time. This continuity can be seen in obedience as well as disobedience. It is seen above all in the fact that the same voice which spoke at Sinai, which called the people forth from Egypt, is also the voice which speaks in his day to strengthen the weak knees and to bolster the sagging spirits.

How would Jews of the first century who read this have reacted? Would they have been insulted? Surely not if they had read Philo. Surely not if they had had contact with the Essenes. Surely not if they had lived in Northern Galilee. For our indications are that the Temple ritual was not as important to people living in that area as it was to people living in Judea and in Jerusalem. Since we do not know to whom the epistle was addressed, when it was written, or who wrote it, we have to try to arrive at the author's value system from within the document itself. It is doubtful, however, that Jews of the first century, even Jews devoutly attached to the Temple, would have had any great difficulty with the epistle to the Hebrews.[33] There were many people who criticized the Temple and its administration and many people who looked for ways in which the presence of God could be more fully assured. It is highly unlikely that Jews of the first century before 70 C.E. would have found this epistle offensive.

The writer's major concern is to make God's presence immediate. The enormous cleavage between heaven and earth has been bridged in the work of Jesus. In this respect the author does not accept Greek values but stands solidly in the Jewish tradition.

---

32 The most thorough treatment of the theme of the relation of the two covenants to each other in Hebrews is by J. De Vuyst, 'Oud en Nieuw Verbond' in de Brief aan de Hebreen (Kampen: J.H. Kok, 1964).

33 S. Sandmel says: "Judaism is not vilified in Hebrews, nor are Jews aspersed ... Hebrews seems concerned not with a relationship to the Judaism or the Jews of the age when it was written but with the ancient Judaism of the Scriptures ..." (Anti-Semitism in the New Testament [Philadelphia: Fortress, 1978], 120.)

Earthly sanctuary, Jerusalem temple, and the heavenly sanctuary do not jux-
tapose each other as above and below, but rather as old and new (10:20) insofar
as the earthly sanctuary is merely earthly, and the new, the heavenly sanctuary,
encloses both heaven and earth. Consequently the world and history are open
towards God.[34]

---

34   Ulrich Luck, "Himmlisches und Irdisches Geschehen im Hebräerbrief," *NovT* 6
      (1963), 192-215, quote from 209.

2

Temple and *Bet Ha-midrash* in the Epistle of Barnabas

Martin B. Shukster and Peter Richardson

The anti-Judaic content of the epistle of Barnabas[1] is not its most disturbing feature. As readers of the New Testament we are unfortunately familiar with—though often inured to—the anti-Judaic themes it rehearses. What disturbs the reader most is the virulence with which these themes are presented. The package is more offensive than the contents. In what follows we will attempt to account for this "packaging," arguing that the stridency of the epistle's anti-Judaism is not the inevitable result of its New Testament patrimony as some believe,[2] but rather that its disturbing tone is related to identifiable historical circumstances.[3] We will first address matters of provenance, and date; then against this historical backdrop we will examine the epistle's major polemical foci on the Temple and the *Bet ha-midrash*.

Provenance

For many years scholars have viewed the epistle of Barnabas as Alexandrian in origin, though recent scholarship has grown increas-

---

1 For the purposes of this paper we will assume that the first seventeen chapters form a discrete unit composed by a single author. Cf. E. Robillard, "L'Epître de Barnabé; trois époques, trois théologies, trois rédacteurs," *RB* 78 (1971), 184-209.

2 R.R. Reuther, *Faith and Fratricide* (New York: Seabury Press, 1974). For a response to the important questions raised by Reuther see A.T. Davies (ed.), *Antisemitism and the Foundations of Christianity* (New York: Paulist Press, 1979).

3 S. Lowy ("The Confutation of Judaism in the Epistle of Barnabas," *JJS* 11 [1960], 1-33), is of much the same opinion, although he is not prepared to specify the historical events which prompted the epistle's composition.

ingly sceptical of this position.[4] The arguments usually proposed for
Alexandrian provenance include (a) the epistle's early currency and
popularity in Egypt; (b) its use of allegory and typology; and (c) its
understanding of *gnōsis* as special insight into scripture. We will contend that these arguments are often more supportive of Syro-
Palestinian provenance,[5] and that other evidence can be marshalled
which makes Syro-Palestine preferable as the location of the epistle.

(1) The epistle's early currency and popularity in Egypt is the strongest
argument in favour of an Alexandrian provenance.[6] This evidence,
however, is by no means conclusive, since the two Alexandrian Fathers
most familiar with the work have known connections with Syro-
Palestine—Clement having visited and been instructed by teachers
from Palestine and East Syria (*Strom*. 1.1.11) and Origen having spent
much of his later life in Caesarea.[7]

(2) The use of allegory and typology was not strictly confined to
Alexandria. Somewhat similar hermeneutical principles were employed at Qumran and by Paul, so we can assume that these principles
enjoyed some currency in Palestine and other regions nearby. The
attempt to locate the epistle on the basis of hermeneutical principles is
further complicated by the work's probable dependence on earlier
Christian *testimonia*,[8] for even if a hermeneutical principle could confi-

---

4   L.W. Barnard, in a series of articles between 1958 and 1966, and R.A. Kraft, *Barna-
    bas and the Didache*, The Apostolic Fathers, vol. 3 (New York: Thomas Nelson &
    Sons, 1965), among others favour Alexandrian provenance. Kraft does, however,
    offer the delightful qualification that Barnabas may have belonged to a school which
    was a "Christianized offspring of a Qumranlike Judaism in Greek dress" (55)! Those
    sceptical of the Alexandrian hypothesis include A.L. Williams, "The Date of the
    Epistle of Barnabas," *JTS* 24 (1933), 337-46; and more recently P. Prigent, in his
    introduction to Prigent and Kraft, *Epître de Barnabé: Introduction, traduction et notes*,
    SC, 172 (Paris: du Cerf, 1971), and K. Wengst, *Tradition und Theologie des Barnabas-
    briefs* (Berlin: de Gruyter, 1971).
5   Though awkward, the designation "Syro-Palestine" is not inappropriate for our
    period. According to the Mishna, Syria's status was a matter of considerable debate,
    with R. Aqiva and R. Eliezer arguing that *halakot* reserved for Israel were equally
    binding for Syria. R. Gamaliel II, it would seem, was of the opposite opinion (*m.
    Šebu*. 6:2 [cf. *t. Šebu*. 4:12]; *m. Ḥal*. 4:7). For discussions of the relevant pericopes
    see C. Primus, *Aqiva's Contribution to the Law of Zera'im* (Leiden: Brill, 1977);
    J. Neusner, *Eliezer Ben Hyrcanus: The Tradition and the Man*, 2 pts. (Leiden: Brill,
    1973); and S. Kanter, *Rabban Gamaliel II: The Legal Traditions* (Chico: Scholars
    Press, 1980). Prigent (Prigent and Kraft, *Epître*, 22-24) also treats Syro-Palestine as a
    unit, though for different reasons.
6   Williams correctly points out that the early citation of a source in a particular region
    is not always helpful in establishing provenance ("Date," 340).
7   For Origen's relationship to Judaism see N.R.M. de Lange, "Jewish Influence on
    Origen," in *Origeniana*, Quaderni di "Vetera Christianorum," 12 (Universita' di
    Bari: Instituto di Letteratura Cristiana Antica, 1975), 225-42, and "Origen and
    Jewish Bible Exegesis," *JJS* 22 (1971), 31-52.
8   See, in particular, P. Prigent, *Epître de Barnabé I-XVI et ses sources* (Paris: Gabalda,
    1961) and H. Windisch, *Der Barnabasbrief* (Tübingen: Mohr [Paul Siebeck], 1920).

dently be limited to a single geographic region that would only prove helpful in determining the provenance of the underlying source and not the work as a whole. Arguments drawn from hermeneutical principles, weak as they are, might succeed if the material examined could be shown to have originated with the author (whom we will call "Barnabas") independent of his other sources. The circumcision of Abraham's servants is one of the rare occasions where Barnabas' own views are plainly in evidence (9:7-9).[9] By means of Gen. 14:14, Barnabas establishes 318 as the number of household members circumcised in Gen. 17:23-27, and then shows, by means of *gematria*, how this number prefigures Jesus and the cross. There is no evidence that a *gematria* exposition of Gen. 14:14, or the transposition of the number 318 to illumine other passages, ever formed part of the common stock of Alexandrian exegesis.[10] By contrast, *gematria* was the preferred rabbinic method of expounding the text in question,[11] while Josephus employs the 318 servants of Gen. 14:14 in his treatment of Gen. 12: 10-12 (*B.J.* 5.380). Barnabas' use of *gematria*, and his transposition of Gen. 14:14 to Gen. 17:23-27 might then be taken as evidence of Syro-Palestinian provenance.

(3) The use of the term *gnōsis* (= $d^c t$) to describe profound insight into the meaning of scripture has parallels in the Pauline and Qumran writings.[12] Of particular note is the epistle's pesher-like historicizing of scriptural prophecies,[13] again a method foreign to the Alexandrian school.

The arguments usually adduced in support of Alexandrian provenance are not compelling. In fact, the cumulative force of these arguments points away from Alexandria to Syro-Palestine as the epis-

---

9 So Prigent, *Sources*, 58-60. Cf. Kraft, *Barnabas*, who views the *gematria* on Gen. 14:14 as an inherited *testimonium*, with the exegetical novelty lying in its transposition to Gen. 17:23-27 (107-108).

10 Philo attaches no significance to the figure of 318, and reduces it to 300 (*Abr.* 39). Clement does know Barnabas' *gematria* but does not relate it to Gen. 17:23-27 (*Strom.* 6.11.84). By contrast, Origen, who knows the epistle, does not use the *gematria*, and instead follows Philo in reducing the 318 servants to 300 (*Hom. Gen.* 2.5).

11 Rabbinic tradition equates the 318 servants with Eliezer, Abraham's steward (*b. Ned.* 32a; *Gen. Rab.* 43:2; *Lev. Rab.* 28:4; *Num. Rab.* 18:21; *Pesiq. R.* 18:3; *Pesiq. Rab. Kah.* 8:2; *Pirq. R. El.* 27).

12 As M. Burroughs (*The Dead Sea Scrolls* [New York: Viking Press, 1955], 256) puts it: "What is meant by knowledge in the Scrolls has to do with the wonders of God's creation, the fulfillment of prophecy, and the meaning of the divine laws man must obey." See also, W.D. Davies, "Knowledge in the Dead Sea Scrolls and Matthew 11:24-30," *HTR* 46 (1953), 113-39, and B. Reicke, "Da'at and Gnosis in Intertestamental Literature," in E.E. Ellis and M. Wilcox (eds.), *Neotestamentica et Semitica: Studies in Honour of Matthew Black* (Edinburgh: T & T Clarke, 1969), 245-55.

13 Prigent (Prigent and Kraft, *Epître*), who dehistoricizes these prophecies (26), takes the "absence" of pesher-like exegesis as an argument against Syro-Palestinian provenance (24).

tle's more likely place of origin. There are a number of additional arguments which seem to tip the balance in favour of the Syro-Palestinian alternative.

In attempting to dismiss circumcision as a sign of the covenant, Barnabas chides his audience saying:

> But you will say, surely the people has received circumcision as a seal? Yes, but [*alla kai*] every Syrian and every Arab and all the priests of the idols have been circumcised; are then these also within their covenant?—indeed even [*alla kai*] the Egyptians belong to the circumcision. (9:6)[14]

Although no textual variation has been preserved, the genuineness of the phrase describing the Egyptians has been questioned on structural grounds.[15] If we accept that the Egyptian reference is an interpolation, the Syro-Palestinian hypothesis is considerably strengthened, since the resultant text deals only with the Syrians and the Arabs. Alternatively, even if the Egyptian reference is authentic, one wonders why it was not given primacy of place for the benefit of an Egyptian audience. In either case the verse's emphasis on the circumcision of the Syrians and the Arabs at the expense of the Egyptians would seem to suggest Syro-Palestine as the epistle's likeliest place of origin.

Two final points can be made in favour of Syro-Palestine provenance. Negatively, Barnabas shows no sympathy with, or interest in, the *logos* theology which is the signature of the Alexandrian school; positively, he does show a marked interest in eschatology which, while lacking for the most part among the Alexandrian exegetes, is a commonplace in works ascribed to Syro-Palestine.

There are then solid grounds for proposing a Syro-Palestinian origin for the epistle. This conclusion is corroborated in part by Prigent, who shows that the *testimonia* and midrashic elements inherited by Barnabas have recognizable affinities with early church writings native to Syro-Palestine.[16] The significance of this claim will become clear later in this paper when an explanation is proposed for the tone of the epistle.

Date

There are two passages that have long been considered capable of disclosing the epistle's date: the quotations from Daniel's vision of the "Ten Kings" in chapter 4, and the statements about the rebuilding of

---

14   Text and translation followed throughout is that of K. Lake, *The Apostolic Fathers*, vol. 1, in *LCL* (London: Heinemann, 1919).
15   See Windisch, *Barnabasbrief*, 354.
16   Prigent, *Sources*. As has already been mentioned the location of the sources does not determine the location of the work as a whole. It is, however, legitimate to use Prigent's conclusions as corroborative evidence.

the Temple in chapter 16. It is sometimes denied that either one or both of these passages can be used for purposes of dating. We have argued elsewhere that evidence drawn from a variety of secular and religious sources converges on a date coherent with the obvious meaning of both passages—a date at the end of Nerva's reign (*c* 98 C.E.).[17] The basic lines of the argument are as follows:

The "Ten Kings"

The "Ten Kings" passage points to a time when three mighty rulers, or "horns," have been humiliated by a less imposing figure whom Barnabas calls a "little offshoot" or "little excrescent horn" (4:5). This "excrescent horn" (clearly the emperor in power at the time of composition), which subdues three kings, has sometimes been identified with Vespasian who superseded Galba, Otho, and Vitellius. But Vespasian's impressive military and administrative career is wholly ill-suited to the term "excrescent horn". A more natural and more attractive candidate is Nerva (96-8 C.E.).[18] He too brings a triumvirate to an end—the glorious Flavian dynasty of Vespasian, Titus, and Domitian—and in his case the term "excrescent horn" aptly describes a frail caretaker emperor who did not even have the support of the army.

Rebuilding of the Temple

Domitian, Nerva's predecessor, had persecuted those attracted to Jewish "superstition," with God-fearers and perhaps even Christians figuring among the victims.[19] This persecution probably turned on the collection of the *fiscus Iudaicus*, a punitive measure introduced by Vespasian to transform the former Jewish Temple Tax into a collection for the Temple of Jupiter Capitolinus. With Nerva's accession, Domitian's harsh measures came to an end, marked in the most public fashion by the minting in his first year of a coin bearing the legend *FISCI IUDAICI CALUMNIA SUBLATA* ("the *calumnia* related to the Jewish Tax is abolished"). The coin's iconography hints that the significance of the Nervan reform may well have been more far-reaching than an exchequer reform of an unpopular tax. Nerva's coin is domi-

---

17 P. Richardson and M.B. Shukster, "Barnabas, Nerva, and the Yavnean Rabbis," *JTS* n.s. 34 (1983), 32-55.
18 Three scholars lean towards a date in Nerva's reign: A.L. Williams, "Date"; F.X. Funk, *Die Apostolischen Väter*, (Tübingen: Mohr [Paul Siebeck], 1901); and W. Hilgenfeld, *ZwTh*, in a series of articles between 1858 and 1871, not available to us.
19 For a recent treatment of Domitian's policies towards Judaism see E.M. Smallwood, "Domitian's Attitude toward the Jews and Judaism," *Class. Phil.* 51 (1956), 1-13.

nated by the figure of a palm tree—the symbol of Judea. It is surely no accident that this iconographic representation contrasts sharply with the *Iudaea capta* series of his predecessors. The majority of these Flavian coins also show a central palm tree, but, as might be expected of coins celebrating the defeat of Judea, the palm is flanked by a seated weeping woman and a standing centurion. By removing the two bracketing figures, Nerva's coin in effect removed the symbols of Judea's prior defeat and subjugation at the hands of the Flavians, and so hinted at a restoration of ante-bellum status.

There are a number of rabbinic traditions datable to the 90s which connect a resumption of the Temple Tax to an abortive attempt to rebuild the Temple. Genesis Rabbah recalls how two enigmatic figures, Lulianus and Pappus, resumed the collection of the Temple Tax appropriated earlier by the Flavians.[20] Significantly, this tradition locates the collection on the Syro-Palestinian coast. Genesis Rabbah further implies that the collection was related to a Roman decision to allow the Temple to be rebuilt, and that this decision can be related in turn to a distinguished rabbinic embassy from Yavneh which other sources place towards the end of Domitian's reign (*c* 95 C.E.).[21] Megillat Ta'anit records a short-lived holiday honouring Trajan, Nerva's designated successor, a holiday which was abolished when Trajan executed Lulianus and Pappus at Laodicea.[22]

From the above evidence we concluded that Nerva had been favourably disposed towards the rebuilding of the Temple. However the brevity of his reign did not allow the matter to move beyond the promissory stage, and the Jews, expecting Trajan to act on the promise of his adoptive father, established the Trajan Day holiday to honour the newly installed emperor, as both a sign of fealty from a once rebellious people and as an expression of proleptic gratitude for the restitution of their national cult. This expression was so vivid in the Syro-Palestine region that some enthusiasts took it upon themselves to resume the Temple Tax collection as a means of capitalizing the project. But Jewish hopes, so eloquently expressed in the establishment of the Trajan Day festival, were abruptly shattered when the new emperor, evidently uncomfortable with the notion of a rehabilitated Jewish people, executed two of the principals involved in the Temple Tax collection.

Thus when Barnabas emphasizes that the Temple is being built now (*ginetai ... nyn kai autoi hoi tōn echthrōn hypēretai anoikodomēsousin auton* [16:4]) he is not, as some suggest, alluding to a spiritual temple of

20 *Gen. Rab.* 64:10.
21 For the major references to the embassy in rabbinic literature see W. Bacher, *Die Agada der Tannaiten*, vol. 1 (Strasbourg: Trübner, 1903), 79 n. 3.
22 *b. Ta'an.* 18b; *y. Ta'an.* 2:13, 66a; *y. Meg.* 2:6, 70c.

the Christian believer,[23] but rather to a Jewish temple "built with hands"; and when he adds that the "servants of the enemy" are rebuilding it, he is alluding to the Yavnean authorities who were no doubt perceived as instrumental in securing and supporting the Roman endorsement of the rebuilding venture.

We would then date the epistle to the end of Nerva's reign when Jewish hopes for the rebuilding of the Temple were running especially high.

Context

A tone of urgency pervades the epistle. Events have recently taken a dramatic and dangerous turn — so dramatic in fact, that unlike many of his other scriptural citations Barnabas can leave the "Ten Kings" prophecy uninterpreted ("You ought then to understand" [4:6]). The movement of recent events has convinced the author that these are "the last days," a "present evil time" (4:9) controlled by the "worker of evil himself" (2:1). A beleaguered Christianity faces its "final stumbling block" (4:3) and Barnabas exhorts his audience to caution and hatred of "the error of this present time" (4:1). Despite these exhortations the author's prognosis for the community is bleak. While scripture may tell the church that it has the authority to rule the world (6:18), Barnabas must concede that in the light of the present situation this eventual triumph has been postponed to an indefinite period in the future when Christians will be "made perfect as heirs of the covenant of the Lord" (6:19). The Christian kingdom will only be realized "through pain and suffering" (7:11).

The "present evil time" which threatens Christianity is not, as Lightfoot believed,[24] the spectre of Nero *redivivus*, but rather the spectre of Judaism *redivivus*! For Barnabas the destruction of the Temple in 70 C.E. had conclusively ended Jewish covenantal claims. In fact the Flavian emperors even seemed to formalize Christianity's inheritance of God's covenant by diminishing Jewish national status through the payment of the *fiscus Iudaicus*. But with the end of the Flavian dynasty came an unexpected improvement in Jewish fortunes. The *fiscus Iudaicus* was reformed significantly by the newly installed emperor, and expectations that the Temple would now be rebuilt quickly followed. Within a Christian context, this apparent rehabilitation of Jewish status raises afresh the question of who possesses the covenant.

---

23 A popular view which has been defended recently by J.J. Gunther, "The Epistle of Barnabas and the Final Rebuilding of the Temple," *JSJ* 7 (1976), 143-51.

24 J.B. Lightfoot, *Apostolic Fathers*, vol. 2, pt. 1 (London: Macmillan, 1890), 506-507.

For Barnabas a change in Roman policy, whether related to the *fiscus Iudaicus* or to the Temple, would threaten to undermine his community's understanding of the covenant by obscuring the political signs of Christian supersession. When some members of his community concede that "the covenant is both theirs and ours" (4:6) we can guess that such a policy change has already begun to work its mischief. For Barnabas any suggestion of the continuity of Jewish covenantal claims is dangerously retrograde, and must be dealt with aggressively.

While Barnabas is dispirited by the events of the 90s, the Judaism he confronts is understandably buoyant. The 90s seem to have been a decade of self-conscious consolidation for the Jewish people. The rising power and prestige of the patriarchate under Gamaliel II, the increased use of the ban to enforce uniformity of belief, the "benediction against heretics," the canonization of scripture, and Aquila's fresh Greek translation—all have been dated to this period. These measures in themselves might seem to pose no small threat to the early church. But with the reform of the *fiscus Iudaicus* and the accompanying expectation that the Temple would be rebuilt, it is easy to imagine that Judaism would seem a formidable adversary and at the same time an attractive alternative to some Christians.[25]

Barnabas directs his polemical attack at two of Judaism's major institutions: the Temple, the reconstruction of which seems to be his most pressing concern, and the *Bet ha-midrash*, the principal vehicle for the rabbis' ascendancy as guarantors of accurate scriptural interpretation. Although for Barnabas the distinction between these two fronts blurs at times, each will be treated separately.

Polemic against the Temple

The Jewish hope that the Temple would be rebuilt is the most important reason for the epistle's composition and provides its basic structure. Not only is the Temple the first and last issue addressed by the author, but references to it also punctuate (often unexpectedly) the epistle as a whole. The rebuilding of the Temple is a sufficiently large concern that it surfaces, perhaps unconsciously, in the introduction. Barnabas tells his audience that they "ought to make a richer and deeper offering (*prosagein*) for fear of him" (1:7). Although it is not immediately obvious, *prosagein* is used here (cf. 2:9) in its LXX techni-

---

25 Some parts of the Johannine literature usually dated to the 90s may also reflect the resurgence of Judaism. See F.M. Braun, "La Lettre de Barnabé et l'Évangile de Saint Jean (simples reflections)," *NTS* 4 (1957-58), 119-24. For the attraction which Judaism stubbornly exercised over Christianity see M. Simon, *Verus Israel* (Paris: de Boccard, 1964).

cal sense of "sacrifice"[26] with the comparatives "richer and deeper" juxtaposed with Jewish practices. This introductory verse anticipates the criticisms of the Jewish cult which follow. God does indeed demand service, but not the service mistakenly practised by the Jews.

According to Barnabas, scripture plainly states that God has no need of sacrifice. The sacrificial system has been abolished (*katērgēsen*) in order that the "new law (*nomos*) of the Lord Jesus Christ, which is without yoke of necessity, might have its oblation not made by man" (2:6). So Barnabas cautions his audience to beware of succumbing to the folly and, it would seem, allure of Jewish cultic notions. God has given the Christians a proper understanding of scripture so that "we should not err like them, but seek how we may make our offering (*prosagōmen*) to him" (2:9).

Barnabas renews his attack on the Jewish cult in the introduction to his christological exposition (chap. 5). Christ's death is described in language appropriated from the sacrificial cult: he "endured to deliver up his flesh to corruption, that we should be sanctified by the remission of sin, that is, by his sprinkled blood" (5:1). The same motif is taken up in the typological treatment of the red heifer sacrifice (chap. 8), where the ashes of the heifer—a type of Christ—are sprinkled on the people "in order that they all be purified from their sins" (8:1). Even the spreading of the redemptive Good News is drawn allegorically from the sprinkling of the people with the ashes of the sacrificial victim (8:3).

The expectation that the Temple would be rebuilt is pressing enough that on occasion Barnabas smuggles it into the discussion even though his scriptural exposition does not require it. When equating Jesus with the "stone" mentioned in a group of biblical texts he adds parenthetically: "Is then our hope (*elpis*) on a stone? God forbid" (6:3), in obvious anticipation of his discussion of the Temple in chapter 16: "I will also speak with you concerning the Temple (*peri tou naou*), and show how the wretched men erred by putting their hope (*ēlpisan*) on the building . . ." (16:1).

Similarly, in his strained exegesis of a "land flowing with milk and honey," the Temple is again plainly in view: "For, my brethren, the habitation of our hearts is a shrine holy (*naos hagios*[27]) to the Lord" (6:15).

The Temple issue also intrudes into Barnabas' treatment of baptism. The Jews "will not receive the baptism that brings remission of sins, but they will build for themselves (*oikodomēsousin*)" (11.1). The object of "build for themselves" (a term used almost exclusively with reference to the Temple reconstruction[28]) either has been lost in

---

26 See K.L. Schmidt, *prosagō*, *TDNT* 1:131-33.

27 Not insignificantly, Barnabas accounts for 14 of the 18 usages of *naos* in the apostolic fathers (E.J. Goodspeed, *Index Patristicum* [Leipzig: Hinrichs, 1907]).

28 Ten of Barnabas' twelve usages of *oikodomeō* (and cognates) occur in chapter 16.

transmission or is to be supplied by the "cisterns of death" of the next verse. In either case, the proof-texts which follow show clearly that Christian baptism leading to the remission of sin is not contrasted with an analogous Jewish baptism, but rather with the expiatory function of the Temple. Barnabas claims that the Jews have committed two sins: "they have deserted me, the spring of life, and they have dug for themselves a cistern of death" (11:2). The scriptural citations which follow connect the "cistern of death" with the destruction of the Temple, not Jewish ritual immersion: "'Is my holy mountain Sinai a desert rock? For ye shall be as fledgling birds, fluttering about when they are taken away from the nest.' (4) And again the Prophet says, 'I will go before you and I will make mountains level, and I will break gates of brass and I will shatter bars of iron ...'" (11:3-4).

Although Isaiah's prophecies refer to Jerusalem only and not the Temple, it is likely that Barnabas believed the Temple was intended. The reference to the "holy mountain" (*to oros to hagios*) is suggestive of the Temple mount, while the "gates of brass" recalls the storied brass gates of the Herodian Temple.[29] These allusions might seem rather distant, but such allusions often spark Barnabas' exegesis as, for example, in the unambiguous proof for the Temple's final destruction in chapter 16: "Again, it was made manifest that the city and the temple and the people of Israel were to be delivered up. For the Scripture says, 'And it shall come to pass in the last days that the Lord shall deliver the sheep of his pasture, and the sheep fold, and their tower (*ton pyrgon*) to destruction'" (16:5). As with the proof-texts in chapter 11, there is nothing in this prophecy that explicitly relates to the Temple, yet it is clear from the context that it was so understood by Barnabas. Like the "gates of brass" of 11:14, the architectural connection of the "tower" (*ton pyrgon*) with the prominent tower of Antonia (*B.J.* 5: 238-46) may well explain Barnabas' choice of this text to illustrate the Temple's destruction.

For Barnabas the mediatory function of the Temple in effecting remission of sin no longer obtains. Christianity, through baptism, the blood of the cross, and even the "sprinkling" of the Good News, is the only means of redemption.

In chapter 16 Barnabas finally addresses the Temple issue directly: "I will also speak with you concerning the Temple (*peri tou naou*)" (16:1). The Jews have erred in putting their hope (*ēlpisan*) in a physical building. Instead of worshipping God in the Temple like the heathens, they should have placed their hope in him. A mixed quotation proves

---

29 The "brass gates," or "Nicanor's Gate(s)" as the Mishna calls them (*Šeqal.* 6:3; *Yoma* 3:10; *Sota* 1:5; *Mid.* 1:4, 2:3, 6; *Neg.* 14:8), was a source of considerable pride to Josephus (*B.J.* 1.201). For rabbinic traditions about the miraculous arrival of the gates, see *t. Yoma* 2:4; *b. Yoma* 38a; *y. Yoma* 3:10, 41a.

the vanity of Jewish hopes by stressing that God's proper abode is heaven. Barnabas then develops two exegetical points hinted at earlier: first, that the Jews have been delivered up to destruction (16:5), from which we are to infer that no legitimate temple is possible, and, second, that the notion of a temple is to be understood spiritually: "I find then that a temple exists" (16:7), but "this is a spiritual temple being built for the Lord" (16:10). By this transformative appropriation the author intends to prove that the Jewish hope in a new Temple, whether it is eventually realized or not, is without foundation. No temple of God can exist other than the spiritual temple which is the Christian believer.

Polemic against the *Bet Ha-midrash*

Barnabas' attack on the Temple is persuasive only insofar as one accepts the underlying premise of the epistle as a whole—Christians alone are capable of understanding God's will because, as heirs to the covenant, they have been vouchsafed the unique gift of interpreting scripture as God intended. Jewish exegetes, on the other hand, misinterpret scripture and as a consequence their exegetically derived practices are mistaken. In the context of a date in the 90s this polemic against Jewish exegesis is understandable. With the rise in power and influence of the rabbis came an accompanying rise in prestige of their exegetical institution—the *Bet ha-midrash*. At the turn of the first century Josephus could write that "the Pharisees . . . have the reputation of being unrivalled experts in our country's laws" (*Vita* 191; cf. *B.J.* 2:162). Barnabas recognized that this reputation as guarantors of correct interpretation posed a considerable danger for Christians, a danger which would only increase once the Temple was rebuilt. He therefore attempts to show that it is Christianity that interprets scripture as God intended, and it is Christian teachers like himself, and not the rabbis of the *Bet ha-midrash*, who should be recognized as the most trustworthy expositors (10:12). In short, it is Christian, not Jewish, exegesis which teaches the believer to act as God has ordained.

The intimate relationship between Christian exegesis and the right action can be seen in Barnabas' introductory remarks:

There are then three doctrines of the Lord: "the hope of life" is the beginning and end of our faith; righteousness is the beginning and end of judgement; love of joy and of gladness is testimony of the works of righteousness [*ergōn dikaiosynēs*]. (7) For the Lord has made known to us through the prophets things past and things present and has given us the first fruits of the taste of things to come; and when we see these things coming to pass one by one, as he said, we ought to make a richer and deeper offering for fear of him. (1:6-7)

The statement about Christian exegetical gifts is bracketed by references to right action: "works of righteousness" standing in contrast to

Jewish "works of evil," and with the "richer and deeper offering" of
the Christian standing in contrast to superficial Jewish cultic practice.
Christian exegesis interprets scripture as God intended, and this correct interpretation should lead directly to correct action. The negative
inference is also to be drawn: errant Jewish exegesis leads to errant
practice.

The relationship between exegetical gifts and right action is
plainly in evidence when Barnabas formally addresses the first issue on
his agenda, the sacrificial cult. Christians are urged to "seek out" (in the
LXX and Aquila *ekzētein* = *drš*[30]), that is "seek out scripturally," "the
ordinances of the Lord" (2:1) which have been hidden from the Jews
but revealed to the Christians: "For he has made plain to us through all
the Prophets that he needs neither sacrifices nor burnt-offerings nor
oblations" (2:4). To conclude the argument Barnabas writes: "We
ought to understand, if we are not foolish, the loving intention of our
Father, for he speaks to us wishing that we should not err like them
(*homoiōs*), but seek (*zētein*[31]) how we should make our offering to him"
(2:9). It is God's intention that scripture be properly understood by
Christians; therefore it is essential that they themselves interpret it so as
to avoid the mistaken conclusions of Jewish exegesis. The same view is
repeated in the next line: "We ought, therefore brethren, carefully to
enquire concerning our salvation, in order that the evil one (*ho ponēros*)
may not achieve a deceitful entry into us and hurl us away from our
life" (2:10). The "evil one" is likely a reference to the "evil angel"
(*angelos ponēros*) who, it is claimed elsewhere in the epistle (9:4), misled
the Jews into their literal practice of circumcision. The "deceitful
entry" of the "evil one" against which Christians must guard themselves
by "careful enquiry" might also be a veiled allusion to the error of
Jewish exegesis.

The second issue Barnabas addresses is Jewish fasting. The argument concludes in much the same way as the earlier argument against
the sacrificial cult: "The long-suffering one . . . made all things plain
to us beforehand that we should not be shipwrecked by conversion to
their law" (3:6). Once again the special gift of Christian exegesis is
offered as an antidote to exegetically derived Jewish practice. As in the
previous argument the warning against Jewish errors is followed by an
exhortation to utilize Christian interpretive gifts: "We ought, then, to
enquire earnestly into the things which now are, and seek out (*ekzētein*)
those which are able to save us" (4:1). This exhortation is immediately
followed by a further warning against drifting into Jewish practices
which may result from associating with Jews: "Let us then utterly flee

---

30   See H. Greeven, *ekzēteō*, *TDNT* 2:894-95.
31   LXX and Aquila also render *drš* by *zēteō*, a term which for Barnabas also seems to
     carry the identical force of *ekzēteō*. See H. Greeven, *zēteō*, *TDNT* 2:892-93.

from the works of lawlessness, lest the works of lawlessness overcome us . . . .(2) Let us give no freedom to our souls to have power to walk with sinners and wicked men, lest we be made like them (*homoiōthō-men*)" (4:1-2).

Similar views are advanced when Barnabas allegorizes Jewish dietary laws in chapter 10: "Moses received the three doctrines concerning food and thus spoke them in the spirit; but they received them as really referring to food owing to the lust of their flesh . . . . (11) See how well Moses legislated. (12) But how was it possible for them to understand or comprehend these things? But we having righteous understanding of them announce the commandments as the Lord wished" (10:9-12). Again Christian—and not Jewish—exegesis is the prerequisite for right action.

As already mentioned, Barnabas believes that Christians have been vouchsafed a unique gift to interpret scripture as a covenantal sign. So when in chapter 9 he comes to interpret the Jewish covenantal sign of circumcision he can easily collapse the two competing signs into one—the "true" circumcision of the believer is nothing other than the true understanding of revelation. God had repeatedly asked the Jews to hear his word but without success. Christians on the other hand can hear his voice clearly because their ears have been circumcised. The covenantal sign of Christian exegesis is the true circumcision: "The circumcision in which they trusted has been abolished. For he declared that circumcision was not of the flesh" (9:4). "So then he circumcised our hearing in order that we should hear the word and believe" (9:3).

As was the case in his polemic against the Temple, Barnabas is prepared to appropriate elements from the very institution he attacks. In chapter 10 he applauds the believer "who has not gone to the counsel (*boulē*) of the ungodly . . . and has not stood in the way of sinners . . . and has not sat in the seat of scorners" (10:10).[32] Then, employing sentiments one usually associates with the rabbinic academy, he urges Christians to associate instead "with those who meditate in their heart on the meaning of the word which they have received, with those who speak of and observe the ordinances of the Lord, with those who know that meditation is a work of gladness, and who ruminate on the words of the Lord" (10:11). Barnabas, much like his opponents, offers up the exegete as the model of the true believer.

In chapter 4 he warns his audience as follows: "Let us flee from all vanity, let us utterly hate the deeds of the path of wickedness. Do not by retiring apart live alone as if you were already made righteous" (4:10). Instead he counsels that Christians "come together (*synerchomenoi*) and

---

32   Cf. *m. 'Abot* 3:2, where R. Hananiah b. Teradyon, a contemporary of Barnabas, interprets the "seat of scorners" of Ps. 1:1 as two men who sit together and do not discuss words of Torah.

seek out [together] (*synzēteite*) the common good" (4:10). *Synerchomai* occurs on only two other occasions in the apostolic fathers, and there in liturgical contexts.[33] Is it then possible that when Barnabas suggests liturgical meetings to "expound together"[34] he is in effect championing an alternative exegetical institution, that of the Christian *Bet ha-midrash*?

We have seen that polemics against both the Temple and the *Bet ha-midrash* run through the epistle. In the work's final verses these two elements converge with surprising, and somewhat bizarre, results.

In Barnabas' view the Christian believer is the temple of God. God himself dwells in the Christian and prophesies through him, "by opening the door of the temple [that is the mouth] . . . (10) For he who desires to be saved looks not at the man, but at him who dwells and speaks in him, and is amazed at him, for he has never either heard him speak such words with his mouth, nor has he himself ever desired to hear them" (16:9-10).

The solutions generated in attacking the Jewish hope of a rebuilt Temple and the rise in power and prestige of the *Bet ha-midrash* have collapsed into one: the spiritual temple is in fact the ecstatic exegete of the Christian *Bet ha-midrash*.

Yet ironically, Barnabas himself bears little resemblance to this model of the ecstatic exegete. He is a teacher (*didaskalos*; 1:8), a functional title which, unlike his description of the ecstatic exegete, seems to carry formal status (1:8; 4:9). As a teacher/exegete he employs some of the formalized vocabulary of the *Bet ha-midrash*.[35] He does not create new and unexpected interpretations, but rather faithfully transmits what he has received (1:5; 4:9), and in so doing is aware enough of his audience's limitations that he tailors his discourse to their ability to understand (6:5). Barnabas is more nearly a teacher/exegete on the model of the very *Bet ha-midrash* he attacks.

This paper has attempted to show that the stridency of the epistle's anti-Judaism can best be understood against the historical backdrop of the 90s, when the Yavnean consolidation and an expectation that the Temple would be rebuilt combined to make Judaism a dangerously attractive alternative to Christianity. Barnabas' warnings not to associate with Jews, his exhortation that Christians themselves search the scriptures, and his repeated cautioning against "becoming like them,"

---

33 Ign. *Eph*. 13:1; 20:2 (Goodspeed, *Index*).
34 See J. Schneider, "*suzēteō*," *TDNT* 7:894-95. Also of interest is A. Schlatter's suggestion that *dwrs* lies behind Paul's use of *sunzētēs* in I Cor. 1:20 (*Paulus der Bote Jesu* [Stuttgart: 1934], cited by H. Conzelmann, *1 Corinthians* [Philadelphia: Fortress, 1975] 43, n. 32).
35 For tannaitic equivalents for expressions such as *ti legei*, *all' ereis*, *heuriskō*, see W. Bacher, *Die bibelexegetische Terminologie der Tannaiten*, *Die exegetische Terminologie der jüdischen Traditionsliteratur*, pt. 1 (Leipzig: Hinrichs, 1899).

all point to the likelihood that for some Christians the attraction of the *Bet ha-midrash* had already proven irresistible.[36] The character of the author is a testimony to just how threatening the resurgent Judaism of the 90s must have been. For in his own way, Barnabas, the teacher/exegete, appears to have fallen victim to the very attraction he warns his audience against—he has "become like them."

---

36   When Barnabas warns against being made like some who heap up sins saying "the covenant is both theirs and ours. It is ours" (4:6-7) we can perhaps infer that Judaism was prepared to accept gentile Christians. The question of the gentiles' place in the covenant was a live one during the tannaitic period. In *Mek. R. SbY.* (*Jethro* 19:1; Epstein and Melamed [eds.], 137) there is a discussion of whether the gentiles were also given the Torah at Sinai. Part of this discussion reads: "I said not: 'It is unto the seed of Jacob' (Is. 45:19)—[that is] it is yours" (cf. *Mek. R. I. Jethro* [Bah] 1; Laut. [ed.], 199).

3

Judaism of the Uncircumcised in Ignatius and Related Writers

Lloyd Gaston

The anti-Judaism which begins in the New Testament becomes much nastier in the writings of the early fathers and in the legislation of the post-Constantinian emperors. At least some of this development, however, must be understood as a misunderstanding by later generations of the polemic of earlier generations. At least some statements which were later understood to refer to Judaism or to Jews or to Jewish Christians were originally made to correct beliefs and practices of Gentile Christians.[1] Two developments were especially fateful. There was the struggle first to appropriate the LXX as Christian scripture without following its commandments, and then the struggle to subordinate this scripture to the emerging New Testament canon.[2] Much of the anti-Judaism of Justin and Tertullian and the *adversus Judaeos* literature may reflect something of this struggle.[3] There was also the necessity of forming and preserving the self-understanding of the church in the context of a society where Diaspora Judaism was flourishing and acknowledged and very attractive. Thus the virulence of a Chrysostom has as its primary target not Jews or Judaism as such but "a

---

1   "It may be possible to reconstruct the emphases of anti-Judaic disputes in such a way that the role of the *intra muros* debates noted above sheds light on the development of *extra muros* anti-Judaism." P. Richardson, "On the Absence of 'Anti-Judaism' in 1 Corinthians," in P. Richardson (ed.), *Anti-Judaism in Early Christianity*, vol. 1 (Waterloo: Wilfrid Laurier University Press, 1986).

2   See H. von Campenhausen, *The Formation of the Christian Bible* (London: Black, 1972).

3   Cf. the important work of D.P. Efroymson, *Tertullian's Anti-Judaism and its Role in his Theology* (University Microfilms, Temple University Ph.D., 1976); "The Patristic Connection" in A.T. Davies (ed.), *Antisemitism and the Foundations of Christianity* (New York: Paulist, 1979), 98-117; "Tertullian's Anti-Jewish Rhetoric: Guilt by Association," *USQR* 36 (1980), 25-37.

disease which is flourishing in the body of the church,"[4] and something similar could be said about the exegesis of Cyril of Alexandria.[5] We shall here examine an early phase of the phenomenon of Christian judaizing.

We begin with Ignatius, partly because he provides us with a title, and partly because he can help us to limit the scope of this inquiry to Western Asia Minor in the period around the turn from the first to the second century C.E.[6] Thanks to the work of A.T. Kraabel and others, we know from excavations and inscriptions something of the position of Judaism in this time and place.[7] It is also the area of an early spurt in the growth of the church.[8] There is the further advantage of avoiding major problems associated with other areas. I refer not only to early Syrian and Egyptian gnosticism but also to the vexed problems of the "Jewish Christianity" of certain gospel fragments and the sources of the pseudo-Clementines. On the other hand, the interpretation of Ignatius is disputed enough to provide us with some important issues.

It is necessary first to define how certain terms will be used in the following. The expression "Jewish Christianity" or some similar phrase is used in so many different ways as to make communication almost

---

4   Homily 1 against the Jews, p. 86 in W.A. Meeks and R.L. Wilken, *Jews and Christians in Antioch in the First Four Centuries of the Common Era* (Missoula: Scholars Press, 1978).
5   See R.L. Wilken, *Judaism and the Early Christian Mind* (New Haven: Yale University Press, 1971).
6   See the area studies of J. Weiss, *Earliest Christianity* (New York: Harper, 1959), 2:774-817; W. Bauer, *Orthodoxy and Heresy in Earliest Christianity* (Philadelphia: Fortress, 1971), 61-94; L. Goppelt, *Christentum und Judentum im ersten und zweiten Jahrhundert* (Gütersloh: Bertelsmann, 1954), 245-67; H. Koester, "GNOMAI DIAPHOROI," *Trajectories through Early Christianity* (Philadelphia: Fortress, 1971), 114-57, 143-57; and many articles by S.E. Johnson, including "Asia Minor and Early Christianity," in J. Neusner (ed.), *Christianity, Judaism and Other Greco Roman Cults* (Leiden: Brill, 1975), 2:77-145. U.B. Müller, *Zur frühchristlichen Theologiegeschichte; Judenchristentum und Paulinismus in Kleinasien an der Wende vom ersten zum zweiten Jahrhundert n. Chr.* (Gütersloh: Mohn, 1976), also confines his study to this area and period, but unfortunately he considers only Revelation and the Pastoral Epistles. While he correctly identifies the opponents in Revelation 2-3 and one front in the Pastorals as enthusiastic ultra-Paulinists, he also assumes that the other front reflected in the Pastorals is a Christian Judaism not unlike the theology of Revelation itself. One way to avoid facing an issue is to say "Über die judenchristliche Herkunft der Gegner kann heute eigentlich kein Streit mehr sein" [actually, there can be no dispute nowadays about the Jewish Christian origin of the opponents (in the Pastorals)] (58). Beginning with Ignatius may help us see the question from a new perspective.
7   See A.T. Kraabel, *Judaism in Western Asia Minor under the Roman Empire* (Dissertation, Harvard, 1968). It would be helpful if someone studied the Sibylline Oracles, Book III, 401-88, from the perspective of Asia Minor Judaism, as was done for Egypt in other parts of the book by J.J. Collins, *The Sibylline Oracles of Egyptian Judaism* (Missoula: Scholars, 1974). We can recall here the estimate by S. Baron that 20 per cent of the population of the eastern half of the Roman Empire were Jews, *A Social and Religious History of the Jews* (New York: Columbia University Press, 1937), 1:171, 370-72.
8   Evidence is found in the classical example of the letter of Pliny to Trajan.

impossible.[9] On the one hand, for Daniélou and others the term is so broad as to cover almost the entire second-century church and therefore becomes meaningless.[10] On the other hand, some definitions are stated in terms of such Christian doctrines as christology[11] or anti-Paulinism[12] as to make the adjective virtually irrelevant. I use the term here in the narrow sense defined by Kümmel[13] and Malina (who calls the phenomenon, wisely I believe, Christian Judaism).[14] I refer then to Christians who not only called themselves Jews but also called themselves that before their baptism. I refer to people who had and continued to have at least some relationship to the Sinai covenant and commandments. I refer to people who came from a community which could be identified as Jewish in some way and whose departure, if they left that community, could have been felt as a loss.[15]

On the other hand, I use the noun "judaizer"[16] and the verb "to judaize" as they are used in ancient texts to refer to the actions of Gentiles. The verb is intransitive, and while it can on occasion be used to describe the forced conversion of Gentiles to Judaism,[17] it more usually designates the adoption by Gentiles of certain Jewish customs without conversion.[18] Those who encourage others to "judaize" may

---

9 See S.K. Riegel, "Jewish Christianity: Definitions and Terminology," *NTS* 24 (1978), 410-15.
10 "Jewish Christianity should be understood to refer to the expression of Christianity in the thought forms of Later Judaism," *The Theology of Jewish Christianity* (London: Darton, Longman and Todd, 1964), 10. When R.N. Longenecker, *The Christology of Early Jewish Christianity* (London: SCM, 1970), 18, speaks of Matthew, John, Hebrews, James, 1-3 John, 1-2 Peter, Jude, and Revelation as "addressed to Jewish Christians or to potentially interested Jews," it is not his definition but his concept which is too broad.
11 So the tradition from Irenaeus to H. Lietzmann, *A History of the Early Church* (New York: Meridian, 1949).
12 G. Strecker, *Das Judenchristentum in den Pseudoklementinen* (Berlin: Akademie, 1958), and Bauer, *Orthodoxy*, 241-85; G. Lüdemann, "Zum Antipaulinismus im frühen Christentum," *EvT* 40 (1980), 437-55.
13 "das der heidenchristlichen Grosskirche vorauf-und parallellaufende palästinische Judenchristentum," *RGG* 3d edition, 3:967-72.
14 B.J. Malina, "Jewish Christianity or Christian Judaism: Toward a Hypothetical Definition," *JSJ* 7 (1976), 46-57. Note that this is the phrase also in modern Hebrew.
15 I have attempted the beginning of a description of early Christian Judaism using only the Pauline epistles as a source in "Paul and Jerusalem," in P. Richardson and J.C. Hurd (eds.), *From Jesus to Paul: Studies in Honour of Francis Wright Beare* (Waterloo: Wilfrid Laurier University Press, 1984), 61-72. Using those minimal data as criteria, one could then add to the material from the Synoptic tradition. The Jewishness of later so-called "Jewish Christianity" should then be studied anew.
16 Council of Laodicea, Canon 29.
17 Esther 8:17 LXX; Josephus, *B.J.* 2.454, in both cases done out of fear. This is certainly not the normal word for "convert to Judaism" in either a transitive or intransitive sense.
18 Gal. 2:14; Josephus, *B.J.* 2.463; Plutarch, *Cic.* 7:6; Acts of Pilate 2:1; Council of Laodicea, Canon 29. Later the word becomes completely detached from Judaism and refers to "heretics who deny the divinity of Christ" (Lampe, *A Patristic Greek Lexicon*, s.v.). We leave Ign. *Magn.* 10:3 aside for the moment.

themselves be Jews or Christian Jews or Gentiles, but for the sake of terminological clarity they should never for that reason be called judaizers.[19]

Ignatius

Ignatius, bishop of a city with a large and influential Jewish population, wrote in haste to five churches, some of which he also had visited, in Western Asia Minor, an area also with a large and influential Jewish population. Nevertheless, any discussion of the relationship between the church and the synagogue will have to be left to other members of the seminar, for there is nothing of the sort in Ignatius.[20] Instead there is reference to certain "heresies," one of which is usually called that of the docetists and the other that of the judaizers. There is debate about whether these heresies reflect the situation in Antioch[21] or the situations in the churches addressed.[22] Even more important is the debate on whether Ignatius is fighting against two separate groups[23] or one group combining both "heresies."[24] If we are convinced that there is only one group, and that in Asia, then a further question concerns whether or not these people should be called Christian Jews.

P.J. Donahue, in the most recent contribution to the subject, believes that the Ignatian "heretics" were Christian Jews. He writes: "Ignatius appeals to a kerygmatic summary not to justify his christology but to justify his rejection of the Law . . . in the context of his dispute with Jewish Christians, such an appeal simply underscores the obsolescence of Judaism . . . . It is the Law which is the fundamental issue

---

19 This distinction should be maintained even if those who encourage others to judaize may for themselves also be Gentile judaizers.

20 "It is significant, moreover, that there is no controversy against Judaism in its orthodox form in the letters of Ignatius, in spite of the fact that the author comes from a city where there was a numerous and respected Jewish colony." H. Riesenfeld, "Reflexions on the Style and the Theology of St. Ignatius of Antioch," *Studia Patristica* 4 (Berlin: Akademie, 1961), 312-22, 313.

21 J. Weiss, *Christianity*; W. Bauer, *Orthodoxy*; V. Corwin, *St. Ignatius and Christianity in Antioch* (New Haven: Yale University Press, 1960); P.J. Donahue, "Jewish Christianity in the Letters of Ignatius of Antioch," *V.C.* 32 (1978), 81-93.

22 E. Molland, "The Heretics Combatted by Ignatius of Antioch," *JEH* 5 (1954), 1-6; L.W. Barnard, *Studies in the Apostolic Fathers and Their Background* (Oxford: Blackwell, 1966), 19-30; C.K. Barrett, "Jews and Judaizers in the Epistles of Ignatius," in R. Hamerton-Kelly and R. Scroggs (eds.), *Jews, Greeks and Christians* (Leiden: Brill, 1976), 220-44.

23 C.C. Richardson, *The Christianity of Ignatius of Antioch* (New York: Columbia University Press, 1935); V. Corwin, *Ignatius*; P.J. Donahue, "Jewish Christianity."

24 J.B. Lightfoot, *The Apostolic Fathers, Part II: S. Ignatius, S. Polycarp* (London: MacMillan, 1885); E. Molland, "Heretics;" L.W. Barnard, *Studies*; C.K. Barrett, "Jews and Judaizers."

which separates Ignatius from his Jewish-Christian opponents."[25] But all of this is to read into Ignatius an outmoded view of Paul's struggles in Galatians! The fact that the word *nomos* occurs only twice in Ignatius, once as a positive witness ("They were not persuaded by the prophecies or the law of Moses or the gospel or, thus far, our own individual sufferings" *Smyrn.* 5:1), and once in the phrase "the law of Jesus Christ" (*Magn.* 2; "the commandments of Jesus Christ" *Eph.* 9:2), hardly speaks for Donahue's thesis. Similarly, when V. Corwin wants to understand one front as Christian Jews in Antioch heavily influenced from Qumran, she is forced into the strange concession: "They are not orthodox Jews, for they do not practice circumcision."[26] Rather than continuing our catalogue of contortions, let us turn to the principal texts themselves. Only two passages have been understood to refer to judaizers.

Ignatius had visited the church in Philadelphia, and it probably is in reference to something he observed there that he wrote the fascinating sentence: "But if any one interpret Judaism to you do not listen to him; for it is better to hear Christianity from a man having circumcision than Judaism from an uncircumcised [man]" (*Phld.* 6:1). If the first man may refer generally to someone from the past such as Paul, the second one is a real person in Philadelphia, a Gentile, whose teachings can be called either by himself or by Ignatius "Judaism." Since phrases like "the wicked arts and snares of the prince of this world" are really not very helpful in determining the nature of the teaching, let us look at the report of an actual confrontation: "I heard some saying, 'If I do not find [something] in the archives, I do not believe [it] in the gospel,' and when I said to them 'It is written [in scripture],' they answered me, 'That is the question'" (*Phld.* 8:2). Ignatius is not the best exegete of what would later be called the Old Testament, and it seems that he lost this argument. Instead he refers once more to Jesus' cross and death and resurrection, as he always does against the docetists. If we are allowed to connect the two passages, it seems that the "Judaism" of Ignatius's uncircumcised, Gentile opponents consists only in their ability to argue their docetic case from the LXX in a way that he cannot refute.

Ignatius did not personally visit the church in Magnesia, but he spoke with their representatives in Smyrna before writing. The warnings are in chapters 8-11:

For if we are living until now according to Judaism, we confess that we have not received grace. For the divine prophets lived according to Christ Jesus. (8:1-2)

---

25   P.J. Donahue, "Jewish Christianity," 87.
26   V. Corwin, *Ignatius*, 58. She is anticipated in this by W. Bauer, *Orthodoxy*, 88, who speaks of "a Jewish Christianity that apparently had abandoned its most offensive demands" and notes that "it can even include the uncircumcised."

If then those who walked in ancient customs came to newness of hope, no longer Sabbatizing but living according to the Lord's Day, on which also our life arose through him and his death—which some deny . . . . (9:1)

It is monstrous to talk of Jesus Christ and to judaize. For Christianity did not believe in Judaism, but Judaism in Christianity. (10:3)

I wish to warn you not to fall into the snare of vain doctrine but to be fully convinced of the birth and passion and resurrection which took place at the time of the procuratorship of Pontius Pilate; for these things were truly and surely done by Jesus Christ. (11:1)

The "Judaism" of which Ignatius complains here again has a docetic christology and is the opposite of the witness of the prophets. Since for Ignatius the prophets were all Christian, it may be that it was the ancient prophets who ceased to keep the Sabbath, as Molland argues,[27] but it is more reasonable to think of contemporary schismatics who hold their own Eucharist apart from the bishop (4:1), that is, on the Sabbath rather than on Sunday. I hardly think that makes them Christian Jews.[28] Of course Ignatius also refers to "strange doctrines and ancient myths" (8:1) and to "evil leaven, which has grown old and sour" (10:2), but nothing but unconscious presuppositions[29] would suggest that these are apt ways for Ignatius to characterize Judaism. In conclusion, then, if we are allowed to combine the situations in the various letters, it seems that Ignatius encountered a group of Asian Gentile Christians with a docetic christology and a disinclination to express the unity of the church around a single bishop and Eucharist. That in two of the letters Ignatius chooses to refer to what are to him intolerable heretics as "judaizers" and their teaching as "Judaism" probably has to do more with their use of the LXX to support their doctrines than with their Christian worship on the Sabbath. The fact remains that this "Judaism" is taught by the uncircumcised.[30]

---

27 E. Molland, "Heretics," 3.
28 Note that *Ign. Smyrn.* 1:2 says nothing whatsoever about the composition of the specific church in Smyrna.
29 "Judaism with its Law is the old, the sour, the evil," P.J. Donahue, "Jewish Christianity," 88.
30 "The 'judaizers' were apparently not born Jews but Gentiles . . . . They are thus gnostics of non-Jewish origin, but with a Jewish secret wisdom—just as, for example, Saturninus developed his doctrine of man from Gen. 1:25" (J. Weiss, *Christianity*, 765). "The judaizers of Ignatius are uncircumcised Gentiles and hence no real Jews . . . (holding) a heresy combining both elements of gnostic docetism and Gentile Judaism" (C.C. Richardson, *Ignatius*, 53, 84). "This uncircumcised Judaism, therefore, cannot be any kind of a Jewish Christian Movement" (E. Schweizer, "Christianity of the Circumcised and Judaism of the Uncircumcised," in Hamerton-Kelly, *Jews, Greeks and Christians*, 245-60). "It is the *Judaeo*-Christians, Christians adopting Jewish practices, not *Jewish*-Christians, i.e., those of Jewish origins, who attract Ignatius' ire" (Meeks and Wilken, *Antioch*, 20). Note the need for some terminological clarity.

Cerinthus

At about the time Ignatius travelled under guard through Western Asia Minor there lived in Ephesus a rather shadowy figure named Cerinthus. He is a good example of the tendency of the church to see Jews where none are present. Irenaeus says of him:

> A certain Cerinthus, then, in Asia taught that the world was not made by the Supreme God but by a certain Power highly separated and far removed from that Principality who transcended the universe and which is ignorant of the one who is above all, God. He suggested that Jesus was not born of a virgin [because that seemed to him impossible], but that he was the son of Joseph and Mary in the same way as all other men but he was more versed in righteousness, prudence and wisdom than other men.[31]

The fathers loved to line their heretics up in genealogies; because of the first statement, Cerinthus gets put in a line with the early Syrian gnostics Menander and Saturninus. Because of a superficial similarity of the second statement to what is reported about the christology of the Ebionites, Cerinthus also gets put in a line with the followers of "Ebion."[32] It is important to recognize, however, that Epiphanius is the first to call him a Christian Jew and even he is hard put to it to explain how someone could live by a law which he thought was given by evil angels. Nevertheless, we still frequently hear references[33] to the famous Christian Jew Cerinthus. It is my conviction that the gnosticizing Christian Jews of Asia ought to be removed from all our history books and put back into the patristic polemical fantasy where they have their only real home.

Asia Minor

A.T. Kraabel's important study *Judaism in Western Asia Minor under the Roman Empire* has unfortunately still not been revised and published.

---

31 *Adv. Haer.* 1.26.1; cited from A.F.J. Klijn and G.J. Reinink, *Patristic Evidence for Jewish-Christian Sects* (Leiden: Brill, 1973), 103.

32 See Klijn and Reinink, *Jewish-Christian Sects*, 8-12, 68, and earlier, C. Schmidt, *Gespräche Jesu mit seinen Jüngern nach der Auferstehung* (Leipzig: Hinrichs, 1919), 403-52.

33 The most recent is H. Koester, *Introduction to the New Testament*, vol. 2 (Philadelphia: Fortress, 1982), 204: "Cerinthus was active in Asia Minor; he advocated gnostic teaching, but seems to have been a Jewish Christian who insisted upon circumcision." This is connected with the "Jewish Christian syncretism" of the opponents in Revelation (204) and Colossians (265), and the "Jewish Christian gnosticism" of the opponents of Ignatius (286) and the Pastorals (304). The prevalence of the concept that Cerinthus was a Christian Jew seems to go back to an influential article by G. Bardy, "Cérinthe," *RB* 30 (1921), 344-73.

Two important conclusions can be stated here. First, Anatolian Jews were well established, independent, numerous, self-confident, and open to Hellenistic society without any compromising of their understanding of Judaism. Asian Judaism must have cast a powerful shadow for the early church to grow under, both in a negative (Melito of Sardis, letter to Diognetus) and positive (Gentile Christian judaizers) sense. Second, "'Jewish Christianity' in the technical sense . . . is a rare thing in Asia Minor."[34] That means that the church related to the synagogue only at a distance if at all. Asian Christianity shares of course the Jewish matrix of the whole church, in Daniélou's sense, but we find little direct influence in Asia. There are certain elements of Asian Christianity, such as millenarianism and Montanism, the prominence of women in positions of authority, angels, and other mediators, often ascribed to Jewish influence, which Kraabel argues can be better explained from Anatolian culture. Rather than looking for parallels from Qumran, we would all be well advised to turn instead to Nilsson's classic study.[35] Other members of the seminar can deal with external polemic in the Asian church. I would like to point to those writers and movements which have no explicit connection with the synagogue outside or Christian Jews inside.

We found in Ignatius no references to Jews or Christian Jews and very little to the LXX but only a kerygmatic Christian tradition directed against docetists. The same is true of Polycarp's letter and of the three letters of John.[36] The Acts of Paul represent a very interesting aspect of Asian Christian piety[37] but tell us nothing about any relationship to Judaism. 1 Peter is concerned about the relationship of the church to the state—not the synagogue—and although the author does use the LXX to appropriate for the church language originally speaking of Israel, it is not in a polemical context at all. Jude and 2 Peter are very polemical but the polemic is directed inwards completely, and it is perhaps significant that the opponents are named after such Biblical Gentiles as Cain, Balaam, the Sodomites, etc. In all of these writings Judaism is completely ignored, perhaps prudently from their minority

---

34   Kraabel, *Asia Minor*, 151.
35   M.P. Nilsson, *Geschichte der griechischen Religion*: 2, *Die hellenistische und römische Zeit* (Munich: Beck, 1961).
36   Recent research on the Fourth Gospel would locate it in a Christian Jewish congregation, but its Judaism has nothing to do with judaizing (in either sense) nor with gnosticism (even if the gnostics were able to use it well for their own purposes). In any case it does not fit within an Asian context but was composed most likely in Syria (So W.G. Kümmel; Alexandria, proposed by J.L. Martyn, is very improbable). The letters, on the other hand, may possibly be directed to Asian congregations, in which case only "the elder" is likely to represent Christian Judaism (cf. Müller, *Judenchristentum*, 29-30).
37   See S.L. Davies, *The Revolt of the Widows; the Social World of the Apocryphal Acts* (Carbondale: Southern Illinois University Press, 1980).

perspective. Even such famous Christian Jews as John (which one?), Philip (which one?) and his daughters, and Aristion, the disciple of the Lord, may have more to do with Asia establishing a line of succession to the earliest church than with any significant migration,[38] and there is no reason at all to connect Papias with Jewish Christianity.[39] Although it was originally planned, it seems unnecessary to devote much time here to the situation of Colossians. Especially since the work of Lohse and Schweizer,[40] it is no longer necessary to argue that the Colossians "heresy" has nothing to do with the Torah or with Christian Jews but is perfectly at home in Anatolian Gentile Christianity. Perhaps the time is not yet ripe to say something similar about Galatians, although that is certainly at the back of my mind.

We also found that Ignatius called the practices and/or views of certain Gentile opponents "Judaism" and the people "judaizers." We do not know whether or not they would have called themselves that. In any case, as M. Simon says, "C'est au coeur de l'Asie Mineur, en Phrygie et en Galatie, que se manifest le plus clairement, en dehors de la Palestine et de la Syrie, le christianisme judaïsant."[41] The best evidence comes from the Council of Laodicea, whose Canon 29 says that "Christians must not judaize by resting on the Sabbath, but must work on that day, rather honouring the Lord's Day; and if they can, resting then as Christians. But if any shall be found to be judaizers, let them be anathema from Christ." That the practice was widespread is shown by another, contradictory Canon 16, "The Gospels are to be read on the Sabbath, with the other Scriptures." That is, Christians are warned not to worship on the Sabbath, but if they do it anyway, they are at least to read the gospels as well. The judaizing which the Council condemns seems to have been a self-conscious deliberate imitation of the attractive synagogue.[42] It is doubtful that such people would accept the

---

38 Similar in intent to the Pella legend, on which see G. Lüdemann, "The Successors of Pre-70 Jerusalem Christianity: A Critical Evaluation of the Pella-Tradition," in E.P. Sanders (ed.), *Jewish and Christian Self-Definition*, vol. 1 (London: SCM, 1980), 161-73. A massive post-70 migration of Christian Jews to Asia as suggested by E. Schwartz and K. Holl (cf. H. Lietzmann, *History*, 1:189f.) cannot be supported by the evidence.

39 Even if "the elders," to whose tradition Papias appeals, may be itinerant Christian Jews.

40 E. Lohse, *Colossians and Philemon* (Philadelphia: Fortress, 1971); E. Schweizer, *Der Brief an die Kolosser* (Zurich: Neukirchener, 1976), and his articles cited on p. 17. Cf. also H. Weiss, "The Law in the Epistle to the Colossians," *CBQ* 34 (1972), 294-314.

41 *Verus Israel; Etudes sur les relations entre Chrétiens et Juifs dans l'Empire Romain (135-425)* (Paris: Boccard, 1964), 382. The whole chapter, "Les judaïsants dans l'Église," 356-93, is important.

42 Cf. also Canons 37 and 39, concerning participation in Jewish feasts, including Passover, and perhaps Canon 7, against the Novatians, Photinians and Quartodecimans. Not relevant, however (pace Simon), are Canons 35, against the worship of angels, and 36, against the use of magical amulets, for *phulaktērion* clearly does not refer here to *tefillin*, in spite of Matt. 23:5.

designation of judaizers, although they might have tried to appropriate the distinguished name of Judaism. We do not know what the attitude of the synagogue was to this imitation by Gentile judaizers. Incidentally, there is also considerable evidence of non-Christian Gentile judaizing in Asia Minor, seen most clearly in the cult of the Hypsistarioi and the Lydian God Sabbatistes.[43] In terms of earlier Christian movements, the Quartodecimans followed the Jewish calendar and of course were accused of judaizing: the lost writing of Clement of Alexandria against them was called *Ecclesiastical Canon against the Judaizers* (Eus. *H.E.* 6. 13, 3). I have not found but could imagine the accusation of judaizing being made against the Montanists, and would also find it probable that Marcion thought of his opponents as judaizers, simply because they read the LXX as scripture as did Ignatius's opponents. We find then in Asia Minor no Christian Jews but a propensity for imitating some aspects of Judaism on the part of some which was castigated as judaizing by the church authorities.

Revelation and the Pastorals

Can the Judaism of the uncircumcised we know from Ignatius also be used to cast light on earlier Asian writings? I believe that it can and will discuss two in descending order of probability. Shortly before Ignatius wrote his seven letters to the Asian churches, John did the same to a list with some overlap with Ignatius. In the letters of Revelation 2-3 we hear that people referred to by the names of the traditional enemies of Israel, Balaam and Jezebel, are encouraging Christians "to eat food sacrificed to idols and to practice immorality" (2:14, 20). It is assumed by most, probably for good reason, that the Nicolaitans designate the same group (2:6, 15). In addition to such libertine practice, we also hear about the "teaching" (2:14, 15, 20, 24) of these people, but the only example given has to do with "knowing the deep things of Satan" (2:24). While it is probable that they would have said rather "the deep things of God" (cf. 1 Cor. 2:10), it is at least conceivable that they are well down the road toward gnosticism and we should take John at his word. Again as with Ignatius the question of a two-front polemic is raised.[44] The reference to a "synagogue of Satan" (2:9; 3:9; cf. 2:13) might suggest rather a single group, and certainly this hypothesis is simpler. It may be that these Gentile gnosticizing libertines actually called their

---

43 See Nilsson, *Geschichte*, 662-67.
44 See E. Schüssler Fiorenza, "Apocalyptic and Gnosis in the Book of Revelation," *JBL* 92 (1973), 565-81, who claims two groups: Gentile libertinists related to the Corinthian theology and local Jews. This is at least better than Koester's attempt ("GNOMAI," 148-49) to speak of judaizing gnostics, for even if they should be Jews there is no evidence of judaizing.

group that, or it may be that again John only indulges in name calling. But in any case, the people involved are Gentiles, for we have to take John seriously when he refers to them as people "who say that they are Jews and they are not [but they are lying]" (2:9; 3:9). Just as in Philadelphia and Magnesia a few years later, so here in Philadelphia and Smyrna we find uncircumcised Gentiles falsely referring to themselves as Jews. John denied the claim, just as he denies their self-designation as apostles (2:2). Once more, we are dealing in Revelation with an inner-Christian polemic against the Judaism of the uncircumcised.[45]

The Pastoral Epistles may speak in the voice of an Aegean Greek complaining about some aspects of church life in the Asian interior. Insofar as the polemic is not just rhetorical,[46] we learn the following about the "opponents": They speculate about myths (1 Tim. 1:4; 4:7; 2 Tim. 4:4; Titus 1:14) and genealogies (1 Tim. 1:4; Titus 3:9). They are excessively ascetic with respect to marriage, food, and wine (1 Tim. 4:3-5; 5:23). They say that the resurrection has already occurred (2 Tim. 2:18). They speak much more highly about the authority of women than the Pastor thinks appropriate (1 Tim. 2:11-15; 5:4; 2 Tim. 3:6-7; Titus 2:5).[47] They teach something they call Gnosis (1 Tim. 6:20). All of this fits more or less with what we know of the situation in Asia Minor at the beginning of the second century, and there would be no problem if we did not have other references which identify the "opponents" as Jews. They (assuming once more a unified group) are also called "those of the circumcision" (Titus 1:10),[48] or "Jewish" (Titus 1:14), or "teachers of the law" (1 Tim. 1:7; cf. Titus 3:9). The explicit references to circumcision and the Law make an Ignatian solution impossible. It looks like we have a strange hybrid, people who are really Jews or Christian Jews holding views otherwise characteristic of Asian Gentile Christianity. The simplest and perhaps the best solution is the literary one proposed by W. Bauer: "It appears to me," he writes, "to be more convincing to understand the peculiar heresy combatted in the Pastorals from the perspective of the mentality of the pseudonymous letter writer—as 'Paul' he must deal with the 'teachers of the law' and

---

45 U.B. Müller (*Judenchristentum*, 34-35, 46-50) makes a good case for understanding the author as an itinerant Christian Jewish prophet from Syria. He is in any case, as Müller emphasizes, not part of an Asian congregation, nor do we find in his work any evidence of Christian Jewish congregations in Asia. The opponents attacked in the letters are hyper-Pauline enthusiasts (pp. 21-26), accused of idolatry and *porneia* in terms of traditional anti-Gentile polemic.

46 See R.J. Karris, "The Background and Significance of the Polemic of the Pastoral Epistles," *JBL* 92 (1973), 549-64; M. Dibelius and H. Conzelmann, *The Pastoral Epistles* (Philadelphia: Fortress, 1972), 65-67; U.B. Müller, *Judenchristentum*, 55-56.

47 See D. MacDonald, "Virgins, Widows, and Paul in Second Century Asia Minor," *SBL Seminar Papers* 1979 (Missoula: Scholars Press, 1979), 1:169-84.

48 Note how quickly these people turn into Cretans, who give testimony against themselves that Cretans are "liars, evil beasts, lazy gluttons" (1:12).

the 'circumcision' but as a second century churchman, he opposes gnosticism."[49] The Christian Jews of the Pastorals then are as fictive as the books and parchments of 2 Tim. 4:13. They look back to the Paul of Acts and not real people in later Asia.[50]

Conclusion

We conclude by referring back to the specific concerns of this seminar. It is clear that Judaism, particularly in the space and time under consideration, has room within itself for a great variety of Judaisms. Nevertheless, not all Judaisms are Jewish, and it is unfair for Jews to be tarred with the brush of Gentile Christian judaizers. It seems that some uncircumcised Christians in Asia referred to their own teaching and practice as "Judaism." It is even clearer that other Asian Christians used the term "judaizing" as a disparaging way to refer to their opponents. One would have to trace the entire history of the church to see whether such references have in fact been the cause of slander of Jews. This paper could not do that, but it did find a number of ghosts in contemporary scholarly literature. I refer in particular to the judaizing,[51] gnosticizing[52] Christian Jew. Whatever be the case elsewhere, such a creature did not exist in Asia Minor and should be dropped from our textbooks. Recognition of the phenomenon of a Judaism of the uncircumcised can help us revise for the better our understanding of Christian origins; it can also remove some of the misunderstandings from the long tradition of Christian anti-Judaism.

49 Bauer, *Orthodoxy,* 89. Cf. also J.L. Houlden, *The Pastoral Epistles* (Harmondsworth: Penguin, 1976), 43, who says, seemingly independently of Bauer, "It is far from obvious that there is much reality in the Jewish quality of these heretics. This is not their dominant characteristic, and the reference may even be a piece of Pauline stage-setting." The Pastorals can best be understood as somewhere on a trajectory between Acts (S.G. Wilson, *Luke and the Pastoral Epistles* [London: SPCK, 1979]) and Polycarp (H. von Campenhausen, "Polykarp von Smyrna und die Pastoralbriefe," *Aus der Frühzeit des Christentums* [Tübingen: Mohr, 1964], 197-252).
50 U.B. Müller (*Judenchristentum,* 67-74) characterizes the opponents as Pauline enthusiasts who cannot yet be called gnostic. His attempt to portray another front, however, comparable to the Christian Jewish theology of Revelation (58-67) cannot be said to have succeeded. On the contrary, on his own showing, the opponents in the Pastorals are much more like the opponents in Rev. 2-3 and therefore not like the author of Revelation.
51 In the modern sense of one who would impose Torah on Gentiles.
52 Although gnosticism proper did not come within the purview of this paper, I refer to the plea made some years ago by H. Jonas in J.P. Hyatt (ed.), *The Bible in Modern Scholarship* (Nashville: Abingdon, 1965), 279-93, not to associate too quickly Judaism and gnosticism. In both cases we need to be a bit more precise in our definitions.

4

Marcion and the Jews

Stephen G. Wilson

About 150 C.E. Justin claimed that Marcion's teaching had spread throughout the whole human race (*Apol.* 20.5-6) and fifty years or so later Tertullian made much the same observation (*Marc.* 5.19). The number of tracts written to combat Marcionite influence (most no longer extant), the extraordinary length of Tertullian's *Adversus Marcionem*—the longest and one of the more tedious things he wrote—and the fact that Celsus knew of only two branches of Christianity, one of them Marcionite (Origen *Cels.* 2.6, 5.54, 6.57, 7.25-26), all reinforce the view that during its heyday in the second century the Marcionite church was one of the dominant forms of Christianity. In some places and at some times it was probably the main form of Christianity known to the inhabitants,[1] and even beyond the second century the influence of Marcion's views continued to be felt. Theodoret, a Syrian bishop in the mid-fifth century, announces with some pride his success in cleaning up pockets of Marcionite resistance in several local villages (*Ep.* 81, 113).

The attitude of the Marcionites towards Judaism is thus an important component in the relationship between Jews and Christians in the second century. Surprisingly, however, this aspect of Marcion's thought has received little attention. There may be a variety of reasons for this. Perhaps Marcion's anti-Judaism is considered to be so obvious and so extreme that it scarcely warrants analysis. There is some truth, too, in the observation that "the real problem for him is posed not by

---

1 See W. Bauer, *Orthodoxy and Heresy In Earliest Christianity* (Philadelphia: Fortress, 1971), ch. 1, on Edessa, and the corrections by H. Koester, "GNOMAI DIAPHOROI: The Origin and Nature of Diversification in the History of Early Christianity," in H. Koester and J.M. Robinson, *Trajectories Through Early Christianity* (Philadelphia: Fortress, 1971), 114-57.

the Jews but—as he saw it—by judaizing Christians."[2] That is, Marcion
was involved in an inner-church dispute, so that problems such as his
connection with gnosticism, his eccentric Paulinism, and his innovative
canon-making have naturally dominated scholarly discussion. It was
moreover Marcion's opponents who won the day and their attitude
towards Jews and Judaism which most influenced the subsequent history of Christianity and, for this reason, D.P. Efroymsen in his recent
thoughtful essay[3] concentrates upon the anti-Jewish strain in the
Catholic reaction to Marcion's teachings. It is also common for Marcion
to be lumped together with the gnostics and, despite well-known differences, to become part of the broader problem of the relationship
between gnosticism and Judaism which, I am happy to say, it is not my
duty to unravel at this point.

On a more general level it is perhaps fair to add that the study of
any theme connected with Marcion is a daunting prospect. On the one
hand, all the evidence which has survived is both secondary and hostile
and this makes any discussion of Marcion an uncertain business.
Moreover, the most important ancient witness to Marcion is Tertullian's lengthy and rather pedantic tract which, while scoring some
telling points and relieved occasionally by a welcome touch of sarcasm,
requires of the reader a considerable degree of concentration simply to
make it through from beginning to end. On the other hand, no discussion of Marcion can fail to be somewhat cowed by the classic work of
modern times published by A. von Harnack in 1921.[4] The result of
some fifty years of labour, into which he put more of himself than into
any other of his voluminous works, it is a brilliant example of collation,
synthesis, and sympathetic portrayal which leaves his successors with
the feeling that there is little to do but pick over the bones. Harnack's
work is, of course, flawed. Inevitably, it reflects the predispositions of
both the man and the liberal theology which he represents. Thus there
is a natural affinity between Harnack's view that the simple gospel of

---

2   K.H. Rengstorf and S. von Kortzfleisch, *Kirche und Synagoge: Handbuch zur Geschichte
    von Christen und Juden* (Stuttgart: E. Klett, 1968), 1:82 n. 139.
3   D.P. Efroymsen, "The Patristic Connection," in A.T. Davies (ed.), *Antisemitism and the
    Foundations of Christianity* (New York: Paulist, 1979), 98-117, especially 100-108.
4   A. von Harnack, *Marcion: Das Evangelium von Fremden Gott* (Leipzig: J.C. Hinrichs,
    1921), *TU* 45. In *Neue Studien zu Marcion* (Leipzig: J.C. Hinrichs, 1923), Harnack
    reviewed some of his reviewers. Some of this material was later incorporated into a
    second edition (1924) which was not available to me. The two major studies since
    then are J. Knox, *Marcion and the New Testament* (Chicago: Chicago University Press,
    1942), and E.C. Blackman, *Marcion and His Influence* (London: SPCK, 1948). See too
    the significant article by B. Aland, "Marcion: Versuch einer neuen Interpretation,"
    ZTK 70 (1973), 420-47. D.L. Balas, "Marcion Revisited: A 'Post-Harnack' Perspec-
    tive," in W.E. March (ed.), *Texts and Testaments: Critical Essays on the Bible and the Early
    Church Fathers* (San Antonio: Trinity University Press, 1980), 95-108, arrived too late
    for full inclusion in the discussion. In general he both concurs with and adds to my
    observations on Harnack.

Jesus had been obscured by a complex overlay of christological dog-
matism and Marcion's notion of a Jewish-Christian conspiracy which
had successfully misrepresented the teaching of both Jesus and Paul.
The radicalism and freshness of Marcion's teaching, and the heroic
individuality which Harnack believed to be rooted in a profound religious experience also greatly appealed to him even though he recognized the distortion involved. He himself, ironically, was far from
comfortable when the closest thing to a Marcionite revolution took
place in his own day with the publication of Barth's commentary on
Romans.[5] It is well known, too, that Harnack went to some lengths to
defend his view that while Marcion's rejection of the Old Testament
was rightly resisted in the second century, the beginning of the twen-
tieth century was a propitious moment for its revival in modified
form[6]—a judgment which was doubtless, in its turn, influenced by the
inadequate view of Judaism and its law which prevailed in the scholarship of Harnack's day. Finally, we can note that Harnack almost
certainly overplays the parallel between Marcion, Paul, and Luther,
and underestimates the influence of gnostic thinkers on his hero.[7] This
brief digression on Harnack is of some relevance to our theme, not only
for the obvious reason that the image of Marcion in our day is to a large
degree filtered through his work but also because, despite dis-
agreements we might rightly have with both Harnack and Marcion,
they both raise the issue of the relationship between Christianity and
Judaism in a sharp and distinctive fashion. Whether their views have, in
some respects, more to be said for them than the solutions adopted by
their contemporaries is a matter worthy of some reflection at a later
stage.

Before we can do this, however, a brief review of Marcion's life and
teaching is required to set the scene.[8] Raised in Sinope, Pontus, and son
of the local bishop, Marcion was apparently banished from the church
by his father. The reason is not known. One rumour, probably circulated by his opponents, was that it was because he seduced a young girl;
but most prefer to think it was a result of his already strange views. He
travelled down through Asia Minor with letters of recommendation
from Sinope (which suggests some division of opinion there) and either
then, or perhaps later in his career, he met with Polycarp, bishop of
Smyrna. When he enquired, "Do you know me?" Marcion received the
immediate response, "I certainly do, you son of Satan."[9] If this represents the general reaction to Marcion in Asia Minor it provided reason

5   See Aland, "Marcion," 421-22.
6   Harnack, *Marcion*, 247-54.
7   It scarcely need be added that the study of gnosticism has changed beyond all
    recognition since Harnack's day.
8   Harnack, *Marcion*, 1-27; Blackman, *Marcion*, 1-14.
9   Irenaeus, *Haer*. 3.3.4.

enough for him to try his luck in Rome. Arriving apparently without fanfare, he subsequently attempted to curry favour with the offer of a substantial sum of money. Around 144 C.E. he attempted to persuade the Roman church to follow his teaching, but he was firmly rebuffed and his earlier gift returned. From then until his death (*c* 160 C.E.) he busied himself with immense energy and success in establishing an alternative church. Some time during his stay in Rome, whether before or after the break is not known, Marcion met and was subsequently influenced by the gnostic teacher, Cerdo (Iren. *Haer*. 1:27.1-3; Tert. *Marc*. 1.2; 1.22; 3.21; 4.17).

Although it has come down to us only at the hands of his opponents, the outlines of Marcion's teaching are sufficiently clear for us to be able to provide a sketch and to draw attention to matters particularly relevant to our theme. It should be remembered, of course, that while some of Marcion's views are marked by what seems to be obstinate rationalism and rigorous logic, not all his positions appear to have been fully thought through. This, at least, is the impression conveyed by Tertullian, and probably has as much to do with the inchoate nature of Marcion's thought as it does with Tertullian's desire to ridicule and rebut him. That this was so is perhaps further indicated by the significant adjustments to Marcion's teaching which his most important pupil, Apelles, felt obliged to make.[10]

There were, in Marcion's view, two gods.[11] The one, creator of the world and all that is in it, is the god of the Old Testament—a fickle, temperamental deity who rules the created order through his law. Sometimes Marcion describes him as wretched and petty, capable of vindictive outbursts and favouritism, but he views him as essentially a righteous rather than an evil god even though he understands the concept of righteousness in an inflexibly legalistic fashion. While Marcion clearly considers this god to be inferior he is never in any doubt as to his reality. The special concern of the creator always has been and always will be his favoured people, the Jews. This portrait Marcion gained largely from an insistently literal reading of the Old Testament which eschewed all attempts to explain away difficulties by the use of allegorical exegesis. The other, the redeemer deity, is radically different: a god of mercy, love and compassion, utterly separate from the creator god and wholly unknown until revealed by Jesus. He is an alien god, alien, that is, to the creator's world and all that belongs to it, and his appearance in the person of Jesus is an unprecedented intrusion. He is the god of the Christians rather than of the Jews. This "stranger" god, the god of love, would bring salvation to unrighteous Israelites (during

---

10 Harnack, *Marcion*, 213-29; 323-39.
11 Harnack, *Marcion*, 135-59; Blackman, *Marcion*, 66-80; H. Jonas, *The Gnostic Religion* (Boston: Beacon, 1953), 137-46 Aland, "Marcion," 425-29, has useful corrections of Harnack.

the descent into hell) but not to righteous Israelites who, bound by their intimate relationship with the creator, would not be able to respond to him.

These two deities, entirely distinct in character and attributes, can be further characterized by the principles law and gospel, which not only belong to different documents but also describe two different modes of operation in the world. According to Tertullian this distinction lies at the root of Marcion's system: "The separation of law and gospel is the primary and principal exploit of Marcion" (*Marc.* 1.19; cf. 4.6; 5.13).

Man, as part of the created order, belongs wholly to this world and its god.[12] In distinction from most gnostic systems, man has no divine spark, no affinity with the saviour god. Salvation originates outside of both man and the world. It is probable that some gnostics spun their fabulous myths for sheer pleasure, but the serious purpose of these stories of devolution, these "epics of decline" (Jonas), was to preserve at however distant a remove a connection between at least some men and the deity who was the ultimate source of redemption. For Marcion there was no such connection. Hope for salvation rested solely upon the intrusion of an alien and hitherto unknown god.

Jesus' irruption onto this scene was unprecedented and unheralded.[13] As the son and revealer of the saviour god he could have no close association with the creator god and his world. He was thus in his earthly existence not a real but a phantom man, appearing only in "the likeness of human flesh." His message about the god of love who cares for the poor and the oppressed (just the way, incidently, in which Harnack portrays the teaching of Jesus in *The Essence of Christianity*) implicitly undermines the Old Testament god though without explicitly attacking him. By his death, caused both by the Jews and the principalities and powers, Jesus provides a ransom (understood, as one would expect, in quite literal fashion) which provides release for the redeemed from the clutches of the creator god and his world—a more realistic understanding of Jesus' death than is usual among Christian gnostics, for whom it was a particularly troublesome issue.[14] Consistent with this, and again different from many gnostics, was the Marcionites' willingness to undergo martyrdom, a fact which probably won them some of their admirers. Precisely how it was that men enslaved totally to the creator god could respond to the message of an alien deity Marcion scarcely makes clear, apart from a few vague references to the impression created by Jesus' words and deeds. That the revelation of the redeemer god through his son Jesus was wholly unpredicted had the

---

12   Aland, "Marcion," 433-37, is especially good on this.
13   Harnack, *Marcion*, 160-80; Blackman, *Marcion*, 98-102; Aland, "Marcion," 437-40.
14   As Aland ("Marcion," 438) points out, Marcion's docetism and his view of the death of Jesus were perfectly suited to his view of the body in the economy of salvation.

interesting consequence that, according to Marcion, Jesus could not be
the Jewish Messiah. He still believed that the Jewish Messiah would
come, but that he would be a Messiah for the Jews alone and his
kingdom earthly and temporary, unlike the universal and eternal
salvation brought by the non-messianic Jesus.

Marcion imposed a rigorous asceticism on his followers. Since the
body belonged to the created order and did not share in the process of
redemption, everything connected with it had to be disciplined and
controlled. It is a commonplace of Christian polemics, from the New
Testament on, that false belief leads directly to immoral behaviour. No,
such charge was made against Marcion or his followers and doubtless
their high moral purpose, as well as their willingness to suffer martyrdom, in part accounts for their appeal. On the other hand, by banning
sexual intercourse, even within marriage, they contributed to their own
decline by failing to breed new members.

Crucial to Marcion's beliefs was his understanding of Paul. He
believed that his own teaching was neither more nor less than a revival
of the true Pauline gospel. Paul's letters are the source of much of his
terminology, the distinctive twist of many of his "gnostic" ideas, and his
conviction that judaizing Christians had conspired to pervert the message of Jesus and Paul. Assuming that Paul's references to "my gospel"
meant that he had used one written gospel, Marcion decided that it was
the gospel of Luke. Since he had abandoned the Old Testament, which
was then the universal Christian scripture, he needed a replacement;
the combination of Paul's letters and Luke's gospel, drastically but not
always consistently purged of all pro-Jewish material, took over that
role. Together with the no-longer-extant *Antitheses* written by Marcion
they became the core of the Marcionite tradition, ultimately provoking
their opponents into providing an expanded canon of their own.[15]

This rather too orderly sketch of Marcion's thought should not be
taken to presume a solution to the persistent dispute about the roots of
Marcion's thought. Was he essentially a gnostic or a Paulinist? How
much did his literal turn of mind and ascetic inclinations contribute to
the overall scheme? Was his view of Judaism *sui generis* or can it be
wholly explained by his gnosticism or Paulinism? It is appropriate to
leave the last of these questions for our concluding paragraphs, but
whatever solution we adopt it is important not to underestimate the
influence of his "gnosticism," his "exaggerated Paulinism," or some
combination of the two on his view of Judaism and the Jews. If Marcion
was by temperament an ascetic or responding to an ascetic trend of his
time, it could explain his revulsion at the world and the flesh and could
have contributed to his reading of certain Old Testament and Pauline

15   By far the best account of Marcion's view of scripture is in H. von Campenhausen,
     The Formation of the Christian Bible (Philadelphia: Fortress, 1972), 73-102, 149-67.

texts, but on the evidence available it is scarcely an all-inclusive explanation. The same holds true of his literal-mindedness, evident in his
reading of the Old Testament and of those New Testament writings he
chose to use. It is an important factor and may in part be a reaction to
the kind of allegorical exegesis found in Justin or, in more extreme
form, in the epistle of Barnabas, but on its own it can not explain
everything.

   We are left with two main, and probably false, options, and it is in
terms of these that the debate is usually cast. Harnack, convinced that
Marcion's views sprang from an intense religious experience, denies
almost all contemporary influences (especially gnosticism) and sees
him as representative only of an exaggerated form of Paulinism.[16] The
reverse has commonly been argued,[17] not only because of the striking
parallels with gnosticism but also because it is held that Marcion's
eccentric reading of Paul is inexplicable unless he was predisposed to
view things in a dualistic fashion. In extreme form neither view is
convincing. The notion of an inferior creator god, the deeply pessimis-
tic view of the world and the flesh, and the deliberate reversal of Old
Testament convictions are so close to gnostic ideas that it is difficult to
think that there has not been some cross-fertilization. On the other
hand Marcion is "a gnostic but not as one of the gnostics." The absolute
separation of the two deities from each other and one of them from the
world, the contrast between the god of justice/law and the god of
compassion/grace, the insistence that man is defined wholly by his
location in his world, and the notion of Jesus' death as a ransom (to take
the more obvious examples) are not typically gnostic and are almost
certainly taken from his reading of Paul. Of course the contrast "gnostic or Pauline" is itself questionable in view of the intense interest in Paul
among gnostic groups, notably the Valentinians. And since it is at any
rate misleading to think of gnosticism in monolithic terms, it may be
simplest to think of Marcion's teaching as one version of gnosticism
among others. When we compare Marcion with other gnostics who
used Paul it is apparent not only that his reading of Paul is eccentric,
even for a gnostic, but also that his Paulinism is proportionately more
influential than in other gnostic thinkers.

   In fact, to read Marcion's thought in the light of the scanty evidence for his career makes a great deal of sense. Ascetically inclined
and with a literal cast of mind, he could well have formed the basis of his
views by a concentrated reading of some of Paul's letters. If Christianity
in Sinope was essentially Pauline, but of a kind in which the sharp edge
and verve of the original Paul had been lost (cf. the Pastoral Epistles,

---

16   Harnack, *Marcion*, 135-36.
17   See the list in A. Lindemann, *Paulus im ältesten Christentum* (Tübingen: J.C.B. Mohr,
     1979), 387, and the comments of Harnack on several of his reviewers in *Neue Studien*,
     1f.

Ephesians, etc.), a reading of some of Paul's letters might well have set him thinking—especially if the letter most familiar to him was Galatians. That the language of Galatians is so influential in his thought, that it stands at the head of his list of the Pauline epistles, and that of all Paul's letters it was addressed to communities closest to Sinope are all things which suggest that this was so. And if the view of Paul which Marcion gets from Galatians is exaggerated, distorted, or truncated, then so is any view of Paul which knows him only through this epistle—as is shown by the difficulty some of us have in bringing the views expressed in Galatians into line, for example, with those expressed in Romans. Marcion edited Galatians as he did all of Paul's epistles but, according to Tertullian (*Marc*. 5.13), his editing of Romans was the most drastic of all, which is what we might expect from someone brought up on Galatians whether he distorted its meaning or not. It may well be, too, that in Asia Minor Marcion had already come across groups who interpreted Paul in a "gnostic" fashion (cf. opponents of the author of the Pastorals, 2 Pet. 2:15-16, etc.). The likelihood, therefore, is that Marcion began as a Paulinist, but with a brand of Paulinism already open to gnostic influence and profoundly affected by his own eccentric reading of Paul. His sessions with Cerdo in Rome presumably exposed him to ideas which were both congenial and suggestive and which could, with some adaptation, be used to articulate and extend the views he had already formed.

We are now in a position to draw together some of the threads which relate specifically to our theme and reflect upon their consequences. We have noted in passing a number of specific comments on Judaism in the reports of Marcion's teaching and it is now time to dwell on them a little further. First, however, it is important to state the obvious: Marcion's teaching in general contains a profound denigration of Judaism and the symbols precious to its life and faith. Whether it is in his view of their god, their scriptures, their law, or in his account of Jesus, Paul, or the Jewish-Christian conspiracy, in each case Judaism appears as an inferior religion. In Marcion's system of dualistic oppositions the things which characterize Judaism always form the darker side of the contrast. Their god is real and essentially righteous, but also severe, capricious, and prone to anger (*Marc* 2.16, 20, 23; Origen *Hom*. vii.i). His plans for the world are supposedly set out in the law—that is, the Old Testament as a whole—yet many of its regulations are complex and pointless (*Marc*. 2.18-19) and he even arbitrarily encourages men to disregard it (*Marc*. 2.21-22), as Jesus did too (*Marc*. 4.12, 16, 27). We also noted Marcion's conviction that while the salvation offered by Jesus could be received by unrighteous Israelites who were cut off from the creator god, righteous Israelites would be immune to his appeal (Iren.*Haer*. 1.27.3; Epiph.*Pan*. 42.4). This looks like a mild form of the deliberately provocative reversal of Jewish beliefs found in some gnostic groups (Ophites, Cainites, etc.), but in Marcion's system it may have a different basis, since it is the logical outcome of his belief that the Jewish god is a real deity with a special attachment to his chosen people.

There is, however, little to suggest that Marcion was deliberately anti-Jewish, for a great deal of what he said seems to be the result of his antithetical turn of mind and his own peculiar form of Christian self-definition. He did not, for example, berate the Jews for the death of Jesus. That event was ultimately the responsibility of the creator and the principalities and powers working under him (*Marc.* 3.24; 5.6) and the Jewish rejection of Jesus was natural since he was an alien and unprecedented figure who did not fit their expectations of a Messiah (*Marc.* 3.6).

This leads to a further interesting observation. In a number of places Tertullian reports that Marcion allied himself with the Jews against received Christian opinion by denying that Jesus was the Messiah of Jewish expectation:

So then, since heretical madness was claiming that the Christ had come who had never been previously mentioned, it followed that it had to contend that the Christ was not yet come who had from all time been foretold: and so it was compelled to form an alliance with Jewish error, and build up an argument for itself, on the pretext that the Jews, assured that he who has come was an alien, not only rejected him as a stranger but even put him to death as an opponent, although they would beyond doubt have recognized him and have treated him with all religious devotion if he had been their own. (*Marc.* 3.6)

It is now possible for the heretic to learn, and the Jew as well, what he ought to know already, the reason for the Jews' errors: for from the Jew the heretic has accepted guidance in this discussion, the blind borrowing from the blind, and has fallen into the same ditch. (*Marc.* 3.7)

Let the heretic now give up borrowing poison from the Jew—the asp, as they say, from the viper. (*Marc.* 3.8)[18]

It is not clear why Marcion reached this conclusion. It could have been the logical outcome of an *a priori* conviction about the unprecedented nature of Jesus' message and the god he represented, as is suggested by Tertullian in 3.6, or it may be that exposure to Jewish arguments about Jesus' messiahship, or even simply a comparison of the discrepancies between the promises and their supposed fulfilment, led Marcion to conclude that Jesus was an unlikely candidate for messianic office. It suited Tertullian's purpose admirably to associate Marcion and the Jews (against whom he also wrote a tract) to their mutual disadvantage, but there is no reason to doubt his report. Marcion apparently believed, with the Jews, that the creator did not prophesy the Messiah's death

---

18   The translation here and elsewhere is that of E. Evans, *Tertullian Adversus Marcionem* (Oxford: Clarendon, 1972).

and would not at any rate have subjected him to that cursed form, crucifixion (*Marc*. 3.18; 5.3); and he agreed that many of the prophecies used by other Christians as christological proof-texts (Isa. 7:14, for example) were inapplicable or had already been fulfilled in past events (*Marc*. 3.13). For Marcion there were two Messiahs and two kingdoms (*Marc*. 4.16). The Jewish Messiah had yet to come and when he did he would bring an earthly kingdom which would incorporate Jews and proselytes: "[Y]our Christ promises the Jews their former estate, after the restitution of their country, and, when life has run its course, refreshment with those beneath the earth, in Abraham's bosom" (*Marc*. 3.24).

There is thus a curious tension in Marcion's view of Judaism. On the one hand it is often implicitly denigrated and always, by definition, seen to be inferior. On the other hand, Marcion apparently allied himself in many crucial respects with the Jewish view of Christian claims (cf. Trypho in Justin's *Dialogue*) and held out for them a future described in their own terms—even though for Marcion it could not compete with the eternal kingdom brought by Jesus. To concede to the Jews their messianic hope and the reinheritance of their land was to reverse the current (and subsequent) Christian view that the loss of their land, following the disastrous rebellions against Rome, was a divine punishment for their obdurate rejection of Jesus as Messiah and their complicity in his death.

What led Marcion to his position? To ask the question is to raise in a particular way the more general problem of the roots of Marcion's thought which we discussed above. But the factors considered there— literal-mindedness, asceticism, Paulinism, gnosticism—important and influential as they are, provide no complete explanation of his view of Judaism. Are there, then, additional factors to be considered?

Blackman, basing himself on one of Tertullian's opening salvoes—that Marcion, like many heretics, was unduly obsessed by the problem of evil—thinks that much of Marcion's thought, including his view of the Old Testament and its god, sprang from a profound disquiet over the problem of theodicy.[19] While he prefers Tertullian's monotheistic solution, he thinks that Marcion may well have had a more profound perception of the problem. If this were so, however, it is not clear why Marcion retained the god of the Old Testament at all, even after his demotion, nor why he characterized him as righteous rather than evil. Nor does it shed any immediate light on Marcion's ambivalent attitude towards Judaism.

Goppelt suggests that Marcion was intent on rejecting the god of the Old Testament rather than the Jews, and thus does not insult the Jews as a people. As a hellenist he takes a cool, somewhat distant view of

---

19 Blackman, *Marcion*, 71-73.

Judaism while at the same time being influenced by certain kinds of Jewish exegetical tradition.[20] This is more a statement of the problem than an explanation of it and it probably underestimates the degree to which contemporary Jewish-Christian relations affected Marcion's thought. Rengstorf takes a slightly different tack when he argues that Marcion's rejection of the Old Testament and Judaism has nothing to do with anti-Semitism because the Jews with whom he disputes are not the Jews of his time but those of the Old Testament and New Testament, insofar as they are people of the Demiurge and belong to him. Quite apart from the logic of this statement, which is not altogether clear and overlooks the obvious denigration of Judaism in Marcion's teaching, there is no evidence that Marcion made such a clear distinction between ancient and contemporary Judaism. Rengstorf goes on to suggest another two, admittedly speculative, reasons why Marcion was fairly favourably disposed towards the Jews.[21] On the one hand, by rejecting Jesus who was not their Messiah, the Jews unwittingly opened up the way for the universal salvation brought by Jesus—against the will of the Demiurge and despite themselves. On the other hand, Marcion's dispute was not with the Jews as such but rather with (as he saw them) judaizing Catholic Christians. These observations are pertinent but they do not explain why Marcion allied himself with the Jews on some matters, unless we are to suppose that it was a mere tactical move to procure any available ammunition for the defence of his position.

Harnack takes a somewhat different tack. His tentative explanation is that Marcion came from a family of proselytes and, like his hero Paul, experienced a dramatic conversion to Christianity which led him to turn on his former religion in anger and disillusionment but without kicking over the traces altogether.[22] Thus Marcion's messianic beliefs are merely a hang over from his Jewish past. We need not accept the questionable view of both Paul and Judaism which this implies, to concede that it has a certain degree of plausibility, although it is entirely speculative. That Marcion's rejection of Judaism is more radical than his predecessors is explained, according to Harnack, by his exaggerated Paulinism and, in the light of our knowledge of the way in which Paul's relationship to Judaism has frequently been distorted, we cannot doubt that this could happen. It might have been equally important that, by the time Marcion wrote, church and synagogue were sufficiently distinct that, for a Jew, conversion to Christianity would almost inevitably have led to a more radical break with Judaism than at the time of Paul.

---

20 L. Goppelt, *Christentum und Judentum im ersten und zweiten Jahrhundert* (Gütersloh: C. Bertelsmann, 1954).
21 Rengstorf, *Kirche*, 65-66, 81 n. 139.
22 Harnack, *Neue Studien*, 15-16.

Indeed, recognition of the complex relationship between church and synagogue in the second century may provide further clues to Marcion's thought. For Marcion, of course, the relationship was not complex. He pressed for a radical simplification of the issue: Church and synagogue, Judaism and Christianity are to be seen as entirely separate entities. Why? Grant suggests that he was driven primarily by the need to reassess the relationship of Christianity to Judaism following the disastrous Jewish revolt under Bar Cochba. After these events any association with Judaism, especially the apocalyptic Judaism that inspired so many of the rebels, would have been a political, social and theological liability.[23] This is not implausible, although there is no clear evidence to indicate that the actions of the rebels in Judea and its environs affected the political and social standing of diaspora Jewish communities in Asia Minor, Rome or elsewhere.

There are other aspects of church-synagogue relationships which may be pertinent too. If Jews and Christians in Sinope and elsewhere in Asia Minor came into contact with each other, friendly or hostile, this could have provided material to set Marcion thinking. We know, for example,[24] of Aquila, an older contemporary of Marcion's from Pontus and a Jewish proselyte, who produced a new Greek translation of the Hebrew scriptures, one purpose of which seems to have been to counter Christian use of the LXX, especially with respect to christological proof-texts. Marcion was convinced that Christianity was both true and superior to all other religious options, including Judaism. The Christianity he knew had appropriated the Jewish god and the Jewish scriptures and doubtless thought of itself as the New Israel. Yet these claims were strongly contested by the Jews who, more anomalously still, continued to thrive. Christian exegetes had to go through considerable contortions to defend their conclusions, not least their claim that Jesus was the Messiah. Among many Christians this probably caused little concern. Justin, for example, in his *Dialogue With Trypho*, rides the waves of Jewish-Christian debate with supreme confidence though fully aware of Jewish counter-claims. But did all Christians react in this way? Could Marcion, for example, have found himself torn between his Christian convictions and the problem posed by the continuation of Judaism and by its alternative exegesis of the scriptures which, in the areas of dispute, may have seemed to his literal mind the more plausible? Could it be that Marcion concluded that the claim that Jesus was the Messiah and the Christian church the True Israel fitted neither the facts nor the predictions, and that the confusion of Christianity with Judaism only served to undermine the distinctiveness of the former?

---

23   R.M. Grant, *Gnosticism and Early Christianity*, (New York: Columbia University Press, 1959), 121-28; followed by Balas, "Marcion," 98-99.
24   Noted by Harnack, *Marcion*, 22.

One more factor has also to be borne in mind. There is a considerable amount of evidence to show that the churches in Asia Minor in Marcion's day had to contend with the problem of Gentile judaizers, that is, Gentile Christians who found themselves attracted to some of the beliefs and practices of Judaism. Ignatius and the author of Revelation, for example, seem aware of and alarmed by the problem.[25] The very existence of such groups would have blurred the distinction between Judaism and Christianity. They would also have compounded the problems caused by Jewish-Christian debates by raising the threat of erosion of the church's identity through a process of "judaization" and, even worse, defection from church to synagogue. One way of responding, found in Ignatius, was to sound the alarm, to threaten and cajole; another might have been to insist upon a radical separation of Judaism and Christianity which left no room for further confusion.

We cannot be sure that these two issues—Jewish-Christian debates and Gentile Christian judaizing—affected Marcion, but they do provide a plausible setting for his extreme solution to the problem of Jewish-Christian relations: leave Judaism for the Jews and let Christianity be seen as a new and superior venture. Conceding to Judaism their God, their Scriptures, their Messiah, and their Kingdom solved in one bold move the dilemmas posed by the survival of Judaism, rival claims to a common scripture and the attraction of Judaism to some Gentile Christians.

There seem to have been three solutions to the Jewish-Christian question in the early Christian period. One was the Jewish-Christian option which was rapidly running out of steam by Marcion's time. Another, arguably the least satisfactory, was the Catholic desire to have the best of both worlds. A third was the radical separation proposed by Marcion, part of the attraction of which perhaps was that it solved with one bold stroke what must have been an extraordinarily puzzling situation for many Gentile Christians in the second century who had rubbed shoulders with the Jews. Far from being surprised at Marcion, we should perhaps be surprised that his enthusiastic and fairly numerous supporters alone came to the same conclusion.

This leads finally to a brief comparison between Marcion's view of Judaism and that propounded by his Catholic Christian opponents. As Efroymsen rightly points out, the Catholic response to Marcion drew upon the *adversus Judaeos* tradition in order to defend its view of the creator god and his dealings with humanity. In place of Marcion's notion of an inferior god they put the notion of an inferior and disobedient people. The character of the god was salvaged, but at the expense of the original people of God. In reply to Marcion's view that

---

25 Ign. *Phld.* 6:2; Rev. 2:9, 3:9. See L. Gaston's article in this volume. Perhaps Marcion should be added to his list of examples.

the arrival of Jesus was wholly without precedent, Tertullian resorts to a heightened emphasis on the clarity of the Old Testament predictions both of Christ and of his rejection by the Jews. And insofar as it is conceded that Jesus and Paul propound a legitimate sense of the newness of the gospel in their conflict with the Jews, this is seen to be consistent both with the endless tussle between God and his disobedient people and with his intention all along to replace the old covenant with the new. Views that are thus familiar enough in the context of the Christian conflict with Judaism are now used in another setting to resolve an internal Christian dispute. The effect is that "Marcion's challenge and threat placed all the anti-Judaic themes in a new apologetic context, appending them to ideas of God and Christ in ways which came perilously close to permanence."[26]

It is clear that both the Marcionite and the Catholic positions involve a denigration of Judaism. Putting it simply, it is as if the Marcionite said to the Jew: "Keep your God, your Scriptures, your Messiah, and your law; we consider them to be inferior, superseded in every way by the gospel." The Catholic said: "We'll take your God, your Messiah, your Scriptures, and some of your law; as for you, you are disinherited, cast into a limbo, and your survival serves only as a warning of the consequences of obdurate wickedness." I would not like to be found defending either view of Judaism. However it might be argued that the one which more obviously belittles Jewish symbols was, ironically, in practice the lesser of two evils. The Marcionite position left Judaism intact, decidedly inferior though it was considered to be. There was a point, as Marcion seems to have noted, in Jews continuing to be Jews, keeping their law, and awaiting their Messiah. And it is of some interest, though perhaps no more than a coincidence, that there is no record of the persecution of Jews by the Marcionite churches. The Catholic position, imperiously defending its proprietal rights to the Jewish God and scriptures, could find only a negative reason for the continued existence of the Jews. The one involved a radical break which left Judaism for the Jews; the other took what it wanted and, in effect, left nothing for the Jews. Or, to exaggerate a little, the one attacked the symbols but left the people alone; the other took the symbols and attacked the people. Judaism is the loser in either case. Whether the Marcionite position, had it prevailed, would have led to the same sad consequences as the view of its opponents is hard to say. But it is worth a moment's reflection. _how supercilious!_

---

26   Efroymsen, "Patristic," 100-108, quotation on 105.

5

Justin Martyr's Argument with Judaism[1]

Harold Remus

Both in his *First Apology* and his *Dialogue with Trypho* Justin Martyr argues with Jewish traditions. However, in the two *Apologies* he is also in conflict with contemporary paganism. That makes possible some comparisons between his argument with Judaism and against paganism and allows one to place the former in a larger context. Similarly, placing the *Dialogue* alongside some of the other dialogue literature produced by Christians, or early Christian references to Judaism, provides further perspective. Such comparisons, coupled with insights from the sociology of knowledge, help illuminate Justin's argument with Judaism.

Justin and Paganism

Justin's attitude to pagan authors is ambivalent. On the one hand, he draws parallels between paganism and Christianity and, through the

---

1 The literature on Justin Martyr is so extensive that one may justly speak of *Justin-forschung*; thus J.C.M. van Winden, *An Early Christian Philosopher: Justin Martyr's Dialogue with Trypho, Chapters One to Nine* (Leiden: Brill, 1971), 1. See the bibliographies in E.R. Goodenough, *The Theology of Justin Martyr* (Jena: Frommannsche Buchhandlung, 1923; reprinted Amsterdam: Philo Press, 1968); L.W. Barnard, *Justin Martyr: His Life and Thought* (London: Cambridge University Press, 1967); N. Hyldahl, *Philosophie und Christentum: Eine Interpretation der Einleitung zum Dialog Justins* (Copenhagen: Munksgaard, 1966); M. Young, "The Argument and Meaning of Justin Martyr's Conversion Story" (Th.D. dissertation, Harvard Divinity School, Cambridge, 1971); D.C. Trakatellis, *The Pre-existence of Christ in Justin Martyr: An Exegetical Study with Reference to the Humiliation and Exaltation Christology* (Missoula, MT: Scholars Press, 1976), who refers (p. x) to George Hunston William's "exhaustive bibliography on Justin Martyr" (unpublished).

My citations from Justin are from E.J. Goodspeed (ed.), *Die ältesten Apologeten: Texte mit kurzen Einleitungen* (Göttingen: Vandenhoeck and Ruprecht, 1914).

logos doctrine, claims the good (and good persons) in paganism for Christianity, thus establishing points of contact between paganism and Christianity. On the other hand, he contends that Christianity roots in a culture and religion antecedent to paganism and that the latter is derivative from those antecedents and, through demonic agency, is in some ways imitative of Christianity. It has been observed that such ambivalence is common to the early Christian apologists: "Before Christianity could be shown to be unique and without parallel, the apologists had to show what it was like, and, by implication, what it was unlike."[2] Thus Christian apologists sometimes seem to fall under the spell of Greek philosophy, affirming its (partial) truth; yet they see it as derivative from Christianity's antecedents and/or turn its weapons against pagan culture.[3] In the conceptuality of the sociology of knowledge, the apologists reorient the social and cultural worlds of contemporary paganism to fit their experience and conception of Christianity.[4]

These general observations may be illustrated by Justin's treatment of pagan miracle claims. Many of his criticisms of these claims can be paralleled from a long tradition of pagan criticism of them. Nonetheless, he expresses these criticisms with reference to Christian data. Thus, he recites shameful details in some of the stories of pagan deities—parricide, sodomy, adultery[5]—and points to the role of these stories in pagan socialization and the deleterious consequences,[6] with the implication that the Christian stories he mentions are free of such shameful details. Later he makes this explicit.[7]

---

2   R.L. Wilken, "Collegia, Philosophical Schools, and Theology," in S. Benko and J.J. O'Rourke (eds.), *The Catacombs and the Colosseum: The Roman Empire as the Setting of Primitive Christianity* (Valley Forge, PA: Judson, 1971), 286; Wilken's phrasing is slightly different in the earlier version of the essay, "Toward a Social Interpretation of Early Christian Apologetics," *Church History* 39 (1970), 456.

3   Cf. the remarks of J. Geffcken, *Zwei griechische Apologeten* (Leipzig and Berlin: Teubner, 1907), 31-32, and the sources and studies cited there. More recently and in more detail see W. Nestle, "Die Haupteinwände des antiken Denkens gegen das Christentum," *ARW* 37 (1941-42), 51-100; G. Klein, "Der Synkretismus als theologisches Problem in der ältesten christlichen Apologetik," *ZTK* 64 (1967), 40-82.

4   To what degree the social and cultural world of the apologists, who were innovators in many ways, coincides with or departs from those of antecedent Christianity is a complex question. In Justin's case, as I have sought to show elsewhere, there is continuity: Justin's philosophical interpretations of pagan philosophy and religion, such as those sketched below, affirm (and proceed from) popular Christian piety at a number of points. See H. Remus, *Pagan-Christian Conflict Over Miracle in the Second Century* (Cambridge, MA: Philadelphia Patristic Foundation, 1983), 151-52, 157-58.

5   E.g., Justin, *1 Apol.* 21.5, 25; *2 Apol.* 12.5; cf. further Tatian, *Orat.* 3, 6, 8-10, 21, 24; cf. H. Chadwick, *Early Christian Thought and the Classical Tradition: Studies in Justin, Clement, and Origen* (Oxford: Clarendon Press, 1966), 11.

6   *1 Apol.* 21.4.

7   Ibid. 25.2: the Christian God was not guilty of adultery or sodomy nor was he possessed by the passions ascribed to Greek deities.

For Justin it is axiomatic that extraordinary Christian phenomena, and they alone, are authentic, despite their similarity to pagan phenomena: "the things we say we have learned from Christ and the prophets who preceded him are alone true [*mona alēthē*] . . . it is not because we say the same things as they [i.e., the pagan authors] that we think we will be acknowledged to be correct but because we speak what is true" (*1 Apol.* 23.1). Thus it is Jesus alone who was fathered by God in an unusual way;[8] he alone is God's logos, his firstborn, and his power (*1 Apol.* 23.2). What is true of his parentage and status is true, by implication, of his resurrection and ascension as well: he alone rose and ascended.[9]

Further indicative of the axiomatic nature of Justin's polemic against pagan miracle accounts is his relativizing and reordering of pagan philosophy and pagan worship. It was from Moses, who antedates all Greek writers,[10] that Plato took what he had to say about moral responsibility (*1 Apol.* 44.8) and about the ordering of primal matter.[11] When Greek philosophers and poets spoke of immortality of the soul, retribution after death, contemplation of heavenly things, and the like, they took their cues from the Hebrew prophets (*1 Apol.* 44.9). Justin thus turns to Christian advantage some of the bulwarks of that culture which one later sees Celsus defending so vigorously. Justin relativizes and reorders paganism's social and cultural worlds further by construing its worship and its extraordinary phenomena as proleptic imitations, demonically inspired, of the genuine, Christian articles. Thus, before Jesus ever became a human among humans, some pagans, incited by the evil demons, were speaking as though the poets' accounts of extraordinary phenomena actually took place (*genomena*) when in fact they had fabricated them (*mythopoiēsantes*).[12] These fabrications of the poets (*ta mythopoiēthenta tōn poiētōn*)—the stories of Zeus's alleged offspring—were put forward by the demons whenever they learned that people were beginning to believe the things predicted of Christ by the prophets (*1 Apol.* 54.1-3). Their intent was to bring it about that

---

8   Ibid. 23.3 (*monos idiōs*); in 22.2 the same word, *idiōs*, is used of Jesus' birth. Cf. further *Dial.* 66.3, where Justin asserts the singularity of virgin birth among Jews: only "our Christ" was born thus.

9   In distinguishing extraordinary elements in the story of Jesus from the pagan counterparts discussed in *1 Apol.* 21-22, Justin does not refer to Christ's resurrection and ascension, but he mentions these at the beginning of the discussion (21.1), and their uniqueness for him may be inferred from his argument in chapter 23 and from his argument from prophecy to the reality of Christ's resurrection and ascension (chap. 45).

10 Ibid. 44.8; similarly, 54.5.

11 Ibid. 59 (Justin cites Gen. 1), 60 (Plato was dependent on Moses but misread him).

12 Ibid. 23.3. Cf. *Dial.* 69.1: among the Greeks the devil (*ho diabolos*) worked wonders similar to the genuine, Christian wonders but did them falsely (*parapoiēsas*); he also worked wonders through Egyptian magicians (*magōn*) and through false prophets (*pseudoprophētōn*) at the time of Elijah.

people would view the things predicted of the Christ by the prophets
as, on the one hand, similar to what the poets had said (and therefore as
not unique) and, on the other hand, as mere telling of tall tales (*teratolo-
gian*).[13] As specific imitations of extraordinary Christian phenomena
predicted by the prophets Justin cites Asclepius' healings and resurrec-
tions[14] as well as other pagan traditions of the extraordinary.[15] The
context of these traditions, namely, popular cultic piety, also has
demonically-inspired features imitative of Christian or Jewish tradition: sprinklings, ablutions, removal of shoes (*1 Apol.* 62), and rites in
the cults of Mithras (*Dial.* 70) and of Dionysus (*1 Apol.* 54.6; *Dial.* 69.2).

That Justin's reorienting of pagan miracle accounts and of pagan
philosophy and piety resists such reinterpretation is indicated by Justin's statement that Plato misunderstood Moses (*1 Apol.* 60), or that
pagans misunderstand the truth (44.10), or that some of the
demonically-inspired imitations of Jewish prophecies are blundered
interpretations of those prophecies (54.4, 7). For Justin, however, these
very misinterpretations and blunderings support his knowledge of
Christianity's scriptures and his trust in them.[16] Indeed, every kind of
evidence—favourable or seemingly unfavourable—counts for Christianity and against paganism. Thus Justin claims for Christianity those
Greeks or barbarians who, though they lived before Christ and were
considered godless (*atheoi*), yet lived in accord with logos (*meta logou*),
for Christ, as God's firstborn (*prōtotokon*), is the logos in which every
people shared.[17] Seeds of truth (*spermata alētheias*) are found among all

---

13   Ibid. 54.2. For Justin's pejorative use of *teratologia* cf. *Dial.* 67.2, where Trypho
     accuses Justin of *teratologia* when Justin argues for the virgin birth of Jesus.
14   *1 Apol.* 54.10; *Dial.* 69.3.
15   Divine fatherhood or virgin birth: Dionysus (*Dial.* 69.2), Perseus (*1 Apol.* 54.8; *Dial.*
     70.5). Resurrection and/or ascent to heaven: Dionysus (*1 Apol.* 54.6; *Dial.* 69.2),
     Perseus (*1 Apol.* 54.8), Bellerophon (ibid. 54.8).
16   *Dial.* 69.1 (*tauta bebaian mou tēn en tais graphais gnōsin kai pistin katestēsen*); the premise
     of Justin's argument is that imitations (in this case, pagan phenomena) prove the
     genuineness of that which is imitated (i.e., prophecies in Christianity's scriptures).
17   *1 Apol.* 46.2-3; among Greeks Justin mentions Socrates and Heraclitus, and among
     barbarians Abraham, Elijah, and the three men in the fiery furnace. In *2 Apol.* 8.1
     Justin speaks of poets and philosophers such as Heraclitus and Musonius who were
     hated and put to death "because of the seed of truth implanted in every race of
     humans" (*dia to emphuton panti genei anthrōpōn sperma tou logou*; cf. similarly 13.5: *dia
     tēs enousēs emphutou tou logou sporas*); in 8.3 and 13.3 he uses the Stoic term *spermatikos*;
     cf. similarly 10.2. On Justin's use of *spermatikos logos* and *to sperma tou logou*, and the
     distinctions between them, see the detailed studies by R. Holte, "Logos Spermatikos:
     Christianity and Ancient Philosophy according to St. Justin's Apologies," *ST* 12
     (1958), 110-68, and J.H. Waszink, "Bemerkungen zu Justins Lehre vom Logos
     Spermatikos," in A. Stuiber and A. Hermann (eds.), *Mullus: Festschrift Theodor
     Klauser* [*Jahrbuch für Antike und Christentum*, Supplementary vol. 1] (Münster: As-
     chendorff, 1964), 380-90, and the critique and exposition in Hyldahl, *Philosophie und
     Christentum* (cited above, n. 1), 70-85. Justin also claims for Christianity those Jews
     who, before Christ came, lived according to the law of Moses: at the resurrection
     they will be saved through him (*Dial.* 45.3-4).

peoples, though the truth has not always been correctly perceived by them (*1 Apol.* 44.10). Those, on the other hand, who prior to Christ lived devoid of logos (*aneu logou*) were enemies of Christ and of those (implicit) Christians who lived according to logos (46.4). As to those things in Christianity considered reprehensible by pagans—notably Christ's crucifixion—they, too, are turned to Christian account by Justin. Suffering and death are not peculiar to Christ; they are attested also for the sons ascribed to Zeus by pagans (22.3-4). The appearance of the cross in many facets of daily life[18] and even in state or civic ritual[19] shows that the crucifixion is the greatest symbol of God's strength and dominion.[20] The cross appears also in Plato's account of cosmogony in the *Timaeus*, but in a mistaken fashion since Plato did not understand clearly (*mē akribōn epistamenos*) Moses' account of the serpent in the wilderness, with the result that he interpreted the *typon* in that account as a chiastic structure of the universe rather than referring it to the cross.[21]

The axiomatic nature of Justin's reorientations of paganism's miracle accounts and of its rites, symbols, and spokesmen is evident. Pagans, says Justin, adduce no proofs when they present the poets' fabrications about Zeus's extraordinary offspring to their youth, who proceed to commit them to memory.[22] Justin, by contrast, devotes considerable space to demonstrating, from fulfilled prophecy, the truth of the words and deeds of Christ (*1 Apol.* 31-53) and to establishing his thesis that the poets' fabrications are demonic imitations of such prophecies (54ff.). Justin's argument from fulfilled prophecy is, of course, inherited. For a number of Justin's contemporaries, both pagan and Christian,[23] such "proofs" did not necessarily constitute proofs. By Justin's account, acceptance of the truth of Jewish prophecy was part of his conversion, a radical resocialization in which Christian social and cultural worlds came to impinge on their counterparts from his pagan socialization, reshaping and reorienting them. The old Christian who, in Justin's narrative, instructs him on that occasion explains that the prophets alone saw and announced what was true. Their method, however, was not demonstration (*ou meta apodeixeōs*) of

---

18   *1 Apol.* 55.3-8; Justin cites sailing, plowing, etc.
19   Ibid. 55.6: the cross appears on trophies or standards used in processions and to it are affixed images of emperors after their death and deification.
20   Ibid. 55.2 (*to megiston symbolon tēs ischyos kai archēs autou*).
21   *1 Apol.* 60.105, referring to *Tim.* 36B-C (specifically *hoion chei* in 36B); for other possible early Christian use of this Plato passage to refer to the cross see J. Daniélou, *The Development of Christian Doctrine before the Council of Nicaea*, vol. 1, *The Theology of Jewish Christianity*, trans. and ed. J.A. Baker (London: Darton, Longman, and Todd, 1964), 285-87 (the *Tim.* passage is erroneously referred to as 26B).
22   *1 Apol.* 54.1 (*hoi de paradidontes ta mythopoiēthenta hupo tōn poiētōn oudemian apodeixin pherousi ekmanthanousi neois*).
23   E.g., Marcion.

the kind familiar in the philosophical schools; rather they were witnesses, deserving of belief (*axiopistoi*), to the truth above all demonstration (*anaterō pasēs apodeixeōs*) (*Dial.* 7.2). In the words of the old Christian, "the truth is as it is" (*to gar alēthes houtōs echei*) and is to be accepted as such: if it has been uttered by a renowned pagan sage such as Plato or Pythagoras, that does not add to or enhance its truth (6.1). What Galen, a contemporary of Justin, regarded as a defect in Christian (and Jewish) argumentation, namely, the lack of demonstration according to commonly accepted canons of logic,[24] is here asserted as axiomatic and as a virtue by the old Christian in view of the nature of the truth involved. In the case of the prophets the old Christian does offer some warrants, but they are different from those accepted in most philosophical schools of the day; they belong to what may be termed popular cultic piety: the prophets' predictions came (and are coming) true, and the prophets performed miracles (*Dial.* 7.2-3). Once accepted, such warrants are employed in argumentation by Justin and other Christians. But they count as warrants only for some, namely, followers of Christ or those sympathetic to them, as Justin implicitly acknowledges in several places. For example, he concludes one lengthy argument from prophecy with the assertion that *perceptive* hearers (*tois ta akoustika kai noera ōta echousin*) will be able to understand that such argumentation differs from that of those who make up fabrications (*mythopoiētheisi*) about alleged sons of Zeus (*1 Apol.* 53.1). The axiomatic nature of Justin's arguments is evident also in another passage where, after reciting a creed of specifically Christian beliefs, Justin states that the *perceptive* person will be able to understand what is here asserted.[25] Those who disagree with Justin on the moral responsibility of persons who lived before Christ are labeled "unreasonable" (*alogistainontes*).[26]

---

24 Cf. the Galen excerpts cited and discussed by R. Walzer, *Galen on Jews and Christians* (London: Oxford University Press, 1949): Moses writes his books without demonstration, simply stating that God commanded, God spoke (pp. 11, 18); in the school (*diatribē*) of Moses and Christ one hears undemonstrated laws (*nomōn anapodeiktōn*) (pp. 14, 16). Galen had written a book *On Demonstration*, and in criticizing Jewish and Christian teaching he assumes that logical demonstration is the way to knowledge; cf. Walzer, 45-48.

25 *1 Apol.* 46.5 (*ho nounechēs katalabein dunēsetai*). Cf., in the much later *Altercatio Simonis Iudaei et Theophili Christiani*, how the Christian assumes that for his Jewish dialogue partner perception of the Christian truth will follow from a desire to understand and to believe. In the edition by A. von Harnack, *Die Altercatio Simonis Iudaei et Theophili Christiani nebst Untersuchungen über die anti-jüdische Polemik in der alten Kirche*, TU 1/3, (Leipzig: Hinrichs, 1883), sec. 4 (p. 16, lines 15-17), "si tu volueris cognoscere, oportet te primum credere et tunc demum poteris intellegere"; sec. 8 (p. 18, lines 21-23), "Erras, Iudaee, nec umquam invenies veritatem, nisi veritatis intellegas originem. Nam si velles credere, poteris et in principio eius invenire, quis est Christus, dei filius." Harnack (p. 15) tentatively assigned the date 430 C.E. to the composition of the work.

26 *1 Apol.* 46.1. H. Chadwick, *Early Christian Thought* (cited above, n. 5), 19-20, aptly summarizes what I have called the axiomatic nature of Justin's argumentation:

Axiomatic statements are those for which one offers no proof except (if pressed) the widespread, common assent to their truth. In the terminology of the sociology of knowledge, such statements belong to the "givens" of a social group—what passes for knowledge in that group and is presented as "objective reality" to its young.[27] Justin faults pagans for offering their youths no proofs of the extraordinary phenomena in pagan culture.[28] But that is just the way the traditions (including the religious traditions) of a group are inculcated during primary socialization. As Reimarus observed, religion is presented to the young as the only, true religion, and most adherents of a religion, therefore, find it to be true, not because it has been "proved" to them, but rather because it is part of the social and cultural worlds acquired by them during primary socialization and made plausible within the social matrices of those worlds.[29] Now, in several passages in the *Dialogue* Justin argues that it is (in Chadwick's words) "the blinding effect of custom and conservatism" that keeps most Jews from accepting Jesus as the Christ so clearly prophesied in their scriptures.[30] That is, Justin perceives the hold that inherited social and cultural worlds have on a person. He does not draw the conclusion, however, that his elaborate (and what he considers convincing) proofs from prophecy are apt to

---

"Throughout his writing he invariably assumes that once the Christian position has been properly set out by an intelligent man, once its way of life has been seen in a faithful disciple, and once it has been seriously attended to by a sincere and open mind, the fulfilment of these three conditions can have only one consequence: the truth will be manifest and forthwith accepted. 'I have no need,' he writes, 'of any sophistical ingenuity, but only to be candid and frank'" (*Dial.* 80.2; 120.6; 125.1).

Roger Brown's description of the operation of the "consistency principle" in social relations is applicable to Justin's statements: "It seems to be a general law of human thought that we expect people we like and respect to associate themselves with ideas we like and respect and to dissociate themselves or disagree with ideas from which we dissociate ourselves. These latter disapproved ideas we expect to find espoused by the wicked and the stupid—those we do not like or respect. The 'goods' in the world in the way of persons, things, and ideas are supposed to clump together and oppose the 'bads,' who are expected to form their own clump. This is a consistency principle. It describes the way the world ought to go, and as long as things work this way nothing much happens to our attitudes. But when a new girl friend dislikes our favorite music or an admired professor ridicules our religious beliefs or an esteemed critic attacks a play in which we are appearing, the mind starts working." Roger Brown, *Social Psychology* (New York: Free Press, and London: Macmillan, 1965), 551.

27 See, e.g., Peter L. Berger and Thomas Luckmann, *The Social Construction of Reality: A Treatise on the Sociology of Knowledge* (Garden City, N.Y.: Doubleday, 1966), 60-61 et passim.

28 See n. 22 above.

29 H.S. Reimarus, "Unmöglichkeit einer Offenbarung, die alle Menschen auf eine gegründete Art glauben könnten," published posthumously by Lessing (Braunschweig, 1777); reprinted in K. Lachmann (ed.), *Gotthold Ephraim Lessings Sämtliche Schriften*, 3d edition, revised by F. Muncker, vol. 12 (Leipzig: Goschen'sche Verlagsbuchhandlung, 1897), 325, 335.

30 Chadwick, *Early Christian Thought*, 131, n. 53, referring to *Dial.* 38-39, 123.6, 125.5.

carry conviction only with insiders (to whom they will be axiomatic) and to persons (like himself at one time) on the way to becoming insiders.

Similar are his statements about the extraordinary phenomena of Christianity. Outsiders who reject those phenomena or Justin's reorientation of pagan social and cultural worlds are, in Justin's view, unreasonable or uncomprehending. Justin's polemic against the miracle accounts and claims of contemporary paganism may thus be viewed as one facet of the conflict between their competing communities and their respective social and cultural worlds. The mode of argumentation tends to be deductive, proceeding, often, from tacit but firmly held axioms—"our" truth.

Justin and Judaism

The situation is not dissimilar in the *Dialogue*. There are many issues that Justin and Trypho take up and discuss—the use and interpretation of scriptures that the two have in common, the nature of God and of religion (e.g., observance vs. ethical conduct), the bases of belief (epistemological questions), christology and messianism, the identity of God's people, and the mutual exclusivity of Judaism and Christianity. These and other issues have been examined in previous studies, with points of agreement and disagreement noted.[31] Rather than rehearsing these issues once again, the remainder of this essay will seek to illuminate Justin's argument with Judaism by focusing especially on the social and cultural rooting and dimensions of that argument and viewing it as an expression of a conflict between competing communities and their respective social and cultural worlds.

Justin's posture towards Judaism is as ambivalent as towards paganism: he claims for Christianity those persons in the Jewish tradition who, even though preceding Jesus in time, lived according to logos (the law of Moses). The logos was active in Jewish history; in Daniélou's summary, "The incarnation represents only the high point of a permanent *oikonomia*."[32] Moreover, as was indicated in the preceding section, Justin draws on the Jewish heritage of Christianity to establish the

---

31   E.g., S. Krauss, "The Jews in the Works of the Church Fathers," *JQR*, Original Series 5 (1893), 123-39; E.R. Goodenough, *The Theology of Justin Martyr: An Investigation into the Conceptions of Early Christian Literature and its Hellenistic and Judaistic Influences* (Jena, 1923; reprinted, Amsterdam: Philo Press, 1968); L.W. Barnard, "The Old Testament and Judaism in the Writings of Justin Martyr," *VT* 14 (1964), 394-406; H. Chadwick, "Justin Martyr's Defence of Christianity," *BJRL* 47 (1964-65), 275-97; P. Richardson, *Israel in the Apostolic Church*, Society for New Testament Studies Monograph Series, 10 (Cambridge: Cambridge University Press, 1969), 9-14.

32   J. Daniélou, *A History of Early Christian Doctrine before the Council of Nicaea*, vol. 2, *Gospel Message and Hellenistic Culture*, trans. and ed. J.A. Baker (London: Darton, Longman and Todd, and Philadelphia: Westminster Press, 1973), 161; for a detailed

antecedence of Christian thought and ritual to paganism and the superiority of Christianity to paganism.

On the other hand, Justin denies continuing theological validity to a Judaism apart from Jesus—*that* Judaism has been superseded, Justin argues at a number of points. Thus, those persons who confess Jesus as the fulfilment of the Jewish scriptures (*Dial.*, passim) and as the new law (11.2) and the new lawgiver (12.1; 14.3) are God's true people (11.5; 135.3, Christians are *Israēlitikon to alēthinon . . . genos*). They have the ultimate revelation (11.2), and much of the *Dialogue* turns on Justin's showing that the God of the Jewish scriptures is the Christian God (e.g., 11.1) and on Justin's imparting to Trypho the true interpretation of those scriptures and explaining how Jewish symbols such as water and leaven now find their true home in Christianity (14.1-3). To be sure, Justin allows a place in God's true people for persons who confess Jesus but practise certain traditional Jewish observances, provided they do not attempt to compel non-observant Christians to do the same (47.2-4). That is to say, Justin recognizes so-called Jewish Christians but, at the same time, characterizes as uncomprehending (7.3; 12.2) and as guilty of wicked behaviour (14.2) those Jews who do not confess Jesus and do not acknowledge the truth of Justin's arguments and instead insist on traditional observances. They will not be saved (47.4), especially not those who anathematize in their synagogues those who believe in Jesus as the Christ (47.4). For Justin, here it is all or nothing: such persons must repent and become as Justin is.

Trypho, for his part, makes some concessions. Justin has Trypho say that he is willing to let Jesus be recognized as Lord and Christ and God of the *Gentiles* (64.1). Trypho considers the possibility that Jesus, born a human, could have become the Christ through anointing because he led a life in conformity to the law (49.1; 67.2) but rejects that possibility because Elijah—who would have done the anointing—has not yet come (49.1). Trypho admits that the passages Justin has adduced as referring to the Christ do indeed have this reference, including the passages that name "Jesus" (the son of Nun; 89.1). He admits that the scriptures state the Christ must suffer but questions whether crucifixion can be the mode of suffering since that is cursed in the law (89.2). He gives no credence to popular slanders of Christianity (10.2), and he praises the difficult precepts in the Christian gospels (10.2)— indeed, they may be too difficult (10.2)! But he and the other Jews who figure in the *Dialogue* insist that the passages Justin cites are not as unambiguous as Justin alleges (51; 56) and that some of Justin's interpretations are contrived (79). Ultimately, Trypho is as uncompromising and as exclusivistic as Justin: if Justin will be circumcized

---

listing of passages in Justin showing the logos active in Jewish history see C. Andresen, *Logos und Nomos: Die Polemik des Kelsos wider das Christentum* (Berlin: de Gruyter, 1955), 315-16.

and observe all that is written in the law, then perhaps he will find mercy with God (8.4). But if, says Trypho to Justin, you desert God and pin your hope on a human being, what sort of salvation will remain for you (8.3)? Although you think you live piously and are distinct from others, you are no different than the Gentiles; you do not keep God's commandments, and yet you hope to obtain some good from God (10.3)—and you seek to persuade *us* as though you know God, even though you do not *do* the things that those who fear God do (10.4).

The upshot of these mutually exclusivistic claims and pleas by Justin and Trypho is an impasse. At the end of the *Dialogue*, following Justin's plea to Trypho and his companions that they should pay no heed to the leaders of their synagogues who teach them to deride Jesus, "the king of Israel" (137.2), and should, rather, turn from rejection to acceptance of him (137.1-2) and to the way of repentance (141.2-3), Trypho politely expresses appreciation for the dialogue and asks that they may part as friends (142.1). Both men remain true to their convictions and to their respective groups.

As was noted in the preceding section, Justin regards what he says as self-evidently true; however, he also has some insight into why Trypho and his followers do not come around to his point of view. Trypho is to be forgiven for what he says about Christianity because he has been misled by teachers who do not understand the scriptures (9.1; 38.2; 68.7; 71.1-2). Drawing on some distinctions made by Robert Merton,[33] one may say that these insights by Justin constitute an adumbration of certain observations made by sociologists of knowledge, in this case the binding—and, for Justin, blinding—effects of socialization: Trypho says what he says because that is what he has been taught.

Why, then, does Justin say what *he* says? He was, after all, not raised in a Christian tradition. Justin's answer to that question would be that God and his Christ granted him the wisdom to understand Jewish prophecy as pointing—holus bolus—to Jesus (7.3; 58.3); to those not granted this divine gift of wisdom, such insight into Jewish prophecy is inaccessible (7.3). Indeed, the prophetic gifts once vouchsafed to the Jews have now been transferred to Christians (82). In the opening sections of the *Dialogue* Justin tells how he came to this wisdom—via conversion, first to Platonism and then to Christianity. The latter has received much attention from scholars.[34] Here it suffices to note that for Justin to move from Middle Platonism to Christianity required a radical resocialization. One finds in Justin's narrative of his conversion

---

33   R.K. Merton, *On Theoretical Sociology: Five Essays, Old and New* (New York: Free Press, and London: Collier-Macmillan, 1967), 9ff.; see H. Remus, "Sociology of Knowledge and the Study of Early Christianity," *SR* 11/1 (1982), 49.

34   See the studies cited and the discussion of some of the problematics of the conversion accounts in Remus, *Pagan-Christian Conflict* (cited above, n. 4), 144-53.

and in certain observations in his *Second Apology* some of the recurring features of modern conversion accounts:[35] Justin, the seeker, finds it implausible that Christians, said to be lovers of pleasure, should so readily give themselves into death, thus forfeiting the pleasures they are said to covet (*2 Apol.* 12.1-2). It has been pointed out that the Christian martyrs' freedom and fearlessness recall Socrates' behaviour, whereas the Platonists would not pass the test of dying for Socrates' teaching (*2 Apol.* 10.8).[36] Likewise, the old Christian in the opening sections of the *Dialogue*, through the force of his logic and perhaps because of his age and his resemblance to Socrates,[37] is for Justin still another of those "significant others" who represent and embody the new mode of life and thought in a plausible way. Justin's conversion is not only to a symbolic universe and a body of teachings but to the Christian group(s) which experienced and embodied those teachings and made them seem plausible for at least some persons on the outside looking in. In such groups, as Lofland and Stark observe, the prospective convert interacts with the members of the group, and the group's "perspective 'comes alive,' "[38] even as (to take a second-century example) for the rhetor Aelius Aristides his circle of friends in the Asclepius temple were important in imparting reality to Asclepius and his revelations to Aelius.[39]

A rite of entry—baptism—also seems to figure into Justin's enlightenment and his commitment to the Christian fellowship. That he was received into a Christian community through such a ritual seems likely from the amount of space he devotes to baptismal ritual and his use of the first-person plural pronoun in his description (*1 Apol.* 61). In another passage he seems to refer to initiation as the next step after coming to know Christ.[40] He speaks of baptism as an "enlightenment" (*phōtismos*), asserting that those who are instructed for baptism are "enlightened in their understanding" (*phōtizomenōn tēn dianoian*).[41] Talk

---

35 See Remus, "Sociology of Knowledge," 47; *Pagan-Christian Conflict*, 146-51.

36 M. Young, "Argument and Meaning" (cited above, n. 1), 206-207. O. Skarsaune, "The Conversion of Justin Martyr," *ST* 30 (1976), 64-65.

37 On the modeling of the old Christian after Socrates see Young, "Argument and Meaning," 30, 32, 34, n. 2, 203-204; Skarsaune, "The Conversion of Justin Martyr," 69, and the secondary literature cited there.

38 J. Lofland and R. Stark, "Becoming a World-Saver: A Theory of Conversion to a Deviant Perspective," in C.Y. Glock (ed.), *Religion in Sociological Perspective: Essays in the Empirical Study of Religion* (Belmont, CA: Wadsworth, 1973), 45.

39 See C.A. Behr, *Aelius Aristides and the Sacred Tales* (Amsterdam: Hakkert, and Chicago: Argonaut, 1968), 47.

40 *Dial.* 8.2, where *teleiō genomenō* may refer to initiation.

41 *1 Apol.* 61.12; that the *phōtismos* refers to prebaptismal instruction in specific Christian credenda and not to illumination gained through the act of washing is indicated by 61.13: the person who is enlightened is washed (*ho phōtizomenos louetai*) in the name of Jesus Christ — crucified under Pontius Pilate — and in the name of the Holy Spirit, who through the prophets proclaimed beforehand all things pertaining to

of enlightenment is not uncommon in the rhetoric and liturgical language of second-century Christianity.[42] The importance of initiation and enlightenment for Justin, personally and as a spokesman for Christianity, is suggested not only by the stress he lays on them in *Dialogue* 61 but also by the contrast between, on the one hand, his (enlightened) views of Jesus and Christianity after he becomes a Christian and, on the other, typically pagan and Middle Platonist views of the same,[43] by the detailed contrast he draws between the behaviour of Christians before and after conversion to Christianity (*1 Apol.* 14; cf. *2 Apol.* 2), and, further, by the important role of initiation rites in socialization and resocialization generally[44] as well as in Mediterranean antiquity down to Justin's day.[45]

After Justin's reception into a Christian group, the communal activities and the significant others of that group (or others like it) would play an important role in the maintenance of the new reality. Justin describes these communal activities in detail—the initiations, the readings, the instruction, the prayers, the ritual kiss, the rite of bread and cup, the offerings, the aid to the poor—and the roles played by the actors in these various dramas: the presider, the deacons, the assembly, the God who is worshipped, and Christ, whose example and commands legitimize various acts in the worship (*1 Apol.* 61, 65-67). The importance of these groups and their communal activities for Justin is evident from his consistent identification with them: this is what "we" do and the way "we" do it.

One element in Justin's conversion is that he should (in terminology sometimes employed by sociologists of knowledge) nihilate his former social and cultural worlds. It is evident in the account of his conversion to Platonism: "within a short time [of becoming a Platonist]," he says, "I *supposed* I had become wise, and *in my stupidity* I

Jesus. In other contexts Justin speaks of being enlightened by the name of Christ (*phōtizomenoi*, *Dial.* 39.1) or by Jesus (*pephōtismenos*, *Dial.* 122.1; cf. 122.5) and of the ability to understand (correctly) the utterances of the prophets as a gift from God (*Dial.* 92.1), i.e., as divine enlightenment; similarly, *Dial.* 119.1.

42 See W. Bauer, W.F. Arndt, and F.W. Gingrich, *A Greek-English Lexicon of the New Testament and Other Early Christian Literature* (Cambridge: Cambridge University Press, and Chicago: University of Chicago Press, 1957), s.v. *phōtizō*, and H. Conzelmann, *phōs, etc.*, *TDNT*, 9 (1974), 310-58. *1 Clem.* 36.2, though not connecting enlightenment with baptism as Justin does, is yet similar in thought and terminology to *1 Apol.* 61.12.

43 Cf. Justin's own description of his change in attitude to Christianity and pagan opinions of it as a result of his conversion, *2 Apol.* 13.1.

44 See M. Eliade, *Birth and Rebirth: The Religious Meanings of Initiation in Human Culture*, trans. W.R. Trask (New York: Harper, 1958).

45 See, e.g., M.P. Nilsson, *Geschichte der griechischen Religion*, vol. 1, *Die Religion Griechenlands bis auf die griechische Weltherrschaft* (Handbuch der Altertumswissenschaft, 5/2/1; Munich: Beck, 3d edition 1967), 653ff.; vol. 2, *Die hellenistische und römische Zeit* (Handbuch, 5/2/2; Munich: Beck, 2d edition 1961), 679ff.; or the well-known enlightenment and initiation of Lucius in Apuleius, *Metam.* 11.

was expecting to behold God at once" (*Dial.* 2.6). In a passage in the
First Apology (2.1) he formulates a hermeneutical principle for such
nihilations: reason (*ho logos*) dictates that truly religious persons and
philosophers should honour and love only that which is true and
decline to follow the opinions of the ancients if these are bad. But what
is "true"? The "true" is apt to be, as was suggested above, that which is
regarded as "true" within Justin's social and cultural matrix.[46]

What is that matrix? Justin's arguments in the *Dialogue* may well
reflect his experience, not only as a seeker prior to his embracing of
Christianity, but especially as a Christian teacher. In the *Acta Iustini*[47]
Justin says that he shared the doctrines of truth with those who wished
to hear them (3.10), and one of Justin's pupils and fellow martyrs says
he received Christian instruction from his parents and further instruction from Justin (4.9-10). George Hunston Williams' characterization
of Justin's school seems apt: it "was something between an advanced
catechetical centre and a one-man philosophical hall."[48] The old Christian in Justin's conversion account, though perhaps a fictitious persona
(modeled after Socrates), may in fact represent a Christian or Christians with whom Justin carried on dialogues before his conversion;
equally likely, he may represent Justin himself after his conversion,
engaging as a Christian teacher in debates with Platonists. It has been
suggested from time to time that the *Dialogue* is the record of an actual
disputation.[49] It is impossible to say with any certainty whether that is
indeed the case, though the promise by Justin (in *Dial.* 80.3) to make a
record of what has passed between himself and Trypho hints at some
such genesis of the writing. The seeming planlessness of the *Dialogue*,

---

46   The Christian reference of "truth" for Justin is seen in passages such as *Dial.* 110.6
      where Justin describes conversion to Christianity as *epignōnai tēn alētheian tou theou*
      (cf. *Dial.* 8.2: if Trypho is concerned about salvation and trusts in God, he should
      come to know the Christ of God, *epignonti soi ton christon tou theou*) and *Dial.* 8.1 where
      he characterizes Christianity as the only trustworthy and beneficial philosophy.

47   In J.C.T. von Otto (ed.), *Corpus Apologetarum Christianorum Saeculi Secundi* (Jena, 3d
      edition 1876-91), vol. 3, *Iustinus Philosophus et Martyr* = Iustini Philosophi et Martyris
      Opera Quae Feruntur Omnia, vol. 2, *Opera Iustini Addubitata* (reprinted, Liechten-
      stein: Martin Sändig, n.d.), 266-79. On the authenticity of the account see
      Goodenough, *Theology*, 75.

48   Williams, "Justin Glimpsed as Martyr Among his Roman Contemporaries," in A.J.
      McKelway and E.D. Willis (eds.), *The Context of Contemporary Theology: Essays in Honor
      of Paul Lehmann* (Atlanta: John Knox, 1974), 108; cf. A. von Harnack, *Die Mission und
      Ausbreitung des Christentums in den ersten drei Jahrhunderten*, vol. 1, *Die Mission in Wort
      und Tat* (Leipzig: Hinrichs, 4th edition 1924), 367.

49   Eusebius, *H.E.* 4.18.6; Krauss, "The Jews" (cited above, n. 31), 124-25; A.L. Wil-
      liams, trans., *Justin Martyr: The Dialogue with Trypho* (London: SPCK, 1930), xxiv
      ("The details of the meeting of Justin and Trypho, and of the emotions with which
      from time to time both they and Trypho's friends are moved, are related too
      naturally to be fictitious." But the *Dialogue* also includes additions from other such
      discussions and perhaps "old notes of his own lectures, or even of his homiletical
      discourses to Christian friends").

on the other hand, may in fact smell of the lamp: The early part of the *Dialogue* may be based on collections of testimonia, with sections 10-29 focusing on texts that treat ritual and cult and sections 30-44 treating messianic prophecies.[50] In the words of Goodenough's summary, "That the arguments of Justin are those generally used in such discussions is highly probable, but the *Dialogue* seems far rather to be a collection of all possible arguments than a report of a discussion in which each argument was actually brought up as recorded."[51] To suggest a lucubratious origin of the *Dialogue* does not entail that the writing is not rooted in Justin's activity as a Christian teacher. Trypho attributes Justin's ready answers to his participation in earlier disputes (50.1), and to Justin's self-deprecation of his rhetorical talents (58.1) Trypho replies that Justin must surely be engaging in understatement (58.2; *eirōneuesthai*); the extended, developed arguments in the *Dialogue* point to significant contact between Justin and Jews, with his arguments hammered out in conversations and disputes with them.

The presence of significant Jewish communities in the Empire at the time of Justin is important in understanding Justin's argument with Trypho. Robert Wilken has assembled a considerable body of evidence from (especially) Christian literary sources, from ecclesiastical canons, from civil legislation, and from archaeology to show that well beyond the second century—on at least into the fifth century—Judaism was a living presence in the Empire, in vigorous communities thriving materially, intellectually, culturally, and religiously, and enjoying the protection of Christian emperors.[52] Commenting on Christian writings about Judaism in this period, Wilken says that:

[W]e are not dealing with Jewish traditions that are background for Christian thinking, nor with Jewish exegetical principles derived from Jewish books. Rather, Christians are being confronted by Jews in their own times who live in the cities alongside of Christians, part of their foreground if you will, and present themselves as rival interpreters of the ancient Jewish tradition which Christians claimed as their own. The Scriptures did not exist in a vacuum. They belonged to particular communities.[53]

For the second century the evidence for such thriving Jewish communities, in the locales where Justin's dialogue with Trypho is perhaps set or where Justin lived and worked, is also solid. If the setting of the

---

50   Thus Chadwick, "Justin Martyr's Defence" (cited above, n. 31), 281-82.
51   Goodenough, *Theology*, 90.
52   R.L. Wilken, *Judaism and the Early Christian Mind: A Study of Cyril of Alexandria's Exegesis and Theology* (New Haven and London: Yale University Press, 1971), chapter 1 (summary, pp. 36-38); "The Jews and Christian Apologetics after Theodosius I *Cunctos Populos*," *HTR* 73 (1980), 451-71.
53   Wilken, "Jews and Christian Apologetics," 467.

Dialogue is Asia Minor, or if Justin was active there for a time,[54] there is archaeological and literary evidence showing the existence of thriving Jewish communities in Ephesus, Smyrna, Magnesia, Philadelphia, and Sardis during this general period.[55] If, as seems likely from the date commonly assigned to the *Dialogue*,[56] Justin composed it in Rome, there, too, the literary and archaeological evidence demonstrates the presence of a number of significant (and diverse) Jewish communities with their own synagogues, burial grounds, and even a rabbinic academy.[57]

Christian dialogue with Jews, one may conclude, was not a mere literary exercise—not in the second century, not even as late as the fifth century.

In a number of passages the *Dialogue* manifests an awareness of continuing contact between Jews and Christians. Trypho has been warned by his community leaders not to enter into discussion with Christians (38.1; 112.4), indicating that such encounters were in fact occurring. Jews, says Justin, curse Christ and his followers in their synagogues (16.4; 47.4; 93.4; 95.4; 133.6) and persecute those followers when given the power to do so (16.4; 95.4; 133.6; cf. *1 Apol.* 31.5).[58] One purpose of such cursing was to expose confessors to Christ who may have been present in the synagogue.[59] Popular literature also sug-

---

54   Eusebius, *H.E.* 4.18.6, sets the dialogue in Ephesus. *Dial.* 1.1, *en tois tou xustou peripatois* is opaque as a geographical reference.

55   E.M. Smallwood, *The Jews Under Roman Rule: From Pompey to Diocletian* (Leiden: Brill, 1976), 508-509; A.T. Kraabel, "Melito the Bishop and the Synagogue at Sardis: Text and Context," in D.G. Mitten, J.G. Pedley, and J.A. Scott (eds.), *Studies Presented to George M.A. Hanfmann* (Mainz: Verlag Philipp von Zabern; and Cambridge, MA: Fogg Art Museum, Harvard University, 1971), 77-85.

56   E.J. Goodspeed and R.M. Grant, *A History of Early Christian Literature* (Chicago: University of Chicago Press, 1966), 101: Justin is in Rome by 150 C.E., the *Dialogue* composed between 155 and 160.

57   The evidence is summarized in Smallwood, *Jews Under Roman Rule*, 519-24; M. Radin, *The Jews Among the Greeks and the Romans* (Philadelphia: Jewish Publication Society of America, 1915; reprinted, New York: Arno Press, 1973), chap. 19, reviews the literary evidence and reproduces a sampling of the symbols and inscriptions; also G. La Piana, "Foreign Groups in Rome During the First Centuries of the Empire," *HTR* 20 (1927), 341ff.; H.J. Leon, *The Jews of Ancient Rome* (Philadelphia: Jewish Publication Society of America, 1960), *passim*.

58   The well-known twelfth of the Eighteen Benedictions which, according to the Palestinian recension and various Christian texts, anathematized "the Nazarenes" alongside the *minim*, may underlie these statements by Justin. On the term "Nazarenes" in the Benedictions see, *inter alia*, Krauss, "The Jews" (cited above, n. 31), 132-34; R. Travers Herford, *Christianity in Talmud and Midrash* (London: Norgate and Williams, 1903), 379-81; G.F. Moore, "Nazarene and Nazareth" in F.J. Foakes Jackson and K. Lake (eds.), *The Beginnings of Christianity*, part 1, *The Acts of the Apostles*, vol. 1, *Prolegomena I: the Jewish, Gentile and Christian Backgrounds* (London: Macmillan, 1920), 426-32; M. Simon, *Verus Israel: Etude sur les relations entre chrétiens et juifs dans l'Empire romaine (135-425)* (Paris: Editions E. de Boccard, 1964), 235-36.

59   Simon, *Verus Israel*, 236: "Comme tous les membres de la communauté pouvaient être appelés à tour de rôle, en l'absence de clergé véritable, à officier dans le culte

gests contact between Jews and Christians, often with no sharp awareness of separation between the two groups.[60] That Trypho, who has
been warned by his leaders against entering into discussions with
Christians, should do so nonetheless seems plausible therefore. Given
the rooting of Jews like Trypho in vigorous Jewish communities like
those just described, it is also plausible—and indeed true to life—that
the *Dialogue* should end in an impasse. As a literary work, it need not
have ended that way. Justin could have embraced Trypho's Judaism
(though the preceding text would hardly motivate such action).
Trypho could have accepted Justin's Christian interpretation of his
scriptures, as commonly happens in the *Adversus Iudaeos* literature.
Both respect philosophy and might have turned their commitment and
energies in that direction. The impasse, however, is the most plausible
ending if one reflects on Justin's odyssey into Platonism and then into
Christianity; for, in order to accept Justin's arguments, Trypho for his
part would have had to pay a similar price—giving up his particular
Jewish identity and, in effect, denying the Jewish fellowship he enjoyed. In short, he would have had to undergo a radical resocialization,
a conversion.

Justin and Anti-Judaism—and Paganism

Is the *Dialogue* anti-Jewish? If one element in the definition of anti-
Jewishness is ignorance and unreality—a fantasized picture of contemporary Judaism and its representatives—then Justin would seem
to be able to plead not guilty. Although Trypho is a straw man in the
sense that "he cannot be identified with any historical character, and is
obviously a tool in Justin's hands,"[61] yet Justin's portrayal of his Judaism
is not simply fabricated; several scholars have specified the accuracy, in
essentials and often in details, of Justin's portrayal of contemporary
Judaism.[62] Nor is Trypho like those straw men in some other Christian

   public, le moyen était sûr: un officiant contaminé par l'hérésie devait nécessaire-
   ment hésiter à prononcer, avec cette bénédiction, sa propre condamnation. Le
   Talmud de dit en toute netteté: 'Lorsque quelqu'un fait une faute dans une quel-
   conque bénédiction, on le laisse continuer; mais s'il s'agit de la bénédiction des
   Minim, on le rappelle à sa place car on le soupçonne d'être un Min'" (*B. Ber.*
   28b-29a).

60   J. Parkes, *The Conflict of the Church and the Synagogue: A Study in the Origins of
   Antisemitism* (London: Soncino Press, 1934; reprinted, New York: Sepher-Hermon,
   1974), 92-94, 144-50.

61   Goodenough, *Theology* (cited above, n. 31), 92.

62   Ibid., 92-96; Barnard, "Old Testament and Judaism" (cited above, n. 31), 400-406;
   P. Sigal, "An Inquiry into Aspects of Judaism in Justin's Dialogue with Trypho,"
   Abr-Nahrain 18 (1978-79), 74-100 (*non vidi*; summarized in *Science of Religion Abstracts
   and Indexes of Recent Articles* 6/1 [1981], 41).

writings of Jewish-Christian dialogue who are knocked down by the ineluctable force of Christian argumentation, only to rise, like Lazarus, and after shedding their Jewish winding sheets enter into eternal life by embracing the Christianity of their *Gesprächspartner*.[63]

If another element in the definition of anti-Jewishness is rancour, then, again, Justin is not egregiously guilty. In *Dial.* 110.2 he describes Jewish teachers as *alogistoi, mē sunientes*, and in 115.5-6 he gives vent to frustration with Jewish polemicists who may find 10,000 Christian utterances well expressed but then light, like a swarm of flies, on one small point. Still, Justin's respect for his learned opponent is apparent throughout the *Dialogue*, and he is willing to give Trypho the benefit of the doubt on his motivations (65.2-3).[64] By way of contrast, one does not find in the *Dialogue* acrimonious accusations of the Jews like those in the *Peri Pascha* of Justin's Christian contemporary, Melito of Sardis,[65] nor scorn and indignation like that which his pagan contemporary, Celsus, heaps on Christianity. And even though Justin is adept at stigmatizing objectionable religious phenomena by ascribing them to demonic agency,[66] he does not, as does the *Dialogue of Timothy and*

---

63 Thus in the *Dialogue of Athanasius and Zacchaeus*, which F.C. Conybeare, "A New Second-Century Christian Dialogue," *The Expositor* 15 (1897), 300-301, dates to the second century; Conybeare's English translation of the Armenian version appears on pages 300-20, 443-63; the Greek text (collated with the Armenian) is given in Conybeare (ed.), *The Dialogues of Athanasius and Zacchaeus and of Timothy and Aquila* (Oxford: Clarendon Press, 1898), 1-64; the conversion of Zacchaeus occurs at the conclusion of the work. Similarly, the conversion of Aquila concludes the *Dialogue of Timothy and Aquila* (Greek text on pages 65-104); A.L. Williams, *Adversus Judaeos: A Bird's-Eye View of Christian* Apologiae *until the Renaissance* (Cambridge: Cambridge University Press, 1935), 71, dates the work to "about the end of the second century of our era." The mss. of these dialogues are of course later than the dates of composition assigned to them.

In the *Altercatio Simonis Iudaei et Theophili* (cited above, n. 25) the condition laid down at the start (sec. 1 [p. 16, lines 3-4]) is that the loser in the debate will embrace the faith of the winner; the Jew is assigned only brief lines, while the Christian makes lengthy speeches; and, as Harnack remarks (in his edition, p. 50), "Fast jede Antwort des Christen befriedigt den Juden sofort; sie lässt ihm nur Raum für neue Fragen, bis er sich am Schluss für überwunden und überzeugt erklärt."

64 Since, as A. von Harnack observes (*Judentum und Judenchristentum in Justins Dialog mit Trypho*, TU 39/1 [Leipzig, Hinrichs, 1913], 92), the *Dialogue* is in effect a monologue inasmuch as Justin puts the words into Trypho's mouth, it is noteworthy that Trypho comes across as favourably as he does. Cf. Williams, *Adversus Judaeos*, 42: "there is no Dialogue as such which is conducted on so high a level of courteousness and fairness until Gilbert Crispin's at Westminster in the end of the eleventh century."

65 O. Perler, ed. and trans., *Méliton de Sardes, Sur la Pâque et fragments*, Source chrétiens, 123 (Paris: Les Editions du Cerf, 1966), paras. 73-75, 78-94, 97. Less biting, though hardly cordial, are the terms employed by the Christian in the *Altercatio Simonis Iudaei et Theophili* to designate his Jewish dialogue partner: disbelieving (*incredule*, 7 [p. 18, line 9] and 16 [p. 25, line 1]; *incredulitas*, 13 [p. 23, line 12] and 14 [p. 23, line 24; p. 24, line 1]); ignorant (*ignorantia*, 12 [p. 21, lines 22, 26]); after his conversion the Jew applies these terms to himself (30, p. 44, lines 3-4).

66 See above, section on "Justin and Paganism," pp. 59-66.

Aquila, say that the devil enters into his dialogue partner and inspires his speech.[67]

If another element in the definition of anti-Jewishness is the assertion that the Jews are being punished for their crucifixion of Jesus, then Justin is guilty, but not to the degree that some other Christian writers are. In *Dial.* 16.3-4 Justin connects Jewish suffering with their crucifixion of Jesus, but other passages do not make that connection. Jesus was "crucified under Pontius Pilate by your people," says Justin (*Dial.* 85.2), but he does not connect that to the destruction of Jerusalem. In saying that the destruction of Jerusalem should lead Jews to repentance (108.2), he does not say that the destruction is the result of the crucifixion, for which he has just blamed the Jews (108.2) and he goes on to say that, even though Jews travel around denouncing Jesus as the originator of a godless and lawless sect (*hairesis . . . atheos kai anomos*) and cursing Christians (108.2, 3), yet Christians do not hate the Jews but, rather, pray for their repentance (108.3; cf. 133.6). In *Dial.* 110.6 Justin sees Jewish defeat in (the recent) war as attested in the scriptures, but, again, he does not connect that with the crucifixion (he cites Isaiah). Justin does say that those who persecuted Christ, and continue to persecute him (in his followers), shall, if they do not repent, have no inheritance in the holy mountain (26.1). In such a passage, Justin would seem to have preserved some of the "eschatological reservation" that has been noted as characteristic of certain early Christian writings[68]—salvation and its benefits are not merely now but also (and definitively) in the future. By way of contrast, one does not find in Justin, for example, the kind of harsh statements about the deserved punishment of the Jews that is set forth in the well-known passage in 1 Thess. 2.14-16 or in Eusebius' account of the Christians' flight to Pella during the first Jewish revolt: Then "God's judgment at last overtook them [the Jews] because they had committed so many crimes against the Christ and his apostles, [the judgment thus] obliterating utterly that generation of the wicked from among humans" (*H.E.* 3.5.3). "It was necessary, then, that in the days in which they had disposed of the Saviour and benefactor of all, the Christ of God, they—shut up, as in a

---

67 *Timothy and Aquila*, fol. 75v-76r (Conybeare ed., 1898, p. 65): "The demon [*daimōn; diabolos* appears in the line preceding], who hates good, seeing that God was being glorified and worshipped but that his own works were being undone and held in contempt, became extremely angry and entered into a certain Jew named Aquila. Just as, in paradise, he entered the weak vessel, the woman, through the snake, so he now entered into a Jew." In the *Altercatio Simonis Iudaei et Theophili* the devil is also adduced as a cause of the Jew's failure to see the Christian truth: 26 (p. 39, lines 3-6); 27 (p. 39, lines 20-22); 28 (p. 40, lines 19-20).

68 On the "eschatological reservation" see J.M. Robinson, in Robinson and H. Koester, *Trajectories through Early Christianity* (Philadelphia: Fortress Press, 1971), 31-35; E. Käsemann, *An die Römer*, Handbuch zum Neuen Testament, 8a (Tübingen: Mohr [Siebeck], 3d edition 1974), 158-59.

prison—should receive the destruction that dogged them from the divine judgment" (*H.E.* 3.5.6). As to Justin's "eschatological reservation," one may contrast with it the kind encountered in the *Dialogue of Papiscus and Philo*, which focuses on punishment of Jews: from the time they crucified Christ the Jews have been dispersed and persecuted and separated from the temple and the observance of the law; they have been "cast out until the consummation of the age" (*heōs tēs sunteleias tou aiōnos*).[69]

To the Gentiles, *Papiscus and Philo* goes on to say, belong the promises.[70] So, too, Justin's *Dialogue:* along with much other early Christian literature it lays claim to "the promises in a book [the scriptures] which was composed of promises and denunciations. The denunciations, therefore, must belong to the Jews."[71] Christians, through their interpretations of the scriptures, "disinherited the Jew from his own sacred books at the very moment [following either of two disastrous Jewish revolts] when these provided his only [sic] comfort. All the law and the promises led on to Christ the Messiah. Rejecting him, the Jew lost all share in them."[72] It is clear from the *Dialogue* that, though Justin manifests little rancour to Jews, for him it is axiomatic that his group and its social and cultural worlds are divinely—and specially—blessed and are therefore superior to Trypho and his fellow Jews and their social and cultural worlds and supersede them. Trypho and his fellow Jews should therefore repent; apart from such repentance (25.6; 141) there is no continuing theological validity, no continuing theological space, for Jewish communities alongside Christianity. In that sense the *Dialogue* may be said to be anti-Jewish.

Living space for Jews is another matter. A recent study by Jeremy Cohen argues that, "Prior to the thirteenth century, Catholic theology

---

69 *Papiscus and Philo* 16, p. 80, lines 1-16, in A.C. McGiffert (ed.), *Dialogue between a Christian and a Jew Entitled* Antibolē Papiskou kai Philōnos Ioudaiōn pros monachon tina (New York: Christian Literature Co., 1889). The composition of the work has been dated to the sixth century; T. von Zahn thought it contained remnants of the lost *Dialogue of Jason and Papiscus* by Ariston of Pella; see Adolf von Harnack, *Geschichte der altchristlichen Literatur bis Eusebius*, part 1, *Die Überlieferung und der Bestand* (Leipzig, 1893; 2d edition, with a Foreword by K. Aland, Leipzig: Hinrichs, 1958), 94.10; E.J. Goodspeed, "Pappiscus [sic] and Philo," *AJT* 4 (1900), 796; Williams, *Adversus Judaeos* (cited above, n. 63), 170, dates the two recensions to the seventh and the eleventh centuries.

70 *Papiscus and Philo* 16, p. 80, lines 16-19, in McGiffert edition.

71 Parkes, *Conflict* (cited above, n. 60), 114; cf. further, pp. 82-85 and the early Christian sources cited there.

72 Ibid., 84. Cutting—in view of Christian attribution of the destruction of Jerusalem to divine judgment, and the resentment such assertions would arouse in Jews—is the statement in *Athanasius and Zacchaeus* (Conybeare Greek ed., p. 44, para. 78; Conybeare translation of Armenian version, p. 449; both cited above, n. 63) that if Jews were not so unfeeling (*anaisthētousin*) they would have felt more anguish (*peponthasin*) at the destruction of Jerusalem than the Egyptians did at the loss of their first-born.

had demanded that the Jews be tolerated in Christendom."[73] This was
an Augustinian view, based on the premise that "God had ordained the
survival of the Jews, in order that their presence and continued observance of Mosaic Law might aid the Church in its mission to the Gentiles,
and so they might convert at the end of days."[74] That is, the conclusion
was not drawn — in a systematic way — that because Judaism had been
superseded by Christianity therefore Jewish communities should cease
to exist. Actions—whether of Christian clergy, councils, or laity, or of
Christian emperors or other officials—did not, of course, neatly con-
form to the Augustinian view; there were many other variables, with
resultant harassment and persecution of Jews and Jewish communities,
forced baptisms, attacks on and confiscation of Jewish property, and
gradual erosion of Jewish legal rights and status.[75] In the earlier centuries, Jews, especially where they were numerous, are also reported as
mounting attacks on Christians or on Christians' property.[76] There is
also evidence, however, of friendly, even close relations between Jews
and Christians,[77] and when Christians physically attacked Jews or their
institutions, various emperors affirmed Jewish legal rights and
privileges.[78] If Cohen is correct, however, beginning in the early fourteenth century the Dominican and Franciscan friars began to advocate
openly that "Latin Christendom rid itself of its Jewish population,
whether through missionizing, forced expulsions, or physical harassment that would induce conversion or flight."[79] It was the friars, then,
who "developed and manned the papal Inquisition, who intervened in
the Maimonidean controversy, who directed the burnings of the Talmud, who compelled the Jews to listen and respond to their inflam-
matory sermons, and who actively promoted anti-Jewish hatred among
the laity of Western Christendom."[80] In drawing from the early Christian premise that Christianity had superseded Judaism, a conclusion
that Justin does not draw and Augustine did not draw, the friars
"facilitated the original vision of a Europe *judenrein*."[81]

---

73 J. Cohen, *The Friars and the Jews: The Evolution of Medieval Anti-Judaism* (Ithaca and
    London: Cornell University Press, 1982), 14.
74 Ibid.; on this Augustinian view see Simon, *Verus Israel* (cited above, n. 58), 119-20,
    270.
75 See the survey of Jewish-Christian relations in the first eight centuries of the present
    era in Parkes, *Conflict* (cited above, n. 60), chaps. 3-10.
76 Ibid., 202-3, 234-35, 258-60.
77 Ibid., 174-77, 189-95, 268-69, 306, 320, 324, 327, 339, 342-44.
78 Ibid., 177, 188-89; 201-3, 207-9, 275-76; see Wilken, "Jews and Christian Apologe-
    tics" (cited above, n. 52), for further examples. App. 1.1 in Parkes, *Conflict*, provides
    a chronological listing for the period 300-800 C.E. of legislation affecting Jews.
    Parkes, 183, 239-43, 255-56, notes, by way of comparison, the harsh treatment of
    heretics which, in the earlier centuries, was often worse than that accorded Jews.
79 Cohen, *Friars and Jews*, 14.
80 Ibid., 13.
81 Ibid., 16.

As a literary work that asserts the superseding of Judaism by Christianity, the *Dialogue*—perhaps in part through its bulk and its detail—may have served as a resource and warrant for such persecution, may have functioned, in other words, as anti-Judaic in an immediate and pressing sense. To investigate such influence goes beyond the scope of this essay. In the *Dialogue* itself, one may observe that the eschatological reservation that might have followed from Justin's assertion of a "second advent" of Jesus (31.1; 49.2; 52.1; 110.2; 111.1), ushering in a millennium (80.5; 81; 139.4) that even Trypho would be forced to acknowledge, is forfeited to a present and emphatic assertion of what Rosemary Ruether has called a "messianic midrash," with an "anti-Judaic left hand" and elevated to "a *new principle of salvation*."[82]

Here it is important to note that, at this remove from Justin and his social and cultural matrices, we are apt to overlook a pressing reason Justin had for making such a move. If the price Trypho and his fellow Jews would have to pay for assenting to Justin's arguments—namely, conversion—is too high for them to pay, think what is at stake for Justin—and other Christians of his and immediately succeeding centuries—in their encounters with Jews. Were Justin to accede to the Jewish communities' interpretations of the Jewish scriptures—and they are indeed the scriptures of the Jews, as Justin plainly states, before quickly claiming them for Christianity since Christians believe them whereas Jews, though they read them, do not perceive their sense (*ou noeite ton en autois noun*; *Dial*. 29.2)—and to these communities' continuing observance of precepts set forth in those scriptures, then not only does Christianity lose its legitimacy over against Judaism but, at least as important, Christianity is subject to attack by pagans as a nouveau sect apostate from Judaism. Celsus, not long after Justin, makes just such an attack and, if Carl Andresen is right, precisely against Justin.[83] Though not fond of Jews either, Celsus notes that they, in contrast to Christians, at least have their own, traditional *nomos*.[84] The scriptures that belong to that tradition are accessible, in Hebrew or Greek, in the library at Alexandria, says Tertullian (*Apol*. 18.8). To prove to a pagan that what Christians said about prophecy was indeed contained in the Hebrew scriptures, Augustine took the pagan to Jews

---

82 R.R. Ruether, *Faith and Fratricide: The Theological Roots of Anti-Semitism* (New York: Seabury Press, 1974), 78 (italics in the original).

83 Andresen, *Logos und Nomos* (cited above, n. 32); Andresen's argument is summarized, with general approval, by Chadwick (cited above, n. 31), 132, n. 59; see also A.D. Nock's review of Andresen in *JTS* N.S. 7 (1956), 314-17, esp. 316, n. 4.

84 Celsus, *Alethes Logos*, in Origen, *Contra Celsum* 5.41 (*ton idion nomon*). In 5.25 Celsus states that the Jews, on becoming a distinct people (*ethnos idion*), made laws befitting themselves, which they preserve along with their worship, as other persons do. Whatever else Jewish worship may be, it is traditional (*hopoian dē, patrion d'oun*). The foil is the Christians.

who could produce the scriptures containing the prophecies.[85] If pagans wanted to learn from the Jewish scriptures—and the well-known attraction of Judaism for pagans should not be overlooked—why should they bother with the Christian middlemen? For the Christians the danger was, as John Chrysostom put it to judaizing Christians in Antioch a couple of centuries after Justin's *Dialogue* was composed, "Don't you realize, if the Jewish rites are holy and venerable, our way of life must be false."[86] In Justin's dispute with Trypho the Jew, paganism is the third—the silent—partner.[87] On the law and the prophets—Christianly interpreted—hang the claims Justin makes for Christianity vis-à-vis paganism.[88] Viewing the *Dialogue* in this light, one may well incline to Goodenough's observation many years ago that the *Dialogue* is really addressed to pagans—and, one might add, to Justin's fellow Christians living vis-à-vis both pagans and Jews—to show that revelation is necessary to come to the truth which philosophy is incapable of attaining and that in the *Dialogue* Justin is seeking to demonstrate to such an audience that the Jewish scriptures and Christian teachings are "a unified production of the single spirit of Inspiration and Revelation."[89]

---

85 Wilken, "Jews and Christian Apologetics," 467-68 (citing Augustine, *Commentary on John* 35.7). Cf. further, p. 468: "In Antioch Jews and Judaizing Christians taunted Christian leaders with the indisputable fact: the Christian Old Testament is a Jewish book. Indeed one thing which drew Christians to the synagogue was that 'the law and the books of the prophets can be found there.' And this, says John [Chrysostom] is the reason I 'especially hate the synagogue' (*Adv. Iud.* 1.5)."
86 *Adv. Iud.* 1.6; cited in Wilken, "Jews and Christian Apologetics," 470.
87 I am grateful to Robert Wilken for this insight.
88 See above, section on "Justin and Paganism," pp. 59-66.
89 Goodenough, *Theology* (cited above, n. 31), 96-100 (the quotation is from p. 99). Earlier, Harnack had observed that the introduction to the *Dialogue*, with its account of Justin's conversion from paganism, "zeigt nun aber, dass das ganze Werk an das griechische Publikum gerichtet ist und nicht, oder doch nicht vornehmlich, auf jüdische Leser rechnete." Harnack (ed.), *Die Altercatio Simonis Iudaei et Theophili Christiani* (cited above, n. 25), 78. Harnack (p. 78, n. 58) notes that F. Overbeck had made the same observation.

6

Melito and Israel

Stephen G. Wilson

Introduction

"Marred by cavalier and superficial use of evidence, as well as by a deplorable harshness of tone . . . ,"[1] said S.G. Hall of an article by E. Werner entitled "Melito of Sardis: The First Poet of Deicide."[2] The "harshness of tone" presumably refers to passages where Werner, a Jew, castigates Melito in no uncertain terms as the author of the accusation that the Jews were guilty of deicide. Harsh words they may be, but scarcely harsher than the words of Melito and certainly milder than the shocking anti-Jewish outbursts of many subsequent proponents of Christianity. Moreover, it could be argued equally well that Hall himself shows an astonishing insensitivity to the anti-Jewish strain implicit and explicit in Melito's *Peri Pascha*. It is remarkable that he, the author of several tightly argued and persuasive articles about Melito and of the best modern edition of the *Peri Pascha*, can in this edition relegate the problem of Melito and the Jews to a passing reference to "the power of the Jewish community in civic life in Sardis," in order to explain the parallels between the *Peri Pascha* and Jewish Passover haggadah, and a laconic footnote to the effect that "Melito shares with the *Evangelium Petri* the tendency to attribute the crucifixion directly and exclusively to Israel."[3]

---

1 S.G. Hall, "Melito in the Light of the Passover Haggadah," *JTS* 22 (1971), 29-46, here 29.
2 E. Werner, "Melito of Sardis: The First Poet of Deicide," *HUCA* 37, (1966), 191-210.
3 S.G. Hall, *Melito of Sardis "On Pascha" and Fragments* (Oxford: Clarendon, 1979), quotations from xxvii and 39 n. 40. All references to *Peri Pascha* and the fragments are based on Hall's text and translation. The text is referred to either by section or by line.

Hall is not alone in this regard for, as A.T. Kraabel noted in 1971, a whole generation of scholars ignored the anti-Jewish polemic in Melito—a fact for which he could provide no ready explanation.[4] A partial explanation is doubtless to be found in the basic hermeneutical principle that what is derived from a text depends to a great extent on the questions the interpreter brings to it. For Christian scholars whose interest is in the theology and liturgical practices of Melito and his community, and for whom the appropriation of Jewish traditions and the assertion of Jewish obduracy and perfidy are natural and necessary concomitants of Christian self-definition, Melito's view of Judaism is likely to be neither an important nor a problematic aspect of his work. Yet, when approximately three quarters of the 105 sections of *Peri Pascha* (1-45, 72-99) deal implicitly or explicitly either with the status of Israel or the charge of deicide, the scholarly silence still remains somewhat puzzling. A notable exception is the sensitive discussion of the charge of deicide by J. Blank[5] but, as we shall argue below, equally important for Melito's view of Judaism is the typological exegesis of the Passover traditions at the beginning of the homily.

Before this material is analyzed more closely, it is important to set the scene with the few extant details of Melito's life and work, all of which will be recalled later as we attempt to explain his view of "Israel." Eusebius (*H.E.* 5.24.2-6) quotes a letter in which Polycrates, the aged bishop of Ephesus, defends (*c* 195 C.E.) the paschal tradition of the Asian churches. It lists the Asian luminaries who had been faithful to this tradition: Philip (called an apostle) and his daughters, the apostle John, Polycarp of Smyrna, Thraseus of Eumenea, Sagaris of Laodicea, Papirius, and "Melito the eunuch whose whole career was in the Holy Spirit, who lies at Sardis awaiting the visitation from heaven when he shall rise from the dead. These all kept the fourteenth day of the Pascha in accordance with the Gospel, in no way deviating, but following the rule of faith." From this we can infer that Melito was a celibate (less likely a full eunuch) and a man of notable prophetic gifts. Eusebius assumes (*H.E.* 4:26.1) that he was bishop of Sardis, which was probably but not certainly the case.[6] Important for our purposes was Melito's adherence to the Quartodeciman tradition of Asia Minor. The Quartodecimans celebrated Easter on the day of the Jewish Passover (14 Nisan), regardless of which day of the week it fell on, rather than on the

---

4   A.T. Kraabel, "Melito the Bishop and the Synagogue at Sardis: Text and Context" in D.G. Mitten, J.G. Pedley, and J.A. Scott (eds.), *Studies Presented to George M.A. Hanfmann* (Mainz: von Zabern, 1972), 72-85, here 81 n. 25.

5   Noted by Kraabel, "Melito," 85 n. 35. See also J. Blank, *Meliton von Sardes VOM PASSA: Die älteste christliche Österpredigt* (Freiburg: Lambertus, 1963), 77-86; K.W. Noakes, "Melito of Sardis and the Jews," in *Studia Patristica* 13 (1975), TU 166, 244-49; R. Wilken, "Melito and the Sacrifice of Isaac," *TS* 37 (1976), 53-69.

6   Hall, *On Pascha*, xii.

first Sunday after Passover as in the so-called "Roman" tradition. It was in response to an attempt by Victor, bishop of Rome, to ban the Quartodeciman dating of Easter that Polycrates wrote his letter. Victor's ban was considered high-handed by some in his day, but his views eventually prevailed despite lingering pockets of resistance.

Melito was a prolific and highly regarded author. Eusebius (*H.E.* 4.26.14) attributes sixteen works to him but, apart from the *Peri Pascha*, only a few fragments have survived and their attribution both to Melito and to specific works in Eusebius' list is often uncertain.[7] There is, however, no reason to doubt that Melito wrote a considerable number of works on a variety of topics, that some of his contemporaries and immediate successors were much influenced by them, and that their influence was fairly short-lived partly because he represented the minority strain of Asian Christianity and partly because his theological views (e.g., his christology) subsequently became suspect. It is probable that some of his works were designed to counter some of the more successful but, to Melito, deviant Christian movements of his day, notably Marcionites, gnostics, and Montanists.

In addition to his various theological tracts Melito addressed an apologetic work to the Emperor Marcus Aurelius in response to some new decrees which had led to confiscation of goods, harassment, and even martyrdom among Asian Christians.[8] Melito seems confident that the Emperor had not authorized these decrees, a confidence based not only on the proven record of Imperial support for the Christian movement (with Nero and Domitian mentioned as notorious exceptions) but on the novel argument that the simultaneous flowering of Christianity and the Roman Empire from the time of Augustus suggested a degree of mutual dependence best nurtured by continuing mutual support: "Our philosophy first flourished among barbarians, but it blossomed out among your peoples during the great reign of your ancestor Augustus, and became especially for your empire an auspicious benefit." The surviving fragments of Melito's apology reveal a concern for the public reputation of Christianity as well as the protection of its adherents, which may well in turn have influenced his view of Judaism—a matter to which we will return below.

Melito was also an accomplished writer and orator. Tertullian apparently considered him to have an *elegans et declamatorium ingenium*

---

7   It is uncertain whether *Peri Pascha* is to be identified with the "two books on the Pascha" mentioned by Eusebius. For full discussion of the list and the fragments see Hall, *On Pascha*, xiii-xxii, xxviii-xxxix and the translations on 62-96. Also Blank, *Meliton*, 15f; O. Perler, *Méliton de Sardes Sur la pâque et fragments* (Paris: Les editions du Cerf, 1966), 11-15.

8   Identification of the "decrees" has remained difficult. Melito says they affected Asia, which need not imply that they affected Asia alone. The confident appeal for Imperial support and the suggestion that the Emperor had not authorized them perhaps suggest a local phenomenon.

(Jerome, *De Viris illustribus*, 24), and the *Peri Pascha* itself provides
ample evidence of his rhetorical and dramatic skills. The repeated, if
perhaps excessive, use of exclamation, question, repetition, antithesis,
anaphora, paranomasia, and a host of other formal devices[9] produced
a work which, whether recited or intoned, could be delivered with
impressive and dramatic effect—as some of the samples quoted later
will show. There are clear signs of Biblical and Jewish influence in the
structure and mannerisms of the homily,[10] but the more telling stylistic
parallels are to be found in the writings of the Asian School associated
with the "Second Sophistic"—especially in Maximus of Tyre—and
from this evidence A. Wifstrand concludes that "the main impression
made by the homily of Melito is that of a genuine Greek rhetorical
production."[11]

Eusebius records (*H.E.* 4.26.14) that Melito paid a visit to
Jerusalem in order to obtain precise information about the number
and arrangement of the books of the "Old Covenant," partly as a
favour for a fellow Christian, Onesimus, who was eager for this information and for a collection of "extracts from both the law and the
prophets concerning the Saviour and all our faith."[12] The list Melito
gives accords closely with the canon established by the sages at Jabneh.
Doubtless natural curiosity and piety also motivated Melito's trip—
some call him the first Christian pilgrim to the Holy Land—but it is
strange that he should need to travel there for information which
presumably was available from the Jewish community in Sardis. Is it
possible that they, as a diaspora community, knew only the LXX? This
seems unlikely even if it was the version they used most. More probable
is that it indicates a lack of contact with the Jews in Sardis, perhaps due
to mutual hostility which discouraged the informal exchange of
information—the sort of hostility in fact which, from the Christian
side, comes to expression in the homily itself.

Peri Pascha

A consideration of Melito's view of Judaism falls naturally into two
parts corresponding to two of the main sections of his work: the

---

9 Detailed analysis can be found in T. Halton, "Stylistic Device in Melito, *PERI PASCHA*," in P. Granfield and J.A. Jungmann (eds.), *Kyriakon* vol. 1 (Münster: Aschendorff, 1970), 249-55. See also J. Smit Sibinga, "Melito of Sardis: The Artist and His Text," *VC* 24 (1970), 81-104; C. Bonner, *The Homily on the Passion by Melito Bishop of Sardis and Some Fragments of the Apocryphal Ezekiel* (London: Christophers, 1940), 20-27.
10 Noted by Werner, "Melito" and Hall, "Passover."
11 A. Wifstrand, "The Homily of Melito on the Passion," *VC* 2 (1948), 201-23, quotation on 214.
12 The *Extracts* may be one of the sixteen books listed by Eusebius, or a separate work altogether.

typological exposition of the Exodus story (1-45) and the charge of deicide (72-99). Our purpose will be to consider both what is explicitly stated and what is implied about the nature and status of Judaism and the Jews. An attempt to explain Melito's position will be reserved for the next section.

Pascha Old and New: From Type to Reality

Melito's homily, preceded by a reading of the story of the Exodus,[13] opens with the bold declaration that the mystery of the Pascha is about to be revealed. Superficially the story is clear—"how the sheep is sacrificed, and how the people is saved and how Pharaoh is scourged through the mystery" (lines 3-5)—but its true and deeper meaning is a "mystery." The word *mysterion*, used several times, not only recalls the terminology of the Mystery cults but also prepares for the mystagogic flights of fancy that characterize Melito's Christian exposition of the Pascha.[14]

The deep meaning of the Passover is, of course, essentially christological; but Melito's ruminations on this theme, while frequently repetitious, introduce a number of subtle variations designed to reinforce the central message. At the heart of Melito's typological exegesis lies a contrast between the old and the new Pascha expressed typically in pairs of contrasting terms: *typos/alētheia, parabolē/hermeneia, nomos/euaggelion* (or *logos*). This terminology is used with a considerable degree of flexibility so that even the pairs do not remain fixed and new terms can be used to express one or other side of the contrast. Sometimes a distinction is drawn between the events and the words of the past:

> Whatever is said and done finds its comparison
> What is said a comparison (*parabolē*)
> What is done a prefiguration (*protupōseōs*)
> in order that, just as what is done is demonstrated
>   through the prefiguration
> So also what is spoken may be elucidated through
>   the comparison.
>
> (lines 219-23)

Broadly speaking, as Daniélou notes,[15] this distinction accords with Melito's use of Old Testament traditions: the events and people of the

---

13 Presumably in Greek and not, as some have suggested, in Hebrew. See S.G. Hall, "Melito PERI PASCHA 1 and 2," in *Kyriakon* (cited above n. 9), 236-48.
14 Blank, *Meliton*, 46-51.
15 J. Daniélou, "Figure et Evenement Chez Méliton de Sardes," in W.C. van Unnik (ed.), *Neotestamentica et Patristica* (Leiden: Brill, 1962), 282-92; Blank, *Meliton*, 60-65.

past are seen as types and the words are seen as promises; type is to reality as promise is to fulfilment—much like the distinction found in Justin (*Dial.* 110:2; 114:1, using *typos/logos*).

The key to Melito's exposition of the Old Testament is found in a bold and unusually self-conscious statement of hermeneutical principle:

> This is just what happens in the case of a
>   preliminary structure:
>   it does not arise as a finished work,
> but because of what is going to be visible
>   through its image acting as a model.
> For this reason a preliminary sketch is made
>   of the future thing
> out of wax or of clay or of wood,
> in order that what will soon arise
> taller in height,
> and stronger in power,
> and beautiful in form,
> and rich in its construction,
> may be seen through a small and perishable sketch.
>
> But when that of which it is the model arises,
> that which once bore the image of the future thing
>   is itself destroyed as growing useless
> having yielded to what is truly real the image of it;
> and what once was precious becomes worthless
>   when what is truly precious has been revealed.
>
> For to each belongs a proper season:
>   a proper time for the model,
> a proper time for the material,
> a proper time for the reality.
>
>   (lines 224-44)

The analogy between model (*typos*) and reality (*alētheia*), between blueprint and artifact, contains *in nuce* Melito's view of Israel's past and the Christian present. All the things of the past—the great figures and events of Israel's history and the promises of their scriptures—are to Christianity as model is to finished product; and, Melito concludes, when the reality appears or the artifact is made, the model which was once "precious" and "marvellous" becomes worthless, defunct and void:

> As then with the perishable examples,
>   so also with the imperishable things;
> as with the earthly things,
>   so also with the heavenly.

For the very salvation and reality of the Lord
  were prefigured in the people,
and the decrees of the gospel were proclaimed in
  advance by the law.

The people then was a model by way of preliminary
  sketch,
    and the law was the writing of a parable;
the gospel is the recounting and fulfilment of
  the law,
    and the church is the repository of the
    reality.

The model then was precious before the reality,
  and the parable was marvellous before the
interpretation;
that is, the people was precious before the church
  arose,
and the law was marvellous before the gospel
was elucidated.

But when the church arose
  and the gospel took precedence,
the model was made void, conceding its power to the
  reality,
    and the law was fulfilled, conceding its power
    to the gospel.

In the same way as the model is made void, conceding
  the image to the truly real,
    and the parable is fulfilled, being elucidated
    by the interpretation,
just so also the law was fulfilled when the gospel
  was elucidated,
    and the people was made void when the church
    arose;
and the model was abolished when the Lord was
  revealed,
    and today, things once precious have become
    worthless,
    since the really precious things have been
    revealed.

(lines 255-79)

Melito's claims are confident and remarkably unambivalent. Not for him the qualms and uncertainties of earlier Christian writers who tried to balance Christian appropriation of Jewish traditions with some sense of their abiding value—the result, no doubt, partly of the different circumstances under which they wrote. The implications for Melito's view of Judaism are to some extent self-evident, but it is worth dwelling on them for a while.

In his meditation on the stories of Israel's past Melito concerns himself with the broad sweep of events rather than with minor details, and with the plain meaning of the stories rather than with any allegorical significance. And even though christological typology is at the heart of Melito's understanding, not all the retelling is done with an eye on its typological significance. He does show a certain relish for dramatic embellishment of the biblical narrative, of which the imaginative portrayal of the horrors that befell the Egyptians is the best example (lines 93-212): the swift and implacable grip of Death in the face of desperate but ineffective ploys of the firstborn to evade it, the bewilderment and grief of mourning parents who, throughout Egypt, become a robe of wailing surrounding the grief-stricken Pharaoh. This is good drama, but its significance may go beyond mere dramatic effect. In the sections dealing with the death of Jesus (72f.) the Jews perform a roughly analogous role to that of the Egyptians in sections 1 to 42: as salvation was miraculously wrought for the Jews, surrounded by their enemies, by the blood of the passover lamb, so salvation was miraculously wrought for Christians by Jesus, surrounded by his enemies, in the true paschal sacrifice. Who were Jesus' enemies? Clearly, the Jews. For Melito the tragedy of the Jews was that in the midst of celebrating their own saving event they were, by an ironic twist, responsible for the death of the true paschal lamb. Those who were once the saved become the enemies of salvation. The interplay of these ideas is seen, for example, in lines 92 to 103:

> But while the sheep is being slain
>   and the Pascha is being eaten
>   and the mystery is being performed
>   and the people is making merry
>   and Israel is being marked,
> then came the angel to strike Egypt,
>   the uninitiated in the mystery,
>   the non-participating in the Pascha,
>   the unmarked with the blood,
>   the unguarded by the Spirit,
>   the hostile,
>   the faithless.

Here, in language which echoes the Christian rites of initiation and unction, Egypt's fate anticipates that of those who do not participate in the Christian mysteries, including the Jews. Likewise the fate of the Jews who were responsible for Jesus' death is described in a series of couplets which contrast their conscious remembrance of the old deeds of salvation with their ignorance of the new deeds of salvation being accomplished in their midst. The language is strongly reminiscent of that used to describe the fate of Egypt:

> So you quaked at the assault of foes;
>> you were not terrified in the presence of
>> the Lord,
>> you did not lament over the Lord,
>> so you lamented over your firstborn;
> you did not tear your clothes when the Lord was hung,
>> so you tore them over those who were slain;
> you forsook the Lord,
>> you were not found by him;
> you did not accept the Lord,
>> you were not pitied by him;
> you dashed down the Lord,
>> you were dashed to the ground.
> And you lie dead,
>> but he has risen from the dead
>> and gone up to the heights of heaven.
>
> (lines 732-47)

It is not altogether far-fetched, therefore, to see an analogy between Melito's view of the "enemies of the Jews" in sections 1 to 45 and the "enemies of Jesus" in sections 72 to 99. To some extent the description of the one spills over into the description of the other and it is one of several links between these two parts of the homily which suggest a degree of interdependence between the claim that Christians rather than Jews are the inheritors of the traditions of Israel and the insistence upon Jewish responsibility for Jesus' death.

It is worth noting, secondly, how Melito's christology affects his assessment of Israel's past. The typological foreshadowing of Jesus in the Old Testament is clearly central, but Melito also resorts to a form of modalism in which Christ is seen to be not only prefigured but also a participant in the events of Israel's past. Not only was Abel murdered, Isaac bound, Joseph sold, Moses exposed, and David persecuted (lines 415-24), but Christ too was murdered, bound, sold, exposed, and persecuted with them (line 479-88). The shift from typological prefiguration to modalist participation in Melito's fluid christology strengthens the claim to Israel's tradition while it compounds Israel's guilt in rejecting Christ: he was not just prefigured in their past, he *was* their past.

Thirdly, while the main purpose of *Peri Pascha* is to appropriate Jewish Passover traditions for Christian belief and practice—to show how Christ is the true lamb and the Christian feast the true Passover—Melito does not stop there. He moves inexorably from consideration of the primary saving event of Judaism to sweeping claims about their other distinctive attributes. It is apparent in the lines quoted above (255-79) that the once-chosen people have been superseded by the church and the law by the gospel. The succeeding lines tell a similar story and illustrate the ease with which Melito moves from the one to the other:

> Once, the slaying of the sheep was precious,
>   but it is worthless now because of the
>   life of the Lord;
> the death of the sheep was precious,
>   but it is worthless now because of the salvation
>   of the Lord;
> the blood of the sheep was precious,
>   but it is worthless now because of the
>   Spirit of the Lord;
> a speechless lamb was precious,
>   but it is worthless now because of the
>   spotless Son;
> the temple below was precious,
>   but it is worthless now because of the
>   Christ above.
>
> The Jerusalem below was precious,
>   but it is worthless now because of the
>   Jerusalem above;
> the narrow inheritance was precious,
>   but it is worthless now because of the
>   widespread bounty.
> For it is not in one place nor in a little plot
>   that the glory of God is established,
> but on all the ends of the inhabited earth
>   his bounty overflows,
> and there the almighty God has made his dwelling
>   through Christ Jesus;
>   to whom be glory for ever. Amen.

(lines 280-300)

The holy city and the Temple go the way of the Passover, the people, and the law—deemed worthless (*atimia*) because superseded. What was once the particular inheritance of the Jews is overtaken by the universal bounty of the Christian faith. The status of the Passover thus epitomizes the status of Jewish tradition as a whole.

It is worth noting, finally, that Melito's evaluation of Jewish traditions is not entirely negative. There is no suggestion, such as we find in the epistle of Barnabas, that the law has no value in itself and was never intended for literal observance or, as in Justin, that the law was given to Israel because they were too wicked to receive a "spiritual law." For the period prior to Christian revelation Melito assigns positive value to the law, Temple, holy city, and people: they were "precious" and "marvelous." When there is nothing but a model or preliminary sketch they are with good reason highly valued. By the same token, however, when the reality or artifact appears the model or preliminary sketch has no value: it is "abolished" (*luō*), "worthless" (*atimia*), "made void" (*kenoō*), "fulfilled" (*plēroō*), or "useless" (*achrēstos*). The terminology may vary

but the conclusion remains singular: Judaism and all it signifies is
defunct. The positive assessment belongs solely to Israel's past, the
negative to its present. This stark contrast between two epochs in
Israel's history is perhaps less dramatic in practice than in theory, i.e.,
not all of the "old" is discarded out of hand; the reading of Exodus 12 is,
after all, the setting for the homily and the law can still function as
christological promise. But insofar as the attributes of Judaism have
continuing value it is by absorption into the Christian reality and not
because of any independent value of their own.

Israel and the Death of God

If for no other reason, Melito is notable as the first Christian writer to
make an unambiguous accusation of deicide. Between the "mystery of
the Pascha" (sections 1-45) and the death of Jesus (sections 72f.) Melito
reflects upon the fall and the arrival of sin and death in its wake
(sections 46-71). We might expect the meditation on Jesus' death to be
related to what precedes and, in fact, consideration of the benefits of
Christ's death takes up the last 40 lines or so of the homily (lines
763-804). The bulk of this final section, however, consists of an impas-
sioned denunciation of the crime of Israel in rejecting and killing her
God (lines 551-762). The proportions reveal where Melito's real interest lay. The following excerpts are typical of the tone, content and
brilliant rhetorical effects of the whole final section:

> and you bound his good hands, which formed you
>   from earth;
> and that good mouth of his which fed you with
>   life you fed with gall.
> And you killed your Lord at the great feast.
>
> And you were making merry, while he was
>   starving;
> you had wine to drink and bread to eat,
>   he had vinegar and gall;
> your face was bright, his was downcast;
> you were triumphant, he was afflicted;
> you were making music, he was being judged;
> you were giving the beat, he was being nailed up;
> you were dancing, he was being buried;
> you were reclining on a soft couch, he in grave
>   and coffin.
>
> O lawless Israel, what is this unprecedented crime
>   you committed,
> thrusting your Lord among unprecedented sufferings,
>   your Sovereign,
> who formed you, who made you, who honoured you,
>   who called you 'Israel'?

But you did not turn out to be 'Israel';
   you did not 'see God',
   you did not recognize the Lord.
You did not know, Israel, that he is the
   firstborn of God,
   who was begotten before the morning star,
   who tinted the light, who lit up the day,
   who divided off the darkness,
   who fixed the first marker, who hung the earth,
   who controlled the deep,
   who spread out the firmament,
   who arrayed the world,
   who fitted the stars in heaven,
   who lit up the luminaries,
   who made the angels in heaven,
   who established the thrones there,
   who formed man upon earth.

                        (lines 562-608)

An unprecedented murder has occurred in the middle
   of Jerusalem,
   in the city of the law,
   in the city of the Hebrews,
   in the city of the prophets,
   in the city accounted just.

And who has been murdered? Who is the murderer?
I am ashamed to say and I am obliged to tell.
For if the murder had occurred at night,
  or if he had been slain in a desert place,
  one might have had recourse to silence.

But now, in the middle of the street and in the
   middle of the city,
   at the middle of the day for all to see,
   has occurred a just man's unjust murder.

Just so he has been lifted up on a tall tree,
   and a notice has been attached to show who has
   been murdered.
Who is this? To say is hard, and not to say is
   too terrible.

Yet listen, trembling at him for whom the earth
   quaked.
He who hung the earth is hanging;
   he who fixed the heavens has been fixed;
   he who fastened the universe has been fastened
   to a tree;
   the Sovereign has been insulted;
   the God has been murdered;

the King of Israel has been put to death by
an Israelite right hand.

(lines 693-716)

The notion that the Jews were responsible for the death of Jesus had a long pedigree in Christian thinking, stretching back at least to the early accounts of Jesus' passion. Prior to Melito, however, no one had made the accusation with such boldness and dramatic skill and no one had transformed the 'crime' of the Jews from responsibility for the death of Jesus to responsibility for the death of God. It is the latter which provokes Melito's incomprehension and horror and which inspires his denunciation, but there are a number of subsidiary themes used to vary the rhetorical effect, bolster the accusation against Israel and compound her guilt.

It is noticeable, for example, that Melito uses the term "Israel" without apparent discrimination: it refers to all Jews. No distinction is made between leaders and people or Palestinian and diaspora Jews, as in some earlier Christian writings, nor apparently between Jews of the past and present. The crime is the crime of all Jews. Some take the sting out of Melito's language by supposing that "Israel" refers solely to the Jews contemporary with Jesus and responsible for his death: " . . . nothing would be more mistaken than to reproach the bishop of Sardis with a low-class and malicious anti-Judaism . . . . The Jews he has in mind and accuses are not the Jews of his time, much less the Jews of his diocese, but the Jews of long ago, the Jews of the first Good Friday in Jerusalem."[16] Despite the confidence of his assertion Rengstorf provides no evidence to support it. In its favour we could perhaps note that most of what Melito says about "Israel" relates specifically to the events of Jesus' public ministry, trial, and death, but in view of the subject matter of this section of the homily anything else would have been anachronistic. Cataloguing the misdeeds of the Jews, especially those surrounding the death of Jesus, is precisely the point of sections 72f. It might also be argued that, for Melito, in a sense there was no real "Israel" to address after these decisive events: she was no longer "Israel" because she did not "see God" (lines 589-91);[17] she had been "dashed to the ground" and "lies dead" (lines 744-45 cf. 662-64). However, it seems improbable that this theologoumenon would lead Melito or his community entirely to ignore the existence of contemporary Jewish communities, not least in their own city, who were in some senses successors to those who "murdered God"—even if he did refuse to grant them the title "Israel." There are, moreover, places where

---

16   K.H. Rengstorf and S. von Kortzfleisch, *Kirche und Synagoge: Handbuch zur Geschichte von Christen und Juden* (Stuttgart: E. Klett, 1968), 1:73.

17   On this false etymology of the word "Israel" see Hall, *On Pascha*, 45 n. 50.

"Israel" is addressed in a manner which suggests something more than a rhetorical flourish addressed to a deceased generation:

> Ungrateful Israel, come and take issue with me
>   about your ingratitude
>   (lines 634-35, cf. 73-74, 519-31)

> Value for me the withered hand
>   which he restored to the body;
> Value for me those blind from birth
>   to whom he brought light with a word;
> Value for me those who lay dead
>   whom he raised from the dead already four days old.
>   (lines 651-56)

> Bitter for you is the feast of unleavened bread.
>   (line 678)

It is unlikely, of course, that Jews are being directly addressed, or that they would have read or heard Melito's homily. But is it likely that he and his audience would in these moments have thought solely of the Jews of the first century who killed Jesus and not of their Jewish contemporaries? This is possible but, I think, unlikely.

The guilt of the Jews is underlined in a number of other ways. Their malevolence contrasts starkly with the non-Jews who eagerly admired and worshipped the Lord:

> But you cast the opposite vote against your Lord.
>   For him whom the gentiles worshipped
>   and uncircumcised men admired
>   and foreigners glorified,
>   over whom even Pilate washed his hands.
>   (lines 671-76)

The action of the Jews is cause not to lament, that they rejected him *despite* his good deeds, but to exaggerate further their strange and perverse behaviour: they rejected Jesus *because* he was just, *because* he did works of compassion (lines 505f., 545f.). When it came to the point of death not only did the Jews participate vigorously to inflict the greatest possible agony, they also had the temerity to crucify him in broad daylight in the midst of the holy city (lines 693f.) while they themselves joyfully celebrated their Passover (lines 566f.)—actions which are underlined by the virtual absence of Romans from the scene. And lest they should attempt to justify their actions by arguing that if Jesus had to die they were merely the instruments of divine necessity (cf. Justin *Dial*. 95:2-3) Melito counters with the claim that it should have been accomplished by the hands of godless, uncircumcised foreigners and not by his elect (lines 537-45).

Finally we can again note the effect of Melito's christology, which is more fully developed in sections 82 to 90 than elsewhere. As before, Jesus is in some strange way seen to be a participant in as well as prefigured by the history of Israel, but he is now also identified with the God of Israel. Thus Israel rejects and crucifies not only a Christ whose significance was deeply embedded in their own past but also God himself, the author of creation and of their election and salvation. In rejecting Jesus they were rejecting their own past and their own God, thus forfeiting their right to be the people of this God. For their shocking ingratitude (lines 635f.) they are punished with bitterness (lines 680f.) and, ultimately, death (lines 744f.). The conclusion is entirely consistent with, and may well have influenced, the hermeneutic which operates earlier in the homily.

Influences on Melito

Melito is a significant figure not only because of what he says but also because of his relationship to preceding Christian tradition and because consideration of the factors influential in the formation of his views introduces by way of a particular example many of the issues which would have to be discussed in any general survey of Jewish-Christian relations in the first two centuries. We shall pick up the threads of biographical information and the various strands of Melito's teaching in order to examine the influences on his thinking. Some things we can deduce from the available evidence with confidence, but for others we must rely on informed guesswork—as we must in weighting different factors once they are identified.

(1) However obvious, it is worth noting that a number of the implicitly anti-Jewish themes in Melito are the reverse side of his attempt to articulate his definition of Christianity. The origins of Christianity as a Jewish sect and the intimate contact between them in the early decades made this inevitable not only for Melito but for all early Christian writers. The adoption of many of the beliefs and structures of Judaism and, above all, of their scriptures meant that it was virtually impossible to assert a Christian understanding of salvation without implicitly denying the Jewish equivalent. Between them, too, there was bound to be a degree of animus lacking in their conflict with other competitors. Christians and Stoics, for example, despite some common ground, offered two distinct and discrete views of the world; but Christians and Jews offered variant interpretations of the same basic tradition. The closer they were the more intense was the competition. It is natural, too,

with the well-established split between church and synagogue and the increasing confidence of the claims of a Gentile church, that the ambivalence and anxiety of a Paul or a Matthew in coming to terms with their Jewish roots should be replaced by a more explicit and categorical rejection of the claims of Judaism—as we find, for example, in the epistle of Barnabas, Justin, and Melito. What we find in Melito can be partly understood in this context, especially the exegetical procedures in sections 1 to 45, but there are features of this exegesis as well as the damning charge of deicide which require further explanation.

(2) Melito's rhetorical skills, probably the result of formal training in the traditions of the Second Sophistic, contribute significantly to the tone, if not the content, of his work. Scarcely a paragraph of *Peri Pascha* is formulated without resort to a formal rhetorical device designed to dramatize and enhance its effect. Excessive dependence on such devices can create a somewhat cluttered effect, and Melito is occasionally open to this charge, but in general he uses them skillfully and to good advantage. The homily is a work of art as well as a work of theological reflection. Would his contrast between Jewish and Christian Passovers have been so stark without his fondness for antithesis, paranomasia, rhetorical question, and exclamation? And would his denunciation of the Jews for the murder of Jesus have been so insistent and exaggerated without his love of repetition, anaphora, and oxymoron and his imaginative capacity to turn the tables of Jesus' accusers by putting the Jews on trial? In both cases, probably not. His skill with language, rhetorical device, rhythm, and phrasing sometimes runs away with him, with the result that contrasts are often bolder and denunciations more vehement and colourful than they might otherwise have been. But there is more to Melito than rhetorical intoxication.

(3) Melito was a Quartodeciman. The adherents of this tradition could justifiably claim that theirs was an ancient tradition, almost certainly older than the Roman tradition that eventually superseded it and with roots that may go back to the earliest Palestinian communities. Lohse's reconstruction of the Quartodeciman festival concludes that it was characterized by intense eschatological expectation and a fast for the conversion of the Jews. Of course, Jesus was seen as the true paschal lamb, but the emphasis was not so much on his death and resurrection as on his glorious return.[18] Most of this is based on later evidence and does not seem to fit Melito's *Peri Pascha*, in which there is little emphasis on eschatological expectation and no hint of a fast for the Jews. Indeed the tone of sections 72f. moves in quite the opposite direction— loading blame upon the Jews rather than longing for their salvation. It

---

18   B. Lohse, *Das Passafest der Quartadecimaner* (Gütersloh: C. Bertelsmann, 1953); cf. Blank, *Meliton*, 27f.; N. Hyladahl, "Zum Titel Peri Pascha bei Meliton," *ST* 19 (1965), 55-67.

is nevertheless clear that while both the Quartodeciman and Roman practices were affected by their association with the weekly and annual festivals of Judaism, the closer association of the Quartodecimans with Jewish practice raised an acute problem: in what way was their Passover to be distinguished from that of the Jews? By insisting on the same dating as the Jews were they not, in effect, judaizing (one of the main objections, apparently, of their opponents)? The accusation would be as natural as the response: a paradoxical determination to distance the Christian from the Jewish festival, the new from the old, the church from Israel, to show that their ostensibly closer connection with Judaism was a case of the "Christianizing" of Judaism rather than the reverse.

Kraabel has noted that none of the other evidence for Quartodeciman practices provides an analogy to, or a theological motive for, the vituperative attack on Israel in section 72f. and suggests that Melito's local circumstances provide the only plausible explanation.[19] Even so, there is no reason to deny the influence of Melito's Quartodeciman convictions on other parts of the homily, especially sections 1 to 45, or the extent to which greater intimacy with Judaism may have led, paradoxically, to a firmer rejection of it. Moreover our other evidence for Quartodeciman practice is very slight and mostly later than Melito, so that we cannot be sure that his views were atypical in the second century.

(4) The positive side of Kraabel's assertion is much more important. It is clear both from the reports of Josephus (*Ant.* 14.235; 16.171) and from extensive archeological excavations "that the Sardis Jewish community was a large one, with a degree of wealth, social status and political power and that the synagogue, on a choice location in the centre of the Roman City, is by far the largest discovered anywhere in the ancient world."[20] The Jewish community was probably active in the rebuilding of Sardis after a disastrous earthquake in 17 B.C.E., a process which took some 150 years, and several of their leaders appear to have been active members of the city council.[21] They were thus a highly visible element in the population, a force to be reckoned with, and it would have been virtually impossible for Christians to ignore them when attempting to establish their own identity and political standing. This provides an additional reason for doubting Rengstorf's conclusion, quoted earlier, that for Melito "Israel" referred exclusively to first-century Jews. Apart from the evidence of the text itself, where the boundaries between past and present are blurred and where ap-

---

19   Kraabel, "Melito," 82-83; though on page 84 he does allow for the added pressure of Melito's Quartodeciman views.
20   Kraabel, "Melito," 77 and n. 5 for literature.
21   Kraabel, "Melito," 83.

peals are apparently made to contemporary as well as past generations of Jews, the political and social realities of life in Sardis suggest quite the opposite. Only when the text is read in isolation from its context can an argument like Rengstorf's appear plausible.

We have no explicit evidence to show how Jews and Christians in Sardis viewed each other. That Melito had to travel to Judea to clarify the content of the Hebrew Bible may suggest that there was little formal contact between them, and perhaps a degree of animosity. It is not improbable that some of the Christians were converts from Judaism or descendants of such. There may also have been traffic in the other direction. In a number of earlier documents there are suggestions that Gentile Christians in Asia Minor were fascinated by and attracted to Judaism (Ign. *Phld.* 6:1; Rev. 2). Justin is aware of this danger (*Dial.* 47), though he blames it on undue pressure from legalistic Jews. A similar phenomenon apparently provoked John Chrysostom, at a later date, into some of the most deplorable anti-Jewish statements in early Christian literature. Here we have moved into the realm of speculation, but a situation in which church and synagogue were separate entities but where occasional traffic flowed in one or both directions, and where there was a need to defend Quartodeciman practice but refute the charge of judaizing, would go a long way towards explaining Melito's hostility towards the Jews. Quite apart from this, however, it is clear that the very existence of a large, visible, and influential Jewish community in Sardis would implicitly challenge any Christian claims to the traditions of Israel, encourage a strident tone, and make it most unlikely that Melito's communities, unless specifically instructed (which they are not), would exclude from the term "Israel" all Jews except those responsible for Jesus' death in the first century.

(5) There are a number of hints that Melito, like many of his contemporaries, tried to counter the increasingly popular teachings of Marcion. Blank notes that the titles of many of the sixteen works attributed to Melito have an anti-Marcionite ring to them[22] and, though caution is required because we can only guess at their contents and even the titles can be differently construed, it seems probable that Melito was conscious of the Marcionite threat.[23] The conscious attempt to clarify the relationship between the two covenants, which shows some points of contact with the gnostic Ptolemaeus,[24] the insistence that the one is fulfilled in the other, and the modalist christology which identifies Christ with God and sees him as an active participant not only in Israel's

---

22   Blank, *Meliton*, 15-17.
23. Werner, "Melito," 206-207; Hall, *On Pascha*, xli.
24   B. Lohse, "Meliton von Sardes und die Brief des Ptolemaus an Flora," in E. Lohse (ed.), *Der Ruf Jesu und Die Antwort der Gemeinde* (Göttingen: Vandenhoeck und Ruprecht, 1970), J. Jeremias Festschrift, 179-88.

history (lines 398f., 451f., 582f.) but also in the creation of the Universe (lines 398f., 590f., 710f.) could all have been developed without reference to the Marcionites, but in the context in which Melito worked it seems unlikely that they were.

It has been argued that Tertullian is more anti-Jewish when writing against Marcion than when writing specifically against the Jews,[25] and there is no doubt that Marcion posed some awkward problems, not the least of which was how to preserve the Old Testament scriptures while resisting Marcion's charge of judaizing—to which, of course, a Quartodeciman would be peculiarly susceptible. Dispute with the Marcionites could have influenced Melito's view of Judaism in two ways: first, by encouraging the preservation of the old covenant by means of its subordination to and fulfilment in the new, with its inevitable denigration of the old and those who continued to live by it; and secondly, in reaction to Marcion's separation of Jesus from the Old Testament God, by encouraging a virtual identification of them which, in turn, transforms the murderers of Jesus into the murderers of God.

(6) Melito's christology, in fact, deserves separate consideration. Whether reacting to Marcion or not, the fluid and not entirely consistent christological statements contribute significantly to his views of Judaism. The identification of Jesus with the character and attributes of God (lines 41-64), the understanding of the incarnation as the enfleshment of the Creator (lines 451-504), and the assertion that "God is murdered" (line 715) fully justify Hall's succinct summary: "Melito does attribute to Christ all the acts of God without exception; he rarely uses expressions which imply a personal distinction of the Son from the Father; where the term *Logos* is used of Christ there is no suggestion of the Middle Platonist ideas which led Justin to think in terms of a *second God*; and Melito addresses his doxologies to Christ rather than distinctly to the father."[26] This identification is also at the root of Melito's view that Christ was not only foreshadowed by, but also a participant in, the history of Israel. The effect on Melito's view of the Jews is dramatic. When they rejected Jesus they were rejecting no upstart Messiah but God himself, the Creator and Redeemer of Israel. Without this conviction there could be no charge of deicide, and the tragedy and guilt of the Jews are compounded because the God they killed was *their* God.

(7) Conflict between Jews and Christians in Asia Minor was not without precedent. The concern of Ignatius and the author of Revelation with the problem of "judaizing" indicates this, but it is the Gospel of John which provides the better parallel. In this gospel not only are "the

25   D.P. Efroymsen, "The Patristic Connection," in A.T. Davies (ed.), *Antisemitism and the Foundations of Christianity* (New York: Paulist, 1979), 98-117.
26   Hall, *On Pascha*, xliii, also the notes on xliii-xliv; Bonner, *Homily*, 27-28.

Jews" seen as representatives of "the world," of all that is demonic and at enmity with the gospel, but there is a chronology of Jesus' death which unambiguously associates Jesus with the Passover lamb. We should not make too much of this: the location of John in Asia Minor, while widely accepted, is not certain; and the association of Jesus with the Passover lamb is clear, if less precise, in the synoptic traditions of Jesus' death which are equally saturated with Passover symbolism. If the connection is allowed, however, and if it is thought that the Johannine tradition in Asia Minor encouraged the development of a Quartodeciman tradition, it may be that the anti-Jewish polemic of that gospel in turn influenced Melito's castigation of the Jews.[27]

(8) As we noted above, Melito's apology addressed to the Emperor was in response to a recent bout of persecution in Asia Minor. Kraabel suggests that this situation would have been exacerbated by the established political status and civic influence of the Jewish community in Sardis over and against whom the Christians would have had to assert their own identity and standing.[28] We also know that Christians were sometimes accused of being upstarts with no venerable ancestry (*Diog.* 1:1) and that one response to this was to claim Jewish antiquity for their own. Is this what Melito means when he says "Our philosophy first flourished among the barbarians"?[29] Are the "barbarians" the empires that preceded Rome, under whom the Jews lived, or are they, as Kraabel hesitantly suggests,[30] the Jews? In an apology the former is perhaps more probable and it would amount to a passing claim for antiquity which is implicitly and more fully worked out in the reflections on Old and New Covenants in sections 1 to 45 of the homily. It is possible, therefore, that the need for an acceptable pedigree, a distinct identity and a respectable status contributed to the manner in which Melito attacks the Jews and asserts the Christian claim to the traditions of Israel.

Conclusion

Melito's view of Judaism can be reduced to two essential elements: first, that Christian symbols, festivals, and beliefs have superseded and abrogated those of Judaism: law is replaced by gospel, the earthly by the heavenly Temple and Israel by the church; secondly, the Jews, in putting Jesus to death, in effect murdered their God. These two convictions are consistent and mutually supportive, for the crime of deicide is,

---

27   Notably Blank, *Meliton*, 35-38.
28   Kraabel, "Melito," 83-84.
29   Fragment 1 in Hall, *On Pascha*, 63.
30   Kraabel, "Melito," 84.

above all others, the reason why Israel was no longer to be considered the people of God.

The implications of the Christian appropriation of Jewish scriptures and traditions for the fate of empirical Israel had to be faced from the earliest days of the Christian movement, and the tendency to blame the Jews and exonerate the Romans is also detectable in the earliest accounts of Jesus' death. Compared with these early traditions, Melito's views are much more sharply and radically expressed, though various intermediate stages can be found in the fourth gospel, the epistle of Barnabas, the apocryphal trial narratives and Justin's *Dialogue*. The one horrendous novelty introduced by Melito is the charge of deicide. This and the other elements in his view of Judaism have no simple explanation. His dependence on Christian tradition in general and the traditions of Asia Minor in particular, his reaction to deviant forms of Christian belief, his intellectual training and rhetorical skills, his need to defend the church in Roman eyes and the pressure of local circumstances probably all played their part, though in what precise mix we cannot be sure.

Melito is a figure whose importance goes beyond the mere antiquarian. We cannot read him and ignore the dark shadow cast by subsequent Christian vilification of the Jews, in which the accusation of deicide played such a dominant and malicious role. For this Melito cannot be blamed, for there is no evidence that his views on this or any other matter were influential for more than a generation or two. He is, however, a prime illustration of the potential mischief in the distortions of even the earliest Christian accounts of Jesus' death and the way in which circumstances can conspire to bring out the worst in them. In particular he unwittingly alerts us to the way in which the temptation to defame Judaism tends to be strongest during the central Christian festival of Easter. This element in Melito's view of Judaism needs to be clearly exposed and firmly rejected for it is, with few exceptions, historically indefensible and, without exception, theologically abhorrent. Perhaps the only positive use for it is to adapt and extend the analogy Melito found between the fate of the Egyptians at the time of Moses and the fate of the Jews at the time of Jesus. It is now the turn of Christians to be warned lest, in the celebration of their foundational saving events, they should by their rejection and defamation of Judaism oppose the will of God and bring punishment on themselves.

The other element in Melito's view of Judaism poses a problem less easily resolved. The adoption of Jewish scriptures and the claim to inheritance of the promises to Israel, which goes back at least to Paul, inevitably sets Christianity on a collision course with Judaism. Melito's views are expressed with a degree of sharpness and finality uncommon in his predecessors and it might be subjected to a form of retrospective modification by a return to the less certain, less coherent but more subtle reflections of a Paul, to whom no simple solution to the dilemma was adequate. In the last resort, however, I suspect Paul will not offer a way out even though some are inclined to attribute to him a two-covenant theory on the basis of Romans 9 to 11.[31] Blank is certainly right in suggesting that Christians should be able to claim the Old Testament for themselves as a source of revelation without vilifying post-Christian Jewry,[32] but this does not resolve many fundamental conflicts. It is perhaps easier for Jews than Christians to accommodate the other positively in a covenantal scheme, but in either case it would seem that one or the other tradition would have to abandon convictions typically held to be fundamental, an expression of the very essence of their faith. There might appear to be a glimmer of hope in a return to the teaching of Jesus and the attitude he apparently had towards his own religious tradition. This, however, would involve a drastic turning back of the clock and it is difficult to harbour optimistic expectations of such a mighty upheaval in so well established a tradition which has, in this as in many other respects, often tacitly ignored the deeds and words of its founder.

31   E.g., L. Gaston, "Paul and the Torah," in *Antisemitism and the Foundations of Christianity* (cited above n. 25), 48-71. His argument extends well beyond Romans 9 to 11.
32   Blank, *Meliton,* 83.

7

Christian Anti-Judaism in its Judaic Mirror: The Judaic Context of Early Christianity Revised

Jack Lightstone

It was originally intended that I should present a paper on the early rabbinic reaction to Christianity and to its anti-Judaism. After some reflection, I decided to tackle a somewhat different theme—the Judaic context of early Christianity and its anti-Judaism—out of a conviction that the tannaitic rabbis had little to say about Christians and went about their work in ignorance (perhaps feigned) of the followers of Jesus. To be sure, this flies in the face of a long scholarly tradition, including much of the work of Moore and Lauterbach, to name but two. But the work on rabbinic reactions to Christianity seemed singularly beside the point and methodologically antiquated, as I will argue.

"The Judaic Context of Early Christianity," my choice of topic, evolved, however, in directions at first not fully expected. Here too the adducing of rabbinic materials in order to elucidate the conceptions and praxis of early Christianity has a formidable history of modern scholarship. But rabbinic evidence impresses upon us a profound sense of distance from the world-views and life of the early church. New Testament and early patristic literature appear far removed in character and geography from the writings of the tannaitic rabbinate. The Jews whom the early Christian writers knew, whose religion posed the threat of judaizing to the church, against whom they strove for self-definition and from whom they were most likely to borrow, were the Jews outside of Palestine. What follows, then, lays out some of the data, such as it is, for those Jewish communities that ringed the Mediterranean basin, beyond rabbinic control or influence. The study strives to describe, in preliminary fashion to be sure, the mythic structure of their world, to define the religious problematic as they perceived it, and to elucidate their solutions to that problematic.

I cannot claim to contribute fresh evidence, or even improved readings and translations of existing texts, which advance our knowledge of Hellenistic Judaism. This study, nevertheless, may shed further light on the data in question, by virtue of asking different questions. Whether I have properly perceived the relevant questions and responsibly addressed them, my readers will have to judge. What follows is an attempt to use the methods of the History of Religions in approaching Judaism, that is to say, to shed light upon the developments within a particular religious tradition by appealing to both data and analytical agenda which transcend the literature under study— without, I hope, skewing the evidence in an overly deductive process. Only the results will vindicate the perspective.

Introduction

Many scholars, past and present, have maintained that Judaic literature met the challenge and vehement vilification from Christian quarters with equal and opposite force. Indeed, according to the *Wissenschaft des Judentums* and its heirs, major structural elements of "post-biblical" normative Judaism developed in direct response to the anti-Judaic claims of early Christianity.[1] Scholars such as Moore view the canonization of the Hebrew scriptures at the Jamnian Council as an attempt to exclude Christian claims for the sacred status of its literature.[2] Rabbi Aqiva and the rabbinic sages of the second century developed theories of eschatology and salvation with an eye to Christian insistence that only in the church and through Jesus could salvation be attained.[3] And, more recently, such scholars as Reuven Kimmelman have attempted to explain numerous rulings of early third century Palestinian rabbis as meeting a Christian challenge on the Palestinian (Galilean) scene.[4] If, then, the gospels tend to find a Pharisee behind every rock and tree waiting for the master to err, then a corresponding tendency abounds among modern scholars of Judaism in the first three centuries C.E.

---

1   See the various relevant essays reprinted in S.D. Leiman (ed.), *The Canon and Masorah of the Hebrew Bible: An Introductory Reader* (New York: KTAV, 1974); G.F. Moore, "The Definition of the Jewish Canon and the Repudiation of Christian Scriptures," 115-41; L. Ginzberg, "Some Observations on the Attitude of the Synagogue Towards the Apocalyptic—Eschatological Writings," 142-62; J. Bloch, "Outside Books," 202-21.

2   G.F. Moore, "Definition"; also Bloch, "Outside Books."

3   Ginzberg, "Observations."

4   In papers on Rabbi Yohanan presented to the Annual Meeting of the Association for Jewish Studies, Boston, December 1976.

Alongside this scholarly trend, oddly enough, one finds the often cited claim that Judaic (i.e., rabbinic) literature of the early Christian centuries is remarkably silent about Christianity, relative to the xenophobia vented upon idolators, Epicureans, magicians, heretics, and assorted others.[5] The apparent conflict between this observation and theories that early Christianity indirectly determined many principal developments in first- and second-century Judaism is lessened by appeal to the phenomenon of Christian censorship and other forms of literary repression. Editors, compilers, and copyists of Judaic (i.e., rabbinic) literature of this period felt from the outset the need to couch their anti-Christianity in euphemisms, *double-entendre*, and generic terms rather than to refer specifically to Jesus and the Christians. For example, G.F. Moore,[6] in order to maintain his notion that the canonization of the Hebrew scriptures was effected in direct response to Christianity, would have us approve such metamorphoses as: *evangelium* from *gilyon*; *min* (heretic) from *ḥiṣon*; Christian from *min*; and, to complete the circle, *haminim* (the heretics) from *hamiras* (Homer). So the books of Homer become the books of heretics, which in turn Moore understands as the books of Christians, namely, the gospels. Likewise references to *gilyonei haminim* evolve into Christian literature as do references to *sefarim ḥiṣonim* (usually understood to be extra-canonical Jewish literature). In a scholarly version of *creatio ex nihilo* a host of Judaic evidence pertaining to early Christianity thereby appears, as if out of nowhere, in Judaic (rabbinic) literature. In defence of Moore, I must point out, however, that in these matters he seems overwhelmingly judicious in comparison with others.

Even if we are not prepared to assent today to this type of scholarly gymnastics—quite acceptable, I might add, in its day—we do not remain without sources altogether. In earliest rabbinic literature, (that is, the Mishna and the Tosefta) are several accounts of persons being healed, to the consternation of the rabbis, by mendicant holy men using the name of one Jesus ben Pantera.[7] One may add to this a number of references to the gospels in still later rabbinic compilations (the Palestinian and Babylonian Talmuds), references which may or may not have circulated in the second century. Indeed, that Jesus ben Pantera is the

---

5 See J. Lauterbach, "Jesus in the Talmud," in *Rabbinic Essays* (Cincinnati: Hebrew Union College Press, 1951), 473-570.

6 G.F. Moore, "Definition."

7 See *t. Hullin* 2:24 (*b. ʿAboda Zara* 16b-17a); *t. Yebamot* 3:3 (*b. Yoma* 66b); *t. Sabbat* 11:15 (*b. Sabbat* 104b; *y. Sabbat* 12:4; *b. Sanhedrin* 67a); *t. Hullin* 2:22 (*y. Sabbat* 14:4; *y. ʿAboda Zara* 2:2; *b. ʿAboda Zara* 27b); see also *b. Soṭa* 47a; *b. Sanhedrin* 107b; *y. Hagiga* 2:2; *y. Sanhedrin* 7:13; see J. Lauterbach, "Jesus in the Talmud." I have no intention of systematically analyzing these sources, as this essay is headed, as it were, in a different direction; I refer the reader to the analysis of M. Smith, *Jesus The Magician* (San Francisco: Harper and Row, 1978), 46-50.
   On the gospels, see *b. Sabbat* 11:62; *y. Sabbat* 16:1 (cf. *t. Sabbat* 13:14; *t. Yadayim* 2:13).

Jesus in question cannot, at least for the earlier sources, be maintained with certainty. Ben Pantera, without any doubt, however, was understood to be Christ by the rabbis of the fourth (and possibly the third) century. In all I am not inclined to remain overly skeptical with regard to these sources; after all, the Jesus ben Pantera stories seem far more likely candidates for source-material than do sundry "heretics" and the like who lurk on numerous pages of the Mishna and Tosefta. But what does this story, probably the only reliable reference to Christians in early rabbinic literature, really tell us? Nothing which we might not already have surmised from elsewhere. The gospels already portray the apostles as exactly this type of mendicant holy man, and the negative reaction of the rabbis could have been surmised without the story of ben Pantera.

It seems that searching for references to Christians and Christianity among the documents of the early rabbis neither elucidates greatly the condition of early Christianity, nor its anti-Judaism, nor, for that matter, the conditions under which second-century rabbinism developed (the ultimate purpose of Moore and others). In view of such benign results we simply must ask different questions.

The study of the Judaic context out of which Christianity arose and with respect to which it developed in the late first and second centuries offers itself as a more immediately encouraging approach. Here, of course, one has recourse to a long modern scholarly tradition, from Strack and Billerbeck's *Kommentar Zum Neuen Testament aus Talmud und Midrasch* through W.D. Davies's *Paul and Rabbinic Judaism* to the more recent work of E.P. Sanders, *Paul and Palestinian Judaism*, to mention just a few. To cite these works in one breath seems, admittedly, hardly fair. They evince different states of the art and different versions of the problematic. The parallelomania (to use Sandmel's now famous term) of Billerbeck and Davies has been carefully avoided by Sanders and others. Rank "historicism" seems another problem evinced by some and overcome by others—one may refer here to the adducing of parallels in Judaic literature, claiming they antedate or are contemporary with the Christian data and, on that basis, asserting that the former bear a causal relationship to the latter. A third factor which has determined the formulation of the problematic is the constant pendulum-swing between the Judaic context and the non-Jewish, Hellenistic milieu in elucidating early Christianity. Here, for example, we see the move from Billerbeck and Davies to Goodenough[8] and back again via Vermes[9] and others.

I have no intention here of entering into any of these debates. Rather I should like to point to some underlying assumptions which

---

8   E.R. Goodenough, *By Light, Light* (New Haven: Yale, 1935).
9   G. Vermes, *Jesus the Jew* (London: Collins, 1973).

appear on the one hand to inform, explicitly or implicitly, all sides of the debate, and on the other hand to be ill-founded. The notion that pharisaic-rabbinic Judaism defines the normative stream of Israelite religion in the first Christian century and beyond in one way or another determines virtually all of this scholarship. Of course one sees this clearly in the work of G.F. Moore,[10] for whom rabbinism equals Judaism, anything else being a mere hiccup of the system. And to be sure the same working assumptions still seem alive and well among some contemporary scholars of Judaism.[11]

The same hypothesis appears at work in a far more subtle fashion, however, in the scholarship even of those who have openly decried claims regarding the normative status of rabbinic (or pharisaic) Judaism. For the assumption survives in the criteria used both to distinguish Judaic from non-Judaic (pagan) evidence and to differentiate properly "religious" data from other socio-cultural products.

An example of the second problem is the case of *Sefer HaRazim*. In the mid-sixties Margolioth pieced together from fragments of the Geniza a document which he named the Book of Mysteries.[12] The document is written in Hebrew but seems influenced considerably by the terminology and praxis of the Greek Magical Papyri. Margolioth dated the book to the first several centuries of the Christian era and thought its provenance to be either the primarily "pagan" coast of Palestine or Egypt. No one has seriously disputed any of this—nor do I. Rather what has been done (or not done) with *Sefer HaRazim* seems to me curious. A major premise of the document is that through knowledge of the various angelic rulers of the heavens and their particular functions one may through the proper rites and words, incantations if you will, produce desired effects on earth. On the strength of this scholars have generally declared *Sefer HaRazim* (merely) a book of magic and, furthermore, the product of the "superstition" of the "common" folk. The upshot is the relegation of *Sefer HaRazim* to the periphery of late antique (or early medieval) Judaism.

I find these claims extraordinary. First, if anthropology has anything to tell us regarding the difference between magic and religion, it is that the lines of demarcation are difficult, if not impossible, to draw. Such distinctions, furthermore, usually amount to the imposition of Western European "tastes" regarding religion upon other periods and other cultures. Indeed, what, for example, is Elisha in the cycle of.

10 G.F. Moore, *Judaism in the First Centuries of the Christian Era* (Cambridge: Harvard, 1958-59).

11 E. Urbach, *The Sages, their Belief and Concepts* (Jerusalem: Magnes Press, 1975); S. Safrai and M. Stern, *A History of the Jewish People in the First Century*, CRINT (Assen: Van Gorcum, 1974-76); A. Oppenheimer, *The Am Ha'Aretz* (Leiden: Brill, 1979).

12 M. Margolioth (ed.), *Sefer HaRazim* (Jerusalem: Yediot, 1966).

narratives of 2 Kings if not an itinerant, mendicant holy-man-shaman? Second, such claims about *Sefer HaRazim* ignore the fact that the document evinces a sophisticated literary activity, which almost by definition cannot have come from the "common folk." Third, the theurgic rites would seem to require the services of a full-time professional. Fourth, scholars tend to ignore the elaborate cosmology and concomitant theology upon which the document expends most of its energies. *Sefer HaRazim* includes, in fact, a vision of the heavenly court and of the enthroned deity, a vision which rivals any I have seen in the mystical texts of the Merkabah from fifth- to eighth-century rabbinism. Finally, even in the theurgic passages of the *Sefer HaRazim* one finds language which in any other context would immediately be recognized as liturgical.

In sum, *Sefer HaRazim* is not "common" at all; rather it bespeaks an elitist editor and reflects the vocation of elitist virtuosi. Assuming, moreover, for the sake of argument, that one may differentiate magic from religion, in *Sefer HaRazim* the so-called magical is nevertheless inextricably bound up with liturgical elements, religious piety, theology, cosmology, and mystical components. That is to say, for the editor of *Sefer HaRazim*, and I suspect for many of his contemporaries, theurgy and piety were integrally interwoven in their experience and world-views.

Given these characteristics of *Sefer HaRazim*, one would expect that document to count among the principal pieces of evidence for late antique Judaic piety and practice. Whence the relative disinterest among scholars of late Roman Judaism? Beneath all, apparently, lurks the supposition that "Judaism" does not admit of prayer and sacrifice to divine intermediaries, nor of compelling these powers to effect such mundane consequences on earth as good health, a rewarding lovelife, the benign countenance of a potentially hostile official, knowledge of what lurks in the minds of one's adversaries, and the like. But surely this amounts to using norms culled in the main from rabbinic texts as criteria for what can or cannot count as Judaism. (Indeed, such views represent a skewed version of even that Judaic stream.) To be sure, for these scholars *Sefer HaRazim* remains a Jewish document—after all it is written in Hebrew—and gives evidence of persons not under the constraints of rabbinic law. Yet in assessing the significance and meaning of the document rabbinic views re-enter through the back door as normative criteria.[13]

One may well speculate on what scholars might have done with *Sefer HaRazim* if it had not been written in Hebrew. I suspect that some

---

13 The consideration given *Sefer HaRazim* by I. Gruenwald in *Apocalyptic in Rabbinic Literature* (Leiden: Brill, 1978), raises some of the issues in the preceding discussion and ranks among the more "enlightened" approaches to *Sefer HaRazim* in other respects.

would vehemently have insisted that it was not Jewish at all, but rather the product of "pagans" heavily influenced by Judaism. The reasons adduced might have been exactly those mentioned above, namely, Judaism (i.e. rabbinism) does not admit of such possibilities. Thus the same rationale used to differentiate between properly religious data and magical practice (and superstition), in slightly altered circumstances, serves to dismiss materials as non-Jewish altogether, albeit from parties with Judaic contacts. But the latter tack like the former treats rabbinism, even if implicitly, as normative, and in turn begs the question anew.

Our hypothetical case finds precise parallel in reality. Many of the Greek Magical Papyri have, to be sure, been thought to be informed by Judaism and, in turn, to have influenced the writer of *Sefer HaRazim*. Nevertheless, the papyri have all been deemed "pagan," that is, outside the normal parameters of the study of late antique Judaism. But not a few of the papyri are in temperament, sentiment and piety indistinguishable from passages in *Sefer HaRazim*, with the difference, of course, that they are in Greek. They may have no more "pagan" allusions than appear as well in *Sefer HaRazim*, and some evince no "pagan" allusions whatsoever. As such the epithet "pagan" in these cases means nothing more than "non-rabbinic."[14] I suspect, moreover, the same to be the case for a number of other phenomena in the Graeco-Roman world of the first several centuries.

Before distilling any programmatic proposals from these methodological considerations, I think it appropriate to introduce two pieces of evidence which will add considerably to the cogency of our argument. First, in those centres where early Christianity was strongest and in which the major elements of patristic thought took shape in the second and third centuries, rabbinism is conspicuous by its absence. The early rabbis flourished in Judea from 70 to 135 and in the Galilee thereafter. Rabbinic influence first obtained in Babylonia at the end of the second century. Rabbinism may never have defined the dominant form of Israelite religion in Palestine, and such power as the rabbinate wielded in Babylonia did not develop until the end of the third century and the beginning of the fourth. While some may quibble with this view of rabbinism's influence in the Holy Land and the East, it remains undeniable that rabbinic power was not exercised in the Jewish com-

---

14   The sole exception to this assessment of the papyri seems to be E.R. Goodenough in *Jewish Symbols in the Graeco-Roman Period* (New York: Pantheon, 1963-68), vol. 2. To a large extent even M. Smith seems to fall short in his classification of the papyri in *Jesus the Magician*, although his more recent methodological statements have greatly informed my own discussion at this point. See "Terminological Boobytraps and Real Problems in Second Temple Judeo-Christian Studies," in P. Slater and D. Wiebe (eds.), *Traditions in Contact and Change*, Proceedings of 14th Congress of IAHR (Waterloo: Wilfrid Laurier University Press, 1983), 295-306.

munities of Syria, Asia Minor, Egypt, North Africa, Greece, Italy, or the islands of the Mediterranean until the seventh century and beyond. But these locales are precisely those areas where early Christianity took firm root and developed. Clement, Justin, John Chrysostom, and so on, in all probability, never met a rabbinic Jew (Eusebius possibly being the sole exception before Jerome).

These facts are nonetheless stunning for being obvious. There remains, however, a second equally self-evident observation that bears upon our case. The demography of Christianity in the late first and second centuries overlays areas of relatively high Jewish settlement[15]—with the notable exception of Jewish communities boasting rabbinic presence. In short, the early church everywhere cohabited with Jews, but never with rabbinic ones.

The upshot of this discussion for the task at hand, namely, reconstructing that Judaic context which elucidates developments in late first- and second-century Christianity in general and Christian anti-Judaism in particular, is severalfold. First, any account of the late antique Judaic background of early Christianity must cease to be written solely or primarily on the basis of rabbinic evidence. To be sure, the Dead Sea documents have contributed immeasurably to the devaluation of rabbinic data in this regard, but the obsession with the influence of Qumran on early Christianity has also obfuscated matters by supplanting one scholarly orthodoxy with another. Second, that Judaic context which remains relevant to our problematic is the world-view and religious praxis of the Hellenistic, non-rabbinic world. The world of Philo, to name just one, ought to interest us more than (or at least as much as) what rabbinic evidence may offer. This, to be sure, hardly represents a novel claim; but with the exception of E.R. Goodenough and some very few scholars, the case has been ignored as often as it has been made. Hellenistic Judaism has simply not been taken seriously, although it is always talked about.

If, finally, we are to act upon our critique of importing rabbinic criteria in evaluating non-rabbinic Judaisms, then we must be open to vastly different definitions of what the "cult of YHWH" may allow and entail. *Sefer HaRazim* cannot be dismissed as mere magic and superstition. Nor can evidence from the magical papyri and other sources (perhaps the Nag Hammadi Codices), hitherto considered to be "pagan," be ignored, especially where documents are shot through and through with Judaic allusions and possess little or no pagan references. Of course what counts as pagan will be as problematic as what counts as Judaic. I cannot give hard and fast rules for drawing the lines of demarcation. That remains a matter of taste and judgment in each case.

---

15   See Philo, *Legatio* 281-82; Acts 2:9-11; 11:19; 13:5, 6; 14:1; 16:2; 17:1, 10, 16; 18:1f, 5, 19; 19:23ff.

There are, of course, good reasons why Hellenistic Judaism has everywhere been talked about but why rabbinic evidence has always in the last resort been utilized. By comparison to rabbinic literature the state of the evidence for non-rabbinic, late antique Judaism is abysmal. With the sole exception of Philo and more recently *Sefer HaRazim* (and perhaps several documents from the Nag Hammadi Library) we have no literature to speak of from the Jews who ring the Mediterranean basin. The literary evidence is fragmentary—a papyrus here, an inscription there; artifactual evidence, such as funerary art and synagogue mosaics, seems rather mute as evidence goes. Other archeological evidence, primarily the architectural remains of tombs and synagogues, present their own difficult hermeneutical problems. In short, there simply is much more evidence from the rabbis and in a format more accessible to scholarly analysis. But that need not stall us altogether. To be sure, barring other discoveries, descriptions of Hellenistic Judaism must be expressed with appropriate reticence. But a "theory" of Hellenistic Judaism which makes sense of the majority of even this fragmentary evidence can be said to be more reliable than one which fails to do so, even if it cannot claim the certitude to which descriptions of rabbinism can aspire.

In the remainder of this essay, then, I should like to lay out a representative sample of the principal types of evidence, fragmentary and episodic though they might be, for Hellenistic Judaism. Second, the discussion offers an account of the basic mythic structure of Hellenistic Judaism, one which I believe helps make sense of these seemingly disparate phenomena. Having accomplished this much, we may then profitably turn to some rabbinic evidence and view the latter in a new light. For rabbinic evidence, even from our programmatic standpoint, aptly elucidates and is elucidated by Jewish life outside the rabbinic circles of the second and third centuries.

Our final task will, of course, bring us back to our point of departure, the Judaic context of late first- and second-century Christianity and its anti-Judaism. I maintain that the picture of late antique Judaism which will have emerged from our discussion provides a more cogent backdrop for early Christian phenomena and demonstrates especially the sense of competition which Christians felt toward their Jewish counterparts. I hope to give some indication that both groups offered different transformations of the same basic mythic structure, offering their systems in lieu of the Temple-centred cult of YHWH, which in the aftermath of 70 lay in ruins. By way of anticipation: the world was conceived as two tiered. The earthly world may be characterized as in need of creative sacred "stuff." The heavens were the repositories of that holy material. The religious problematic was one of mediation, the transportation, as it were, of goods and services between the two realms.[16] What characterizes the religious world-view, as we shall see, of post-70, late antique Judaism is twofold. First, movement between the two worlds is through mediators. Persons either go up to perform this necessary function or are capable of attracting through various means the requisite sacred stuff to earth from the heavens. Second, in either case these mediators were individuals and were judged holy, divine, or saintly, insofar as they were believed to effect this desired movement. As we review the disparate and discrete evidence which follows, we confront this basic pattern again and again albeit in different modes. Why this cult of the individual should have developed in the late Roman empire is difficult to say and best left postponed. We may turn, then, to the data at hand.

Judaic Evidence

A. Philo and the Question of Jewish Mysteries

In terms of documentary evidence for Hellenistic Judaism, Philo Judaeus, of course, provides the lion's share. For this reason alone his writings provide an appropriate departure in our survey of the data. But more to the point, for our purposes, is the thirty-five-year debate concerning the existence of a Judaic mystery as proposed in E.R. Goodenough's interpretation of Philo.[17] Goodenough, much like myself, believed that the Judaic context of early (Gentile) Christianity ought to be found not in pharisaic-rabbinic Judaism, nor immediately in Hellenistic religions, but rather in a Hellenistic Judaism which provides early Christianity with an antecedent model for syncretizing biblical and Hellenistic religious constructs. That argument, of course, is entirely *a priori* as it stands, since Christianity could have produced such a hybrid just as easily as diaspora Judaism. And if its Judaic (Old Testament) roots made the task difficult for early Gentile Christianity, then all the more so for Jews in the Hellenistic world. Still, Goodenough's reading of Philo as a Jewish mystery does not rest on his *a priori* statement, and an assessment of it will help us toward our own ends.

---

16   See in particular A.F. Segal, "Heavenly Ascent in Hellenistic Judaism," in H. Tem-
     porini and W. Haase (eds.), *Aufstieg und Niedergang der Römischen Welt*, 2:23:2,
     (Berlin/New York: De Gruyter, 1981), 1333-94.
17   E.R. Goodenough, *By Light, Light* (New Haven: Yale, 1935); see A.D. Nock, "The
     Question of Jewish Mysteries," in *Gnomon* 13 (1937), 156-65, reprinted in Z. Stewart,
     (ed.), *A.D. Nock: Essays on Religion and the Ancient World* (Cambridge: Harvard, 1972),
     vol. 1. See also E.R. Goodenough, *Jewish Symbols*, vol. 12, 3-22; see also M. Smith
     "Goodenough's Jewish Symbols in Retrospect," *JBL* 86 (1967), 53-68.

To summarize Goodenough's position: the religious goal for Philo was to loosen one's ties to this physical world of corruption through the rejection of worldly cares, and allow one's intellect or spirit to receive into itself divine incorporeal ("intelligible") light, which flows as a stream from the deity through his Logos and the lesser powers of the incorporeal world to this world below. On this stream the eternal (rational) soul may ascend from the world to the realm of incorporeal things, whence it came. Here one may attain a vision of divine entities, bask in the light-stream and join with and contemplate eternal beings. This ascent may be accomplished in life, and in so doing prepares the soul in death to rest eternally in these blessed origins.

How is this to be accomplished? Here, as Goodenough points out, Philo is replete with terminology of a *mystērion*. The way of Torah represents a *mystērion*, entry into the "secrets" into which one is "initiated" by such cultic officiants as the patriarchs and principally Moses, portrayed both as a divine man and a hierophant. To be sure, the image of the mystery cult seems blatant and intended by Philo. But the presence of mystery language in itself hardly seems probative, at least not without evidence of an actual *mystērion*.

If by the term *mystērion* Philo alludes to such cults as Isis and Osiris, Dionysus, and the like, then the terminology of Philo can be nothing more than metaphorical. A *mystērion* in the context of Hellenistic mystery religions refers to a secret rite administered by a hierophant to a society of initiates; by means of the *mystērion* the initiate is transformed in nature, usually through union or identification with a saviour figure, in whose death and resurrection to eternal life the initiate thereby participates. In Philo, however, the "mysteries" of Judaism seem to concern the very much exoteric life of Torah; his initiates include the entire Jewish world; and his hierophants are no living priests, but the great men of Israel's past. Philo's mystery, then, is the public life of Judaism as he knows it in Alexandria.

There appears, however, for Philo a Jewish mystery which transcends the life under the law. Nevertheless, here again we discover no *mystērion*, but the contemplative ambitions of a middle Platonic philosopher, who through philosophic contemplation may attain, as an individual, a religious goal unavailable to the vast majority of his fellow "initiates" into the life of Torah. In this Philo reflects not the cult of Isis and Osiris or any other mystery; rather, he anticipates Plutarch, who in his *Isis and Osiris* does for that group's rituals and myths what Philo does for Moses and Torah.[18]

Philo, then, evinces no Jewish mystery in the sense which Goodenough asserted. The evidence cited by Goodenough, however, does aptly construct a picture of a Hellenistic, philosophic mysticism in

---

18   A.D. Nock, "Jewish Mysteries."

a Jewish mode. Seen now in this new light one may profitably return to those passages in Philo highlighted by Goodenough.

Philo, we must remember, remains in the main an allegorist, bound to his text. As a literary style this mode does not lend itself well to a systematic account of a religious world-view. Still, in a number of passages Goodenough seems correct in maintaining that Philo gives voice to his most basic religious goals and to the view of the universe upon which they depend. Thus, for example, *Qu. Ex.* 2.39:

> (Exod. 24:11b) [What is the meaning of the words], "They appeared to God in the place and they ate and drank"?
> Having attained to the face of the Father, they do not remain in any mortal place at all, for all such [places] are profane and polluted, but they send and make a migration to a holy and divine place, which is called by another name, Logos. Being in this place through the Steward they see the Master in a lofty and clear manner envisioning God with the keen-sighted eyes of the mind. But this vision is the food of the soul, and true partaking is a cause of a life of immortality.[19]

This vision of God attained by being situated in his Logos seems for Philo no mere metaphor, as was the case with mystery language. For he continues in *Qu. Ex.* 2.40:

> (Exod. 24:12a) [What is the meaning of the words], "Come up to Me to the mountain and be there"?
> This means that a holy soul is divinized (Armenian: *astouacanal*) by ascending not to the air or to the ether or to heaven [which is] higher than all but to [a region] above the heavens. And beyond the world there is no place but God .... For those who have a quickly satiated passion for reflexion fly upward for only a short distance under divine inspiration and then immediately return .... But those who do not return from the Holy and divine city, to which they have migrated, have God as their chief leader in the migration.

Here we are faced with the language of ascent. More startling, however, is the clear reference to apotheosis. The one who ascends not only attains a vision unavailable to others but also, if we are to take Philo's language seriously (and I see no reason not to), has undergone a change in nature, passing from human to divine status. Far from being atypical of Hellenistic Judaism, however, Philo only reflects here a notion which one finds over and over again in Jewish theurgic ("magical") documents.

Qu. Ex. 2.40 alludes to the way in which, for Philo, this divinization and ascent are achieved, namely, "reflection." But as other passages demonstrate, there is more to Philonic mysticism than either

---

19   All citations of Philo are from the Loeb Classical Edition (Cambridge: Harvard), H. Colson (ed.); for *Questions and Answers on Exodus*, however, I have used R. Marcus (ed. and trans.), *Philo* (Cambridge: Harvard, 1953).

philosophic contemplation or the same coupled with the life of Torah. In the autobiographical passage in *Spec. Leg.* 3.1ff., Philo adds what seems to be an ascetic dimension:

There was a time when I had leisure for philosophy and for the contemplation of the universe and its contents, when I made its spirit my own in all its beauty and loveliness and true blessedness, when my constant companions were divine themes and verities, wherein I rejoiced with a joy that never cloyed or sated. I had no base or abject thoughts nor grovelled in search of reputation or of wealth or of bodily comforts, but seemed always to be borne aloft in the heights with a soul possessed by some God-sent inspiration, a fellow traveller with the sun and moon and the whole heaven and universe. And then I gazed down from the upper air, and straining the mind's eye beheld, as from some commanding peak, the multitudinous world-wide spectacles of earthly things, and blessed my lot in that I had escaped by main force from the plagues of mortal life.

Again in *Qu. Ex.* 2.51:

For if, O mind, thou doest not prepare thyself of thyself, excising desires, pleasures, griefs, fears, follies, injustices and related evils, and doest [not] change and adapt thyself to the vision of holiness, thou wilt end thy life in blindness, unable to see the intelligible sun. If, however, thou art worthily initiated and canst be consecrated to God and in a certain sense become an animate shrine of the Father, [then] instead of having closed eyes, thou wilt see the First [Cause] and in wakefulness thou wilt cease from the deep sleep in which thou has been held. Then will appear to thee the Manifest One, who causes incorporeal rays to shine for thee . . . .

In part, then, for Philo "initiation" constitutes expunging one's own passions, a prerequisite for the contemplative ascent or, as in this passage, for the descent of incorporeal light to the mystic.

Philo represents a particular type of Jewish holy man in the Graeco-Roman world. Through asceticism (mild, perhaps) and philosophic contemplation the Philonic mystic either ascends to the incorporeal world, there to join the Logos, or alternatively attracts to himself God's incorporeal light. In either case one achieves self-divinization and immortality. There seems no way to determine whether Philo remained one of a kind among Hellenistic Jewry. And there is no indication that *qua* philosophic mystic he assumed a particular social role within the Jewish community. To be sure, by his own admission he held public office; however, it was more an obstacle to his religious goal than a consequence of his religious achievements. Wealth and aristocratic ties, not divine status, suited him for public responsibility and office. Such is not the case with other types of Jewish holy men in the Hellenistic milieu, to whom we now turn.

B. The Magician as Holy Man

From our remarks earlier in this chapter, it should surprise no one that the New Testament and other early Christian documents make virtually no reference to rabbis—Jesus being the most notable exception. Gamaliel gets passing mention in Acts, but while known as a Pharisee he bears no rabbinic title in Christian literature. When, furthermore, one turns one's attention to religious virtuosi among Jews of the Hellenistic Diaspora, early Christian evidence presents no likely candidates for the rabbinic title at all. But the New Testament does know of Judaic holy men outside Judea and, what is more important, the documents seem remarkably consistent in their portrayal of them.

A classic (Judaic) rival, of course, of the apostolic holy men remains the figure of Simon (Magus) of Samaria. Acts, Justin Martyr, Irenaeus and Eusebius all deem him worthy of comment. And the tradition about Simon in Acts 8:9ff will serve us well as an introduction to the issues pertaining to these Judaic figures.

Now there was a certain man named Simon who formerly was practising magic in the city, and astonishing the people of Samaria, claiming to be someone great; and they all, from smallest to greatest, were giving attention to him, saying, "This man is what is called the Great Power of God." And they were giving him attention because for a long time he had astonished them with his magic arts.

The context of this passage is the success of Philip's mission in Samaria, a success, it must be stressed, based on his capacity to exorcise unclean spirits and heal the paralyzed and lame. The story of Simon now ensues. One cannot escape the conclusion that Simon did much the same thing as Philip before the latter's arrival. And just as Philip's talents won recognition of Jesus as a divine being, so Simon's exploits had earned for himself divine status. Acts, however, clearly qualifies Simon's success. Philip's exploits were real, that is, divine power acted through him; Simon's, in spite of the recognition he had achieved, were based on illusion and trickery. The former, then, was a holy man, the latter a *goes*, a magician.[20] But when we cut through the obvious layer of polemic in these passages, it appears that Philip and Jesus, on the one hand, and Simon, on the other, cut much the same figure as religious virtuosi. Thus "divine men" like Simon were more likely than the traditional priesthood of the Jerusalem cult to be the Jewish opponents

---

20   I am particularly indebted here to M. Smith's informative and careful account of the "magician" in the Hellenistic world in *Jesus the Magician*, 68-80, for me, at least, the most cogent section of this book.

of apostolic Christianity. These hypotheses are further borne out by the curious story in Acts 19:11ff.:[21]

And God was performing extraordinary miracles by the hands of Paul, so that handkerchiefs or aprons were even carried from his body to the sick, and the diseases left them and the evil spirits went out. But also some of the Jewish exorcists, who went from place to place, attempted to name over those who had evil spirits the name of the Lord Jesus, saying, "I adjure you by Jesus whom Paul preaches." And seven sons of one Sceva, a Jewish chief priest, were doing this. And the evil spirit answered and said to them, "I recognize Jesus, and I know about Paul, but who are you?" And the man, in whom was the evil spirit, leaped on them and overpowered them, so that they fled out of that house naked and wounded. And this became known to all, both Jews and Greeks, who lived in Ephesus; and fear fell upon them all and the name of the Lord Jesus was being magnified. Many of those who had believed kept coming, confessing and disclosing their practices. And many of those who had practised magic brought their books together and began burning them in the sight of all; and they counted up the price of them and found it fifty thousand pieces of silver.

As with the story of Simon, when the polemical and apologetic aspects of the tradition are accounted for, the general picture remaining paints a vivid scene of competition between Paul and itinerant Jewish holy men. Both work the "same side of the street" and in much the same way. Acts does not know of, or at least seems uninterested in, any other type of Jewish religious virtuosi in the Hellenistic Diaspora.

In view of these two accounts in Acts it appears particularly enlightening that, with the exception of Philo's corpus, the overwhelming majority of literary evidence for Hellenistic Judaism of the late first, second, and third centuries remains so-called "magical" documents. To these, then, we may turn more fully to understand the religious worldview of men with whom Philip and Paul (and, no doubt, other Christian charismatics) came into conflict.

The theurgic (magical if you will) documents left to us by Hellenistic Judaism evince roughly two distinct categories of holy man: the priestly-magus and the divine man.[22] *Sefer HaRazim*, for example, sees as its practitioner a priestly-magus figure. Such a Jewish magus knows intimately the hierarchy of divine beings and their functions. He, therefore, may enlist their aid through incantations, symbolic rites, prayer, and sacrifice. By means of his expertise the priestly-magician mediated the powers of heaven and directed them to highly specific ends. But sacred power continues ultimately to reside in heaven, even while being called upon by the skill and knowledge of the holy man to use below for specific tasks. Typical, then, of *Sefer HaRazim's* praxis is:

---

21   See A.D. Nock, "Paul and the Magus," in F. Jackson and K. Lake (eds.), *The Beginnings of Christianity* (London: McMillan, 1935), 5:264-88, reprinted in Z. Stewart (ed.), *A.D. Nock, Essays*, vol. 1.

22   My typologies here rely upon M. Smith, *Jesus the Magician*, 68-80.

If you should wish to inquire of the spirit of the dead stand before the grave and recount the names of the angels of the fifth camp [in the first heaven]. And in your possession [let there be] oil and honey mixed together in a new bowl (*py'ly*) of glass. And speak thus: I adjure you [O] Spirit Kriphoros [i.e., Hermes] who dwells among the tombs above the bones of the dead, that you might accept from me this offering (*mnḥḥ*) and [that] you may do my bidding and bring to me *x* the son of *y* who died, and stand him before me that he might speak with me without fear, and [that] he might tell me truths withholding nothing (*kḥd*) and I will not fear him. And he will answer my query which I require of him . . . . (*Sefer HaRazim* 1:176-82)

Characteristic of this brand of praxis seems the admixture of theurgic elements with more liturgical and cultic aspects. On the one hand, Kriphoros-Hermes is bound by the oath imposed upon him. On the other, the priestly magus entreats the spirit and bears an offering to please the supernatural being.

Far from being simply a peddler of potions and amulets the priest-magus, like the shaman of the Amerindians, through his intimacy with heavenly beings may aspire to a communality with the divine world unavailable to ordinary believers. That is, a certain prowess as mystic accrues from his knowledge; and, probably, these mystic accomplishments were believed to make his theurgy more effective. It should not surprise us, then, that *Sefer HaRazim* has been cast, in part, as a journey of ascent through the seven heavens with incantations and theurgic rites interpolated into the account of the heavenly worlds. The mystical (quasi-gnostic) vision of the seventh heaven and its doxology of the deity on his throne seem an entirely appropriate part of the document:

The seventh heaven is entirely of light—sevenfold [in brilliance]—and its light illumines all of the dwelling places. And in it is the throne of glory set upon the four beasts of glory (see Ezek. 1). And there are the treasuries of life and the treasuries of the souls. And there is no limit nor end to the great light which is there, and the plethora of light (*'wr hmmwlh*) will light all the world. And angels hold pillars of light. And their light is like that of *Noga* and will not be put out, for their eyes are like sparks of lightning; and they are supported upon wings of light and praise in awe of Him who sits upon the throne of glory. For He alone sits in His Heavenly abode, demanding justice and searching (*mpls*) righteousness, judging in truth and speaking in righteousness, and before him are open books of fire, and rivers of fire flow . . . .

The ecstatic vision replicates in part the hierophanies of Ezek. 1 and Isa. 6. Finally the magus-visionary breaks into a song of praise:

Blessed is His name in His seat of glory
    and to be blessed in the splendour of His might.
Blessed is His name in the treasury of snow
    and to be blessed in the rivers of flame.
Blessed is His name in the mists of magnificence
    and to be blessed in the clouds of glory.

Blessed is His name among the tens of thousands of chariots,
  and to be blessed among the thousands of Shin'an. (Ps. 68:18)

Blessed is His name alone in his throne,
  and to be blessed in the resting place of His might.
Blessed is His name in the mouth of every soul,
  and to be blessed in the song of every creature.
Blessed is YHWH for ever and ever,
Amen, Amen,
Hallelujah.

Thus in the traditions of *Sefer HaRazim*, the figures of theurgic practitioner, mystic visionary, and inspired liturgist all come together in a single holy man located among Hellenistic Jewry. Whatever we may feel to be the inner contradictions in this *mélange*, they obviously represented no insurmountable obstacle either for the practitioner or for his intended clientele. To be sure, *Sefer HaRazim* seems dependent upon various and varied sources, but the units of tradition themselves reflect, I think, a social context in which Jewish holy men did bring together within themselves these diverse concerns. These men entreated and compelled the powers above to make manifest redemption below, while at the same time they might transport themselves aloft in mystical ascent. Still they remained essentially human and distinct from their supernatural helpers, which was not so with a second type of Jewish holy man-magician, the divine man.

Such divine men, common among various groups in late antiquity, differ from the priestly magician in that the former has no need of rites and incantations to make manifest heaven's power on earth. To cite Morton Smith's concise characterization:

...the friends of a higher class practitioner would be apt to claim that he was not a magus, but rather, a "divine man." The "divine man" was a god or demon in disguise, moving about the world in an apparently human body. He could do all the beneficent things a magus could, and he could also curse effectively— though of course he would curse only the wicked. He did his miracles by his indwelling divine power and therefore did not need rituals or spells. This was the critical test by which a divine man could be distinguished from a magician—so at least his adherents would argue. The magical papyri describe a number of rites by which one can obtain a spirit as a constant companion. A magician who has such a spirit at his service can also dispense with rites and spells, he need only give his orders and they will be obeyed. Moreover, there were some magical rites that were supposed to deify the magician, either by joining him with some god in a permanent and perfect union (as Paul claimed to be joined with Jesus), or by changing the form, nature, or power of his soul so as to make it divine. A magician who had been deified would thereafter be a divine man and would perform miracles by his own power, not by a spirit.[23]

---

23   M. Smith, *Jesus the Magician*, 74-75.

Smith here has hit upon the precise nature of the controversy between the followers of Simon and those loyal to Philip (Acts 8:9ff.). Simon's adherents claim that he is just such a divine man as has been described. Christians would demote him from divine man to *magus*, if not to a *goes*, a carnival trickster. But Simon the Samaritan was obviously not the only Judaic pretender to the status of divinity. For, fragmentary as the evidence may be, not a few papyri preserve rites of self divinization from Judaic circles, albeit not from rabbinic ones. Thus the following from the magical papyri:

> But Thou, Lord of life, King of the heavens and the earth and all those that dwell therein (3 Macc. 2:2), whose righteousness is not turned aside, ... who has irrefutable truth, whose name and spirit [rest] upon good men, come into my mind and my vitals for all the time of my life and accomplish for me all the desires of my soul. For you are I and I am you. Whatever I say must happen.... For I have taken to myself the power of Abraham, Isaac, and Jacob and of the great demon-god Iao [i.e., YHWH] Ablanathanalba (PGM xiv, 784ff.; xxi).[24]

To some, claiming to be YHWH himself may have seemed overly pretentious or theologically unsound, since other rites aimed solely at making oneself "an angel upon earth," an "immortal" among the throngs of YHWH's supernatural aids.[25]

It seems stunning that with the exception of some very few scholars (primarily Goodenough and Smith) papyri such as the one cited at length above have remained outside the ken of studies of Hellenistic Judaism, usually because they are branded as non-Judaic on *a priori* (i.e., rabbinic) grounds. The rite in question and others like it are consistently devoid of those pagan elements which might disqualify them as Jewish. Indeed the opposite is the case, for as Smith notes:[26] "It is remarkable that no names of historical persons from Greek, Egyptian, or Persian tradition are used in the papyri as names of deities in spells, although many such persons are named as authors of spells or magical books." On the other hand, "Jesus's name was used in spells as the name of a god. So were the names of Adam (*PGM* 3:146), Abraham, Isaac and Jacob, and of Moses and Solomon who were famous as magicians." For Smith this suggests "that magical deification may have been unusually prominent in Jewish tradition (as exorcism seems to have been)."

Whether by priestly magus or by divine man the Jewish communities of the Hellenistic West had recourse to sacred, creative power

---

24 References to PGM refer to K. Preisendanz and A. Henrichs (eds.), *Papyri Graecae Magicae*, 2d. ed. (Stuttgart: Teubner, 1973-74). Translations by Smith, *Jesus the Magician*, 102.

25 PGM 2:148f.; see E.R. Goodenough, *Jewish Symbols*, 2:203.

26 M. Smith, *Jesus the Magician*, 114.

from the heavenly and angelic realms. In these men, heaven and earth could meet, the one drawing sustenance from the other in a world constantly under attack by unclean and evil forces. That these men played defined roles within the social fabric of Jewish life seems incontrovertible, or so our meagre evidence from Acts would indicate. But the fragmentary and episodic nature of the data will hardly allow us to draw a picture with any specificity.

The Jewish Cult of the Dead

Not all who performed these mediating functions still walked the earth in flesh and blood. By the second or third century at the very latest, the dead among Israel had been enlisted in the struggle to maintain open lines of communication between heaven and earth. To be sure, the dead had always played a role in informing the living. Necromancy was a widespread phenomenon in ancient Israel (otherwise the biblical injunctions against the practice would be senseless). In general, however, for ancient Israel the dead could not play any mediating role between heaven and earth. For as the Psalmist (Ps. 120:15) states, "The dead do not praise YHWH / Nor do all who descend in silence." God was in his heaven or his sanctuary; the dead remained in the netherworld of *She'ol*.

With the Hellenistic age the dead assume an entirely new trajectory.[27] They ascend to heaven, where they have heavenly beings as compatriots. It should little surprise us, then, that the dead—being in the neighbourhood, as it were—should become enlisted in the ongoing attempt to keep the upper and lower realms in communication and in contact. While to some extent all dead could, and as we shall see did, perform this function, deceased holy men could do so more effectively. For the latter had in life already been closer to the deity. We shall thus follow the careers of the dead on both planes, elitist and "commoner," beginning with the former.

In the Hellenistic period perhaps the earliest clear instance of pilgrimage to tombs of Israel's great occurs in the reign of Herod, in the latter half of the first century B.C. Among the various building projects undertaken in his lifetime was the construction of a large-scale mausoleum in Hebron at the traditional site of the tombs of the patriarchs, the cave of *Maḥpela*. Architects constructed a level platform over the area, enclosed the whole in a wall and within the courtyard set six stone blocks in lieu of the tombs themselves. A typical Herodian water system collected rainwater for pools within the structure. The courtyard by all accounts was intended to accommodate in comfort large crowds of pilgrims.

---

27   A. Segal, "Heavenly Ascent" (cited above, n. 16).

In terms of architecture what seems most striking about the structure at Hebron is that the mausoleum replicates exactly Herod's Temple in Jerusalem as Josephus describes it. The one is a scaled-down version of the other,[28] with one major difference: in place of the sanctuary which occupied the centre of the Temple compound, one finds in Hebron the six raised tombs of the mausoleum. These facts invite the conclusion that the mausoleum, and in particular the tombs therein, were considered by its pilgrims as analogous in character and function to the Temple cult itself. Here, as in the Temple, heaven and earth met and goods and services between the two realms might efficaciously be exchanged.

The "argument-from-architecture" admittedly remains suggestive only. But in the Byzantine period we have more direct evidence of the function of the mausoleum of the patriarchs.[29] Although banned from setting foot on the Temple Mount, Jesus received permission to pray at the mausoleum. On the basis of this act of conciliation, one may reasonably suppose that praying at the site had been a longstanding practice. Indeed it continued to be even after the rabbinization of the area, this in spite of the corpse-uncleanness which would have been contracted by anyone visiting the compound. That Jews, rabbinic or otherwise, would willfully contract corpse-uncleanness in order to offer prayers to the heavenly realm seems a stunning reversal of the biblical ethos.[30] For the Hebrew Bible, divine sacred power and powers of uncleanness could not co-exist. The sacrificial altar must remain free from the encroachment of unclean power, lest the link between the sacred realm and this world, terminating at the altar-site, should sustain irreparable damage. Having a tomb filled with uncleanness of the most virulent kind as the termination-point of such a link represents a conceptual revolution.

That tombs may assume such a function, I suspect, has more to do with what has transpired to the surviving spirit of the deceased and the possible services that spirit may render than with any integral holiness adhering to his or her entombed bones. The spirit of the patriarch (or other holy men) seems in some fashion to be both in his tomb and in

---

28   See Josephus' description of Herod's Temple in *B.J.* 5.187f. and in *Ant.* 15.280f.; see also Josephus, *B.J.* 4.532, and Mishna *Middot*. The similarity between the Temple and the mausoleum at Hebron is asserted by M. Avi-Yonah primarily on the basis of his archeological finds coupled with available literary evidence; see S. Safrai and M. Avi-Yonah, "The Temple," in *Encyclopaedia Judaica* (Jerusalem: Keter, 1972), 15:959ff.; M. Avi-Yonah, *Sefer Yerushalayim*, 1 (Jerusalem: Mossad Bielick and Dvir, 1956); M. Avi-Yonah's article in J. Neusner (ed.), *Religions in Antiquity: Essays in Memory of E.R. Goodenough* (Leiden: Brill, 1969), 327-35.

29   Joseph Braslavi, "The Cave of Mahpelah," in *Encyclopaedia Judaica* (Jerusalem: Keter, 1972), 11:670ff.; M. HaKohen, *The Cave of Mahpelah in Sources and Tradition* [in Hebrew] (Tel Aviv: 1965); O. Avisar (ed.), *Sefer Hevron* (Jerusalem: Keter, 1970).

30   M. Douglas, *Purity and Danger* (London: Routledge and Kegan Paul, 1966); J. Neusner, *The Idea of Purity in Ancient Judaism* (Leiden: Brill, 1973).

heaven. He is thus privy to the requests of supplicants and himself has, as it were, the ear of the deity. That the deceased constitutes an active intermediary, rather than a passive instrument of communication, seems evident in that prayer may be addressed to the deceased rather than to a divine being. More properly put, the deceased has become a divine being in some serious sense, and therefore, like God or an angel, may be efficaciously beseeched in prayer.

The matriarch, Rachel, seems a case in point, surviving even in rabbinic Judaism. It remains customary for barren women to visit the tomb of Rachel to pray for progeny. The efficacy of this tomb in overcoming barrenness has to do with the particular person (and biography) of the entombed who herself, according to the biblical narrative, long remained barren. In short, the specificity of function here alerts one to the active role played by the deceased; she above all ought to understand the problem. Indeed, supplicants usually addressed their prayers directly to her.

Pilgrimages to tombs of famous holy men were not limited to these few instances, even within rabbinic Judaism. The (alleged) tombs of David, Maimonides, and Rabbi Simeon Bar Yoḥai (to name but a few obvious examples) were all objects of such piety among rabbinic Jews, although the specific world-view which makes sense of these practices has been rigorously ignored (or suppressed) by the rabbis. The survival of such rites in a rabbinic environment attests to their entrenchment among late antique Jews (and their rabbinized descendants).

With regard to the "common" dead, the evidence is at once more abundant and more complex. Here we face a variety of data each with its own problems. We may begin with literary evidence (oddly enough preserved by a perturbed late antique rabbinate). The plethora of archeological and artifactual Hellenistic-Jewish evidence about the dead and their necropoli may then more profitably be considered.

The late antique rabbinic document *Maseket Semaḥot*[31] preserves some suggestive information about the ongoing function which the dead may have played among late Hellenistic Jewry. Evidence attests to strewing food on the bier of deceased young adults ("brides" and "grooms") during the funeral procession. Food may also have been spread along the way of the cortège and perhaps at the burial itself. The tractate mentions as well the piping of wine and oil "before" these dead, a practice out of which the classical commentaries can make no sense.[32] Of course, these practices replicate the wedding feast the "bride" and "groom" would have had, had they survived. But one cannot help but see here at least something reminiscent of *ex voto* offerings to the saints so common in early medieval Christianity. And

31 D. Zlotnick (ed.), *The Tractate Mourning* (New Haven: Yale, 1966).
32 *Sem.*, 8:2ff.

the existence of communal meals with the dead remained a familiar aspect of Hellenistic religions.[33] Even the apparently obscure piping of wine and oil finds its parallel in the pagan catacombs of Rome, where pipes were driven down from the surface into the catacombs and libations thereby poured into the tombs.

None of these parallels, admittedly, need be significant; indeed they smack of parallelomania—that is, in and of themselves. Still we do know that the *elite* dead were the loci of a Jewish cult (at least of prayer). The use, furthermore, of foodstuff, wine, and oil as media of communion has antecedents both in ancient Israelite religion—in the form of the sacrificial cult—and in such Jewish sects as Qumran and Pharisaism. Cultic meals, finally, exist everywhere among non-Jewish Hellenistic religions outside of the context of the dead[34] and (may) constitute the basis for the early Christian eucharist. Hence there existed a cultural milieu, among Jews as well as among non-Jews of the Hellenistic world, in which communing with the dead via offerings of food, wine, and oil would make considerable sense.

In this light *Semaḥot* 8:1 seems particularly to the point: "One may go out to the cemetery for thirty days to inspect the dead for a sign of life without fear that this smacks of heathen practice." Evidently the "heathen practices" so disturbing to the rabbis entail regular ongoing visits to the tomb within and beyond the thirty-day period.[35] The interdiction, moreover, hardly strikes at non-Jews; rather the passage clearly implies that Jews themselves engaged in these ongoing pilgrimages to the grave-site and did so no doubt as Jews, not as participants in pagan ritual. To the rabbis, of course, any non-rabbinic activity would be worthy of the title, "heathen practice." The language evinces a rabbinic polemic. In all, then, one is left with the impression that (non-rabbinic) Jews regularly engaged in religious rites of some sort at the tombs of their deceased. That is, the tomb had become a cultic locus. Unfortunately, *Semaḥot* does not give further interdictions about what *not* to do at the grave-site.

Again, what late antique rabbinism attempted to suppress, medieval rabbinism clearly evinces. Regular visits to the tombs of family remain commonplace among traditional, rabbinic Jews. There one customarily addresses the deceased, asking that he or she intercede with the divine powers on behalf of surviving relatives.

---

33 See P. Brown, *The World of Late Antiquity* (London: Harcourt Brace Jovanovich, 1971), 62; H. Lietzmann, *The Era of the Church Fathers: A History of the Early Church*, vol. 4 (London: Lutterworth, 1951), 128; E. Rhode, *Psyche: The Cult of Souls and Belief in Immortality Among the Greeks* (London: Routledge and Kegan Paul, 1950), 196, n. 87; see also *m. 'Abot*, 3:3.

34 See, for example, F. Cumont, *Oriental Religions in Roman Paganism* (New York: Dover, 1956), 68-69.

35 See S. Lieberman, "Some Aspects of After Life in Early Rabbinic Literature," in *H.A. Wolfson Jubilee Volume on the Occasion of His 75th Birthday* (Jerusalem: American Academy of Jewish Research, 1965), 511.

The artifactual and archeological evidence for Hellenistic Jewry indicates as well that the common tomb functioned as a portal to the realm of the divine[36]—initially, at least, for the deceased and perhaps therefore for the prayers of the living. Parallel to the new conception among Jews of Hellenistic and Roman times that the dead ascend to heaven, rather than descend to the nether world, one finds the development of new modes of burial and of a remarkably consistent vocabulary of funerary art. Here we may hope to review only the more important data.

Typically, the deceased Jew of late antiquity would have been anointed with oils and spices, taken to a rock-hewn chamber, and left in a *koch*, a coffin-like excavation cut perpendicular to the wall of the chamber. A chamber might have from half a dozen to a dozen such *kochim*. Here the corpse was left to decay until at some later period (11 months in some traditions) the relatives collected the bones, anointed them with wine, oil, and herbs and deposited the remains in a miniature sarcophagus (an ossuary). The bone-boxes were left in one corner of the chamber; the *koch* could be reused.[37] Again, given the taboo against contracting corpse-uncleanness, whatever was believed to have been accomplished by this "secondary burial" obviously outweighed the interdictions about uncleanness (even for Jews living in close proximity to the Temple).

It is tempting to suppose that each of the two burials represents a distinct rite of passage for the dead on their journey from earth to heaven, with the secondary burial effecting the final ascent to the divine realm. For the most blatant distinction between the first and second entombments seems to be the presence of flesh at the former and its absence at the latter. To the Jewish mind, whether rabbinic or non-rabbinic, flesh, more than bones, represented that part of the individual most susceptible to the powers of chaos and the demonic. Thus early rabbinic law, saddled with the biblical notion that both flesh and bones of a deceased contaminate, nevertheless clearly distinguishes, where it can, the virulence of one source of uncleanness from the other. Flesh, for example, in any amount contaminates by overshadowing; only the greater part of the skeleton, however, has the same effect.[38] In early rabbinic homiletical texts, moreover, flesh seems to be the medium of susceptibility to the forces of the corruptible and the corrupting.[39] Here, then, even rabbinic thought mirrors a negative

36 Bernard Goldman, *The Sacred Portal* (Detroit: Wayne State, 1966).
37 See E.M. Meyers, *Jewish Ossuaries: Reburial and Rebirth* (Rome: Biblical Institute Press, 1971); *Sem.* 12, 13; Matt. 27.55ff.; Mark 16:46; Luke 24:53ff.; John 19:38ff.
38 *m. Ohol.* 1:11ff.; see J. Neusner, *A History of the Mishnaic Law of Purities*, Parts 4 and 5 (Leiden: Brill, 1975).
39 See *m. 'Abot* 2:7; some later evidence: *Tanhuma Bereshit* 38 (ed. Buber); see also W.D. Davies, *Paul and Rabbinic Judaism* (London: SPCK, 1952), 17-36; see also *Avot de R. Nathan* 2, 16 (ed. Schechter).

assessment of the flesh so often found in early Christianity (gnostic, Pauline, and ascetic) and in Hellenistic religions.[40] That Philo, from the non-rabbinic side, will also have shared this general evaluation of the corporeal hardly requires argument. Perhaps then at secondary burial the deceased, now free from the last anchors to this realm — their flesh — may ascend to the divine world as transformed beings. Clean bones attest to freedom from this lower abode and the demonic powers which rule it.

The funerary art commonly associated with ossilegium lends further support to our interpretation of secondary burial. Representations on the ossuaries evince a remarkably consistent and limited artistic vocabulary. All bone-boxes exhibit a double portal or circular devices, and more frequently both.[41] Neither representation, I might add, appears solely on bone-boxes. They are commonplace themes in funerary art, along with such other devices as the palm-branch, grapevines, grape-clusters, wreaths (really another circular device), candelabras, *shofar,* and incense shovels.[42] Symbols borrowed from the Temple cult are immediately recognizable among the representations, an observation not to be taken for granted. A host of traditional themes and ritual objects (other than cultic) will have offered themselves to Palestinian and diaspora Jews as candidates for religious art. The Temple, moreover, played no active role in the life of Jewry after 70 C.E.; for diaspora Jews that situation had ensued already for several centuries prior to the cult's demise. The curious choice of sacrificial objects as funerary art thus seems deliberate and significant.

Such Temple symbols may be apocalyptic in nature. In much of late antique eschatological theory the rededication of the Temple figures as part of the end of time. The dead who will rise at the *eschaton* will participate in the new cult. Still, without ruling out this view of matters altogether, it fails to satisfy entirely. First, one cannot say how widespread assent to these particular apocalyptic views was, in Palestine or beyond. More important, Judaism in the Hellenistic age and in particular in the late antique world evinces, as we have already seen, a hearty interest in the immediate *post mortem* careers of the dead. Persons in Hellenistic Judaism survive death as bodiless spirits ascending as "transfigured" beings to heaven.[43] That Hellenistic Jews would have looked forward to some future descent from heaven and near-divine status to resume life in the flesh seems hardly likely. Indeed, I know of little evidence for Hellenistic Jewry indicating assent to the notion of

---

40   See H. Lietzmann, *History*, 128f.; F. Cumont, *Oriental Religions*, 40f., 50f., 157; P. Brown, *Late Antiquity*, 96-109.
41   E. Myers, *Jewish Ossuaries*; B. Goldman, *The Sacred Portal*; E.R. Goodenough, *Jewish Symbols*.
42   E.R. Goodenough, *Jewish Symbols*.
43   See A. Segal, "Heavenly Ascent," 1352ff.

resurrection. It appears, therefore, difficult to associate the use of cultic objects in the funerary art of Hellenistic Jewry with apocalyptic eschatology.

Surely an equally (if not more) plausible explanation offers itself. Hellenistic Judaism associated the tomb with the cult per se. At both Temple and tomb heaven and earth meet. That is why the dead can ascend to heaven. Cultic symbols, then, are salvific in character, but not (necessarily) in apocalyptic terms. The tomb is like an altar, and the dead mediate at the sacred locus which joins the realms. At least they mediate for one transformation, one exchange between the worlds, namely, the ascension of themselves, just as the smoke ascended to the deity from the altar of the sanctuary.

This interpretation of cultic themes in funerary art dovetails with the other (so-called non-Jewish) representations found in Hellenistic Jewish tombs; grape clusters, vines,[44] portals, and the like all find their parallels in the symbols of Hellenistic salvation-religions and mystery cults.[45] Wreaths, branches, grapes, and vines have their provenance in the Dionysiac mysteries. The double-arched portal again is commonplace, particularly in the art from the cult of Isis and Osiris. But in the "pagan" context, the portals are not empty. Under the arches stand the deity and her consort ready to welcome the now liberated initiate. In the Jewish context the portal is in all likelihood the gate to heaven and YHWH. Both cultic and non-cultic symbols on Hellenistic Jewish tombs, therefore, communicate the same message in their idiomatic ways: the tomb constitutes an opening to heaven and the divine.

The archeological and artifactual evidence in itself cannot indicate precisely the functions of tombs and the dead in late antique Judaism. That tombs were links between heaven and earth says nothing about whom they served or how. To be sure we must surmise that the dead constituted the principal traffic along the artery. Whether the tomb had utility for others, art cannot say. Still the little literary evidence at hand strongly suggests that the tombs and the deceased served the living. And the art, to be sure, further explains how the tomb could play such a role, in that the burial place was the gate to heaven, a new altar-site.

Synagogues and Their Offices: Correcting our Perspective

This essay aims, as explained earlier, at elucidating some of the basic structures of the religion of late antique Jews. It does not, however, purport to give an exhaustive account of these phenomena. Still, some

---

44   The grape symbolism is assimilated to the Jerusalem cult already before 70 C.E. See references to Josephus in n. 28.

45   E.R. Goodenough, *Jewish Symbols*.

few brief remarks seem called for regarding the late antique synagogue in view of the (often stated) centrality of the institution in late antique Judaism in general and in the Hellenistic Diaspora in particular. That centrality, however, has in some serious sense been overstated, particularly in regard to the synagogue's function as a substitute for the cult. By way of concluding the review of the data for (non-rabbinic) Judaism in the late Roman world, I shall briefly attempt to relocate synagogues within this structure.

The existence of synagogues in Palestine and the Diaspora is already well attested by the first and second centuries of our era.[46] Yet for all the claims about the importance of the institution across the "Jewish world" (and putting aside for the moment rabbinic sources), we know surprisingly little about the synagogue's function in mediating the sacred. That prayers were offered within the synagogue we may confidently surmise, although direct evidence to that effect is more sparse than one might expect.[47] Acts of course knows of reading the Law and the Prophets in the synagogue (cf. Acts 15:20) and also informs us of homiletic activities (mostly by Christian preachers).

The synagogue, though a locus for prayer, and hence in some sense a link between the divine realm and the world, had no resident holy man who guaranteed this mediation. Synagogues had their officials, a council of elders (*gerousia*), an *archon*, or both.[48] Still these persons were "aristocratic" lay leaders, administrators more than holy functionaries. Indeed tannaitic literature could not even imagine the rabbi as a resident holy man of the synagogue, although Mishna and Tosefta seem quite able to contemplate other equally fictional loci of rabbinic power in the community.

The late antique synagogue, then, seems akin to the early Christian communities (no doubt the former will to a large extent have constituted the model for the latter). The Didache (15:1-2) sees the presbyterate and its sub-offices as lay administrative posts. The status of holy man by contrast appears reserved for charismatics of various sorts, in many cases clearly understood to be mendicant (Did. 11:1-12). The presbyterate guaranteed not a mediating link between heaven and earth, but only an institutional context which safeguarded the existence and continuity of the community of believers for those moments

---

46   See Philo, *Leg.* 20, 132, and *Flacc.*; references in Acts in n. 15; inscriptions from synagogues in Egypt in V. Tcherikover and A. Rucks, *Corpus Papyrorum Judaicarum*, vol. 3 (Cambridge: Harvard University Press, 1957-64), and for elsewhere in the Graeco-Roman world in J.B. Frey, *Corpus of Jewish Inscriptions* (New York: KTAV, 1975), reprinted from the 1936 edition published in Rome by the Pontifical Institute; John Chrysostom, *Homily I Against the Jews* (*Patrologia Graeca* 48: 846ff.).

47   See *Ep. Diogn.* 3:1-46. This passage vilifying Jewish worship knows, oddly enough, nothing of synagogue liturgy, but polemicizes against the (already defunct) sacrificial cult.

48   See n. 41.

when that link could be had. In the hierarchy of mediating moments between heaven and earth, the eucharist was the most frequent and, for that same reason, probably felt to be among the least effective. The visit of an itinerant charismatic of some repute seems to offer mediation of the most efficacious kind—as proven by concomitant healings, exorcisms, and the like.

In view of what we know of the organization of the late antique synagogue, I am tempted to paint for that institution a picture similar to the state of affairs in the early church. The lay leaders maintained a stable community to which moments of mediation were made available, first, but least effectively through prayer, at other times, and more intensively, through visiting holy men whom we have discussed above. This view of matters makes eminent sense of the overwhelmingly bureaucratic character of the evidence which survives for the life of the synagogue and the role of its functionaries.

Christians, Rabbis, and Other Jews

Late antique Judaism, at least in the data from Hellenistic Jewry here reviewed, seems to have had as its basic model of "world" a two-tiered structure. The lower realm upon which mortal men walked and lived was a somewhat precarious place, it would seem. Supernatural (or primeval) malevolent forces constantly attempted to impinge upon what little life-sustaining order existed here below. Only constant recourse to creative, sacred "stuff" from the abode of the deity and his angelic aids kept the powers of chaos at bay. With the power of heaven (the holy spirit if you will) disease, demons and other life-threatening forces might be vanquished. Thus the basic problematic evinced by our data appears to be the mediation between the realms. Those religious structures which address the question thus offer loci whereby the necessary links may be found, the (Jewish) priest-magus, the divine man, the sacred dead, and the philosophic-mystic. These persons join the worlds either with their capacity to ascend to heaven and direct back to earth the sacred power of that realm or, as in the case of the divine man, because they represent incursions of the divine realm into this plane of existence.

Neither early Christians nor early rabbis will have found either the problematic or those religious structures which respond to it foreign to them. In fact quite the contrary is the case, and herein lies the ground for the intense theological and institutional competition (and hatred) among these various expressions of Yahwehism. Each group having essentially the same view of reality (the two-tier universe) and the same conception of the needs of this world (mediation between the realms) offered its idiomatic holy men who in character and especially function will not have greatly differed from those of the competition. The theological apologetic which early rabbinism and Christianity offered in defence of the authority of their holy men remains readily available to us. Unfortunately, nothing comparable survives in the fragmentary evidence for Hellenistic Judaism, with the possible exception of Philo.

Until recently modern scholarship has not tended to view early rabbinism as an instance of this larger Hellenistic pattern of religion. The rational-legal and bureaucratic aspects of rabbinism assumed considerable importance for the *Wissenschaft des Judentums* whose historiography oftentimes served apologetic purposes. The lawyer-homileticist-rabbi which emerged from nineteenth-century histories constituted the perfect instance of the "religion of reason." In an age in which Jews sought respectability, the *Wissenschaftliche* historians offered the classical rabbi as a prototype of the nineteenth-century enlightened believer.

But such a view of the character and function of the early rabbis can stand only by systematically ignoring a host of data preserved in rabbinic literature.[49] Rabbis were not mere interpreters of the law; they professed to constitute the very embodiment of Torah. That Torah, moreover, comprises not only the Pentateuch, the written Torah, but an oral Torah as well, vouchsafed to Moses ("our Rabbi") on Sinai, and "incarnated," as it were, in the rabbis of late antiquity. Torah for the rabbis seems in certain respects to have been much like the Logos for Philo, and like the holy spirit for the early church. The law expressed God's sacred order of "world" on this plane of existence; but Torah was also the first creation, the firstborn of YHWH and through Torah the world was created. "When it came time to create the world, He looked into Torah and created the universe." Torah, for the rabbis, therefore, linked heaven and earth, constituting that principle or power which created order out of chaos and which in the life of the rabbinic Jew maintains that order against the onslaught of the powers of chaos. The rabbi, not a set of documents, mediates the heavenly Torah on earth; as a walking, living Torah, he constitutes the locus of the sacred power of the deity.

Understood in these terms, rabbis, among other things, ought to be able to perform many of the same functions and feats as the non-rabbinic priestly magi and divine men in Hellenistic Judaism, and as the charismatics of the early church. Indeed, according to rabbinic literature, rabbis could bless and curse efficaciously, resurrect the dead, exorcise the demons, heal the sick, interpret dreams, make those dreams come true (or the opposite), and kill, if need be, with a look.

---

49   See J. Neusner, *A History of the Jews in Babylonia*, vols. 4 and 5 (Leiden: Brill, 1965-70); W.S. Green, "Palestinian Holy Men," in H. Temporini and W. Haase (eds.), *Aufstieg und Niedergang der Römischen Welt*, 2:19/2 (Berlin/New York: De Gruyter, 1979), 619-47.

The rabbinate, of course, opposed magic and decried its practice by (other) Jews; yet they did much the same thing, designating their own behaviour as acts of Torah. Surely this seems a case of Philip and Simon revisited; what my holy man does is by the power of heaven; what yours does is mere magic, or illusion and trickery.

As an embodiment of Torah the rabbi did not remain earthbound. Thanks to Scholem[50] we now have detailed knowledge of earlier rabbinic esoteric (gnostic-like) traditions, the goal of which was to ascend through the heavens past the angelic guards to attain a vision of the demiurge upon his throne of glory. Consistent with these mystical ascents described in the *Hekalot* texts, we possess in *Sefer Yeṣirah* an early medieval rabbinic document which professed to reveal that configuration of letters and numbers which comprise the substratum of creation. Scholem has convincingly argued that *Hekalot* traditions date at least to the (early) second century C.E., that is, to nascent rabbinism itself. Thus while traditions in *Sefer HaRazim* described a vision of the Seventh Heaven, and not too long after Paul who "in Christ was caught up to the Seventh Heaven," rabbis too had their praxis of ascent to the palace of the Throne of Glory.

Even in death the rabbi seems to have remained a locus of sacred power. We have mentioned above the pilgrimages of early medieval times to the tombs of great rabbinic personages. One may add here the tradition preserved in the Babylonian Talmud that when Rav (the early third-century Amora) died, the "common" folk would come to his grave-site for handfuls of dirt. The earth from his tomb was believed to possess medicinal qualities.

Early Rabbinism, Hellenistic Judaism, and early Christianity each offered its own holy men as mediators between heaven and earth, having in all three cases, it would seem, similarly defined the religious problematic of their worlds. All three communities proposed their idiomatic transformations of the same structure in lieu of the Temple cult in Jerusalem, which until the first century (or so) had provided (for many Jews) that point where heaven and earth met and the rites by which mediation might be had. In attempting to come to grips with life without a Temple, Hellenistic Jews, rabbis and early Christians turn to individuals, not geographical locations or (national) institutions as modes of mediating the sacred. "Map" is no longer maintained by recourse to sacred "territory" in the late Roman world.[51] And in this our three groups appear typically late antique.

50   G.G. Scholem, *Major Trends in Jewish Mysticism* (New York: Schocken, 1941); G.G. Scholem, *Jewish Gnosticism, Mekabah Mysticism and the Talmudic Tradition* (New York: Jewish Theological Seminary, 1965); D. Blumenthal, *Understanding Jewish Mysticism* (New York: KTAV, 1979); I. Gruenwald, *Apocalyptic*.
51   J.Z. Smith, "The Temple and the Magician," in J.Z. Smith, *Map Is Not Territory* (Leiden: Brill, 1978), 172-89.

What now of Jesus and early Christians in the Talmud, our point of departure? Jesus ben Pantera and the mendicant charismatics who heal in his name, play in rabbinic literature the role of a Christian Simon Magus, or at least of the seven sons of Sceva, to a rabbinic Philip or Paul. For, after all, one good turn deserves another, among people "playing the same game" in the "same ballpark."

8

Judaism, Christianity, and Gnosticism

Alan F. Segal

Two Powers in Heaven

The rabbinic references to heretics who believed in "two powers in heaven" present a promising start for uncovering the vexed relationship between Judaism, Christianity, and gnosticism because some kind of dualistic doctrine seems inherent in the designation[1] and several scholars have seen a relationship between two powers and Christianity. However, when one turns to the rabbinic evidence itself, one finds that the texts define "two powers in heaven" from a confusing variety of perspectives. Furthermore, the texts were written over a long period of time, probably referring to a variety of different phenomena, so only an outline of the complete problem can be presented here.[2]

The best way to begin is to turn to some characteristic occurrences of the designation and try to outline the history of the heresy. The most significant passage may be found in several places in midrashic literature and is alluded to in many more. The tradition occurs often in different versions in the *Mekhiltot*. A simple form of the tradition occurs in Mekilta of R. Simeon b. Yohai (= MRSbY). In Mekilta of R.

---

1   The study of rabbinic heretics (the *minim*) has had several distinguished forebears. See, for example, M. Jöel, *Blicke in die Religionsgeschichte zu Anfang des zweiten christlichen Jahrhunderts* (Breslau: Schottlander, 1880), 2:71f; T. Herford, *Christianity in Talmud and Midrash* (London: Williams and Norgate, 1903), 362f; M. Simon, *Verus Israel* (Paris: de Boccard, 1964), 216f; S.M. Wagner, *Religious Non-conformity in Ancient Jewish Life* (Unpublished dissertation, Yeshiva University, 1964); A. Marmorstein, *Religionsgeschichtliche Studien: Die Bezeichnung für die Christen und Gnostischen im Talmud und Midrash* (Schotsam: Selbst Verlag des Verfasser, 1910), 1:66-81; A. Buchler, "The Minim of Sepphoris and Tiberius in the Second and Third Centuries," in *Studies in Jewish History* (Oxford: Oxford University Press, 1956), 245-74.
2   For further details, the reader is directed to my book, *Two Powers in Heaven: Early Rabbinic Reports about Christianity and Gnosticism* (Leiden: Brill, 1977).

Ishmael (= MRI) the passage occurs in two places (Baḥodesh 5 and Shirta 4) in virtually identical form. In Baḥodesh alone, a closely related tradition, adduced in the name of R. Nathan, was added because of its obvious relevance. Finally, the tradition was known and discussed in Pesiqta Rabbati (= PR), but there it has undergone considerable development.[3] Two of the versions can be compared:[4]

MRSbY	MRI
The Mekilta of R. Simeon b. Yohai, p. 81. Bashalah 15.	The Mekilta of R. Ishmael, Baḥodesh 5, Shirta 4
Another interpretation: *YHWH is a man of war, YHWH is His name.*	*I am YHWH your God*: Why is this said?
Because, when the Holy One Blessed be He was revealed at the sea, he appeared to them as a young man making war. *YHWH is His name.* He appeared to them at Sinai like an old man, full of mercy:	Because When He was revealed at the sea, He appeared to them as a mighty hero making war. As it is said, *YHWH is a man of war.*
	He appeared at Sinai like an old man, full of mercy, as it is said: *And they saw the God* of Israel. (Exod. 24:10)

---

3   *PR* I, pp. 421f. (Braude) Piska 21 100b; see also Pesikta rabbati de Baḥodesh, Exod. 20:2, together with Deut. 5:4:
     (Another comment: *Face After Face*) R. Levi said: God faced them in many guises. To one He appeared standing, and to one seated; (see Gen. 28:13 and Isa. 6:1) to one as a young man, and to one as an old man. How so? At the time the Holy One, blessed be He, appeared on the Red Sea to wage war for His children and to requite the Egyptians, he faced them as a young man, since war is waged best by a young man, as is said *The Lord is a man of war, the Lord is His name* (Exod. 15:3). And when the Holy One, blessed be He, appeared on Mount Sinai to give the Torah to Israel, He faced them as an old man, for Torah is at its best when it comes from the mouth of an old man. What is the proof? The verse *With aged men is wisdom, and understanding in length of days* (Job 12:12); and therefore Daniel said: *beheld till thrones were placed, and one that was Ancient of days did sit* (Dan. 7:9). In regard to God's guises R. Hiyya bar Abba said: If a whoreson should say to you, "They are two gods," quote God as saying in reply: "I am the One of the sea and I am the One of Sinai."
     (Another comment) R. Levi taught at Sinai the Holy One, blessed be He, appeared to them with many faces, with a threatening face, with a severe face, with an angry face, with a joyous face, with a laughing face, with a friendly face. How so? . . . In regard to God's many faces, R. Hiyya bar Abba taught: Should a whoreson say to you, "They are two gods," reply to him, Scripture does not say "The gods have spoken . . . face after face" but *The Lord has spoken with you face after face.*
4   The Mekilta of R. Simeon b. Yohai, p. 81, Bashalah 15. The Mekilta of R. Ishmael, Baḥodesh 5, Shirta 4 (trans. Lauterbach).

	And of the time after they had been redeemed what does it say? *And the like of the very heaven for clearness.* (Exod. 24:10)
I beheld 'til thrones were set down. (Dan. 7:9)	Again, it says, *I beheld 'til thrones were set down.* (Dan. 7:9) And it also says *A fiery stream issued and came forth from him* etc.
So as not to give an opportunity to say "There are two powers in heaven." Rather *YHWH is a man of War.* (Another interpretation:) *YHWH is a man of War.* YHWH fought in Egypt. YHWH fought at the Sea. And He is at the Jordan, He is at the Arnon streams.	Scripture would not give an opportunity to the nations of the world to say "There are 'two powers,'" but declares *I am YHWH your God.* (Exod. 20:2) I was in Egypt. I was at the Sea. I was in the past, I will be in the future to come.
And He is in this world, And He is in the world to come. He is in the past and He is in the future to come.	I am in this world, I am in the world to come.
As it is said: *Behold now, that I, even I, am He*, etc. (Deut. 32:39) *Thus says YHWH, the king of Israel*, etc. *I am YHWH, the first and the last*, etc. (Isa. 44:6)	As it is said: *Behold now, that I, even I, am He*, etc. (Deut. 32:39) *Even unto old age I am the same.* (Isa. 46:4) *Thus says YHWH the king of Israel and his Redeemer the Lord of Hosts, I am the first and the last.* (Isa. 44:6) And it says *Who has wrought and done it? He that called the generations from the beginning. I, the Lord who am the first, and to the end I am He.* (Isa. 41:4)

In MRSbY the subject is introduced as an exegetical comment on the two statements made about YHWH in Exod. 15:3. The exegesis notes the repetition of the name YHWH in Exod. 15:3 and explains its significance. "YHWH is a man of war" is to be interpreted as a descriptive statement referring to God's manifestation as a young warrior when He destroyed the Egyptians at the Red Sea. "YHWH is His name" is necessary because, at Sinai, He will reveal Himself as an old man, showing mercy. Hence, it is important for the Israelites to realize that the same God is speaking in both places, though the manifestations look different.[5]

The text in MRI is even more complex and obviously the result of a long history of redaction. First, one has to notice that the issue is no longer merely the repetition of the divine name of YHWH. In this case, the dangerous doctrine is the idea that there are two different manifestations of God—one, a just young man, appearing at the sea; the other, a merciful old man, appearing at Sinai.[6] Neither MRI nor MRSbY can itself be the ancient tradition. However, it can easily be seen that both are variations of the same tradition. The most ancient layer, which we shall later show to be tannaitic, must be carefully uncovered in comparing them.

The common tradition must have been an exegesis of the meaning of divine names, probably also centred around the Sinai theophany. A common proof-text against the heresy is Dan. 7:9f. However, it is also likely to be the locus of an heretical argument since the passage describes two different figures in heaven in Daniel's night vision. Of course, the rabbis objected to such an idea, saying that the repetition of divine names and the change in divine appearances were planned by one God. From the rabbinic perspective repetition of the divine name did not identify "two powers"; it only emphasized that the Israelites would have to recognize God in different forms throughout their history. In attempting to identify the heresy we should look for a doctrine which did associate "two powers" with the different names of God.

Other interesting details emerge from this passage. It is clear that the heretical doctrine in this particular case involves believing in two corresponding or co-operating deities. This means that the heretics who provoked this response from the rabbis are not likely to have been dualists. Nor can they have been Marcionite Christians or extreme gnostics. Rather, we have to look among the sects contemporary with

---

5   See J. Lauterbach, "Some Clarifications of the Mekilta" (in Hebrew), in N.H. Torchyner, A. Tcherikover, A.A. Kubeck and B. Shortman (eds.), *Sefer Klausner: A Collection of Science and Belles-lettres gathered for Prof. Klausner on his Sixtieth Birthday Celebration* (Tel Aviv: Va'ad Ha Yovet, 1937), 181-88, especially 184-88. See also Judah Goldin, *The Song at the Sea* (New Haven: Yale University Press, 1971), 126f.
6   Space does not allow a complete discussion of the passage. But it should be noted that the rabbinic doctrine of the two *middoth* or "measures" of God is implicit in this discussion in MRI. This aspect was missing in the version occurring at MRSbY. MRI has developed a special tradition about the discussion of God's attributes of justice and mercy, though the actual technical terms do not appear. The theme of God's justice and mercy is very important for dating the whole rabbinic tradition. We shall see that Philo and the Mishnah both record similar traditions about God's justice and mercy. For more detail on this aspect of this passage, see N.A. Dahl and Alan F. Segal, "Philo and the Rabbis on the Names of God," *JSJ*, 9 (1978), 1-25.

the rabbis for theologies with two complementary figures in heaven to find candidates for the heresy. This would include one of the many apocalyptic systems where a figure, like Michael, Melchizedek or even a "Son of Man" were important partners of God in bringing redemption. No doubt many varieties of Christians were also included, for Christianity was exceptionally interested in the interpretation of Dan. 7:9f. Though Christianity's theology was to become explicitly trinitarian, this would not have been clear in the early centuries. For one thing, Christian mention of the "Holy Spirit" would neither have been considered unique nor heretical by the rabbis. For another thing, Christianity of the period was much more concerned with the relationship between the Father and the Son. The concept of the "Holy Spirit" did not provoke the same degree of speculation.[7]

The rabbinic response to the heresy is also clear. The rabbis appeal to scripture to show that God is unitary. Deuteronomy 6, Isaiah 44 to 47, and Exodus 20 are used to show that God is unique. These verses are probably employed against heretical interpretations of Dan. 7:9f.; they are certainly used to oppose the idea that the names of God denote different divinities. This pattern of scriptures is characteristic both of the heresy and the defence against it. It will be especially important for reconstructing the history of the heresy and for understanding the radicalization of gnosticism.

However, other aspects of the heresy are more mysterious. Determining the identity of the groups in question remains a serious problem. MRI describes those professing belief in the doctrine as "Gentiles." PR calls a person with such beliefs either a "whoreson" or a "son of heresy" depending upon the translation. There can thus be no precise identification of the heresy from the terminology in the rabbinic writings. There is some evidence for connecting it with a rabbinic polemic against Christianity. Elsewhere, PR 22 comments on "My God, My God, why has thou forsaken me?" which, in Aramaic translation, are supposed to have been Jesus' last words (Matt. 27:48). The rabbis say that the first "my God" refers to the sea while the second "my God" refers to Sinai. Since no other heretical group found this verse relevant for their doctrine, one may suppose that Christianity was identified as a "two powers" heresy; but the rabbinic charge of "two powers" may not have been originally or exclusively used against them. The many different descriptions of the heresy in the different versions of the tradition suggest that the charge was used against several groups of heretics in different places. This conclusion can be demonstrated more fully later, as more evidence is revealed.

---

7 Jaroslav Pelikan, *The Christian Tradition: A History of the Development of Doctrine* (Chicago: University of Chicago Press, 1971), vol. 1, especially 172-225.

In these passages, one becomes aware of the development of the tradition over a vast period of time. Traditions with so many different layers present immense dating problems, and only approximate dates can be given for each layer. Although these texts occur in the "tannaitic" midrashim, recent scholarship has shown that the traditional attributions should not be accepted without question.[8] The traditions may go back as far as the first century but the texts are not equally ancient. Even so, parts of the early layers of the tradition may be isolated.

With external evidence, it is possible to push the origin of this tradition back much further. Philo attests to the pervasiveness and antiquity of the problem of God's appearances as well as His different aspects. His doctrine of the *logos* commands our attention first, because Philo explicitly calls the *logos* a second God (*deuteros theos*) in several places.[9] He even mentions Jews who are so naive as to believe that this "second God" is the Existent One himself.[10] At the same time, Philo stresses that there is no God besides God the Most High and uses Deut.

---

8   For more information about the new attempt to date rabbinical traditions see, e.g., Jacob Neusner, "The Rabbinic Traditions about the Pharisees Before 70 A.D.: The Problem of Oral Transmission," *JJS*, 22 (1971), 1-18. Also see some of his longer works, such as, *From Politics to Piety: The Emergence of Pharisaic Judaism* (Englewood Cliffs: Prentice-Hall, 1973); *The Rabbinic Traditions about the Pharisees Before 70 A.D.* (Leiden: Brill, 1971); *Eliezer ben Hyrcanus: The Man and the Legend* (Leiden: Brill, 1973).

9   For instance: "Yet there can be no cowering fear for the man who relies on the hope of the divine comradeship, to whom are addressed the words 'I am the God who appeared to thee in place of God' (Gen. 31:31). Surely a right noble cause of vaunting it is, for a soul that God deigns to show himself to and converse with it. And do not fail to mark the language used, but carefully inquire whether there are two Gods; for we read 'I am the God that appeared to thee,' not 'in my place' but 'in the place of God,' as though it were another's. What then are we to say? He that is truly God is one, but those that are improperly so-called are more than one. Accordingly, the holy word in the present instance has indicated Him who truly is God by means of the article, saying, 'I am the God,' while it omits the article when mentioning him who is improperly so called, saying, 'who appeared to thee in the place' not 'of the God' but simply 'of God' " (*Som.* 1.227-29, trans. Colson).

    "Why does [Scripture] say, as if [speaking] of another God, 'In the image of God He made man' and not 'in His own image?' Most excellently and veraciously this oracle was given by God. For nothing mortal can be made in the likeness of the Most High One and father of the universe but [only] in that of the second God, who is His *logos*. For it was right that the rational part of the human soul should be formed as an impression of the divine *logos*, since the pre-*logos* God is superior to every rational nature. But He who is above the *logos* exists in the best and in a special form—what thing that comes into being can rightly bear His likeness? Moreover, Scripture wishes to show that God most justly avenges the virtuous and decent men because they have certain kinship with His *logos*, of which the human mind is a likeness and image." (*Quest. in Gen.* 2. 62, trans. Marcus)

10 *Som.* 1.230-33. Here, the issue for Philo is the meaning of scriptural anthropomorphisms. This is a theme which runs throughout Philo's discussion of the "second God." See also *Mig.* 86-93 where Philo speaks of extreme allegorizers. The issue in that place, however, is loyalty to the commandments.

4:39, as the rabbis do, to deny that any other figure can be considered a God:

> But let Melchizedek instead of water offer wine, and give to souls strong drink, that they may be seized by a divine intoxication, more sober than sobriety itself. For he is a priest, even Reason, having as his portion Him that is, and all his thoughts of God are high and vast and sublime: for he is the priest of the Most High (Gen. 14:18), not that there is any other not Most High—for God being One "is in heaven above and on earth beneath and there is none beside Him" (Deut. 4:39)—but to conceive of God not in low earthbound ways but in lofty terms, such as transcend all other greatness and all else that is free from matter, calls up in us a picture of the Most High.[11]

In this particular case, Philo denies that any other being can be God's agent, for there is only one God. It is interesting that Philo picks the allegory of Melchizedek as *logos* to discuss this issue, since elsewhere he allows that the *logos* can be considered as a "second God" and divine mediator. It appears as though Philo is opposed to some concepts of mediation, even while he maintains the agency of the *logos*.[12] Philo also knows that the names of God connote His aspects of mercy and justice, just as the rabbis do. But Philo identifies the divine names *kyrios* and *theos* (= YHWH and Elohim) with the aspects of God in exactly the opposite way from the rabbis. Generally Philo equates YHWH with the attribute of strict justice and Elohim with the attribute of mercy, the opposite of the standard rabbinic doctrine. Philo's system, however, uses the same configuration of terms that underlies the MRI passage.[13] That Philo knows the issue of a "second God" and the themes of justice and mercy suggests a possible origin well before the birth of Jesus. But Philo's writings also suggest that we are dealing with something broader than a single, continuous issue. By employing very similar scripture, he indicates the existence of a widespread scriptural tradition, since the rabbis, a century later, know nothing of him directly and are not indebted to him for their exegesis. In fact, Philo elsewhere credits some of his exegetical information to traditions that he has learned from the elders.[14] Preliminary indications are, therefore, that many parts of the Jewish community in various places and periods used traditions which, according to the rabbis, contain an heretical concep-

---

11 *Leg.* 3.81.
12 Melchizedek was a heavenly figure of note in Qumran. See Fred L. Horeton, Jr., *The Melchizedek Tradition: A Critical Examination of the Sources to the Fifth Century A.D. and in the Epistle to the Hebrews* (Cambridge: Cambridge University Press, 1976). See M. Friedlander, *Der vorchristliche jüdische Gnosticismus* (Göttingen: Vandenhoek und Ruprecht, 1898), 30-33. See also B. Pearson, "Friedlander Revisited: Alexandrian Judaism and Gnosticism," *Studia Philonica*, 2 (1973), 26, for a discussion of this important text.
13 See *Cher.* 9, 27-28; *Fug.* 18, 95, 100; also Wolfson, *Philo*, I, 223. See Dahl and Segal, "Philo and the Rabbis," 1-25.
14 *Vit. Mos.* beginning.

tion of the deity. This is certainly in line with our previous discovery that Christianity must have been accused of believing in "two powers in heaven." Christianity was vitally concerned with the concept of the *logos*, though, unlike Philo, Christians associated a definite personality with the mediating figure. Furthermore, the Jews of the Gospel of John are represented as opposing Jesus because he claims to be equal with God.[15] *Logos* theology also interested many church fathers.

A passage in the Mekilta, immediately after the first one we have studied, reveals some interesting information about gnosticism.

> Rabbi Nathan says: From this one can cite a refutation of the heretics who say: "There are two powers." For when the Holy One, Blessed be He, stood up and exclaimed: "I am the Lord thy God," was there any one who stood up to protest against Him? If you should say that it was done in secret—but has it not been said: "I have not spoken in secret," etc. (Isa. 45:19)? "I said not unto the seed of Jacob" (ibid.) that is, to these alone will I give it. "They sought me in the desert" (ibid.). Did I not give it in broad daylight? And thus it says: "I the Lord speak righteousness, I declare things that are right" (ibid.). (*Mekilta Baḥodesh* 5)[16]

R. Nathan's argument follows immediately after the first passage that we have studied.[17] Indeed it assumes an exegesis of Exod. 20:2 for it is a further comment on the idea that one God gave the law. At the giving of the Ten Commandments, he argues, no other deity contradicted YHWH's statement that He is Israel's God. Since he made his statement openly and was not contradicted, there could be no other deity. R. Nathan uses another quotation from Isaiah (45:19) to show that the statement in Exod. 20:2 was spoken publicly and openly. This is a theme mentioned elsewhere in the Mekilta as well.[18] The rabbis often emphasize that the law was given to all; the stubborn alone have refused to hear it. But there the argument by the critics of the law is stronger still. From R. Nathan's defence one can infer that the criticism on the part of those who believe in "two powers in heaven" was that the God who gave the law acted secretly or deviously. It becomes necessary to posit an opponent for R. Nathan who believed that the God of Israel did something in secret. The context of the Isaiah passage is creation, so the rabbis appear to want to emphasize creation as well as the giving of the law. This further suggests that the heretical group believed in other deities above the God of Israel. It seems apparent, then, that the God of Israel has been demoted to the role of a demiurge for the heretics. Among those whom the rabbis had constantly opposed for believing that the law was not a universal gift, there seem to have been

---

15   See John 10 as well as 5:18-21 and 8:58-59. See below, pp. 154-55.
16   Mekilta *Baḥodesh* 5 (trans. Lauterbach).
17   See above, pp. 134ff.
18   See MRI, *Baḥodesh* 5 (Lauterbach, 2:234.), not far beyond R. Nathan's comment.

some, here called "two powers in heaven" heretics, who denigrated the God of Israel as a demiurge alone. The most likely groups to have been opposed by the rabbis in this fashion are the extreme gnostics. R. Nathan's remark may thus oppose gnostic sectarians, i.e., dualists rather than the corresponding "binitarians" of the earlier passage, but it is not possible to define whether they are of a Christian or a non-Christian variety.

R. Nathan directs his remarks against the *minim* or sectarians, who are obviously viewed as heretics by the rabbis. However, gnostic Jews or Jewish-Christians could still be included under the rubric of "sectarian" or "heretic" (as opposed to "Gentile") at the end of the second century. Since we know from previous passages that "two powers" referred to Christians and moderate gnostics but not to radical gnostics, we have to conclude that "two powers" was a catch-all term for many different groups—including Christians, gnostics and Jews. The strategy of the rabbis in using this term was quite sophisticated. First, there is a sense in which the designation is apt. Christians and gnostics did posit a second divine hypostasis. Secondly, the rabbis subsumed many different groups under one category. This policy implies that the rabbis wanted to view various sectarians not as different groups but as one group sharing a single, basic misunderstanding. Putting all these heretics into one category and dismissing them is an effective way of dealing with opposition. One did not have to delve too deeply into the heresy. Even Zoroastrians could be included, if necessary. Thirdly, although the designation is apt from the rabbinic perspective, it is also exaggerated from the Christian one. In fact, neither the apocalyptic, mystical, nor Christianized Judaism affirmed two separate deities. They understood themselves to be monotheistic, giving special emphasis to one divine hypostasis or manifestation.[19] Only radical gnosticism posited two different and opposing deities. In effect, the rabbis were classifying the other groups together with extreme gnosticism and treating them all alike. This tactic was effective because it was based not only on a plausible description but also on one which was a heinous charge from both the rabbinic and Christian perspectives. In calling the sectarians "those who say there are two powers in heaven," the rabbis were stating that the sectarians violated the most basic tenet of Israelite faith—the

---

19   There is an interesting use of the term "ditheism" within the church fathers. Hippolytus (*Ref.* 9.11.12) notes that one of the charges made against him by Callistus was that he was a ditheist. It is a logical charge for Patripassionists and modalists to make against the "orthodox." So too Julian accuses Christians of having given up monotheism (*C. Christianos*, 2133). On the other hand, Origen, in his *Dialogue with Heracleides* 2.3, agrees that Christianity can be said to believe in a second God, though only in a special way. It is quite clear then that the rabbis were not alone in debating Christianity's adherence to monotheism with the terms "second God" and "two powers."

unity of God. This ought to make clear that there were times when the rabbis were interested in defining Jewish theology quite carefully.[20]

But there is some further information to be gained by looking at this material. Of all the groups opposed by the rabbis with the term "two powers in heaven," only one, the extreme gnostics, had an opposing configuration of divinities. Within the rabbinic reports there is some helpful information about how gnosticism became radicalized and how the demiurge came to be denigrated. One has to pay very careful attention to the structure of the scriptural defences against this heresy in order to see the clue. The rabbis fight all of the various heresies with the scriptures which emphasize God's unity and uniqueness. They rely heavily on Exod. 20:2, the first of the Ten Commandments, Deut. 6:4, the Shema, and Isaiah 44 to 47, to mention only the first few. We know that these scriptures were used quite early in the battle.

The Opposition to Rabbinic Judaism

The relevance of rabbinic texts for the development of Christianity has been pointed out in the course of the essay. Though the rabbis did not enter into detail about their Christian opponents, they certainly seized upon a principal point of the kerygma of the primitive church—that Jesus had ascended to the Father and received the title "Lord," one of the titles reserved for God in rabbinic tradition. Every document in the New Testament agrees that this ascension took place as part of Jesus' exaltation, though Paul, in Philippians, probably states it most succinctly: "Therefore God has highly exalted him and bestowed upon him the name which is above every name, that at the name of Jesus every knee should bow in heaven and on earth and that every tongue confess that Jesus Christ is Lord to the glory of God the Father" (Philippians 2:9-11).

It seems unlikely, however, that the rabbis invented the argument to counter Christianity. The notions of a split in the Godhead existed in Philo and there is little that is specifically anti-Christian in the rabbinic exegesis. Rather the rabbis and Philo both appear to reflect an exegetical issue which had taken on primal importance in the development of Jewish-Hellenistic thought—albeit that they each witness to the issue at a different stage of development and in a different social context. But the issue at the core seems to be the same—the names of God are not to

---

20 Of course, the rabbis were not alone in doing so. Monarchians and modalists used the same arguments in their battles within Christianity. See J.N.D. Kelly, *Early Christian Doctrines* (New York: Harper and Row, 1958), 109-26. See note 19.

be understood as separate hypostases of God. This argument was then put to use by the rabbis to counter Christian claims about the meaning of Jesus' divine name.

Justin, the Gentile Christian, is the one church father whose relationship to the "two powers controversy" has been noted previously by several scholars.[21] Justin Martyr was born at the beginning of the second century in Shechem, then called Flavia Neapolis, in Samaria. He called himself a Samaritan, which meant only that he was descended from people living in that part of the country and not part of that religious sect,[22] because he stated that he was uncircumcised.[23] Nevertheless, the details of Justin's life and his familiarity with a variety of exotic Jewish doctrines add supporting evidence for the relationship which some have surmised between the Samaritans and early Gentile Christianity. Justin's *Dialogue with Trypho* also evinces polemical use of almost all the scriptural exegesis which the rabbis thought dangerous.

The setting for the *Dialogue* was Ephesus, whence Justin had migrated in his Christian mission. The date for the *Dialogue* must have corresponded closely with the Bar Kokhba Revolt, for Justin mentions it often[24] and Trypho is described as a Jewish fugitive who escaped from the turmoil. Justin's use of midrashic traditions has sometimes been taken as evidence that the *Dialogue* is fictional, serving as a purely literary framework for presenting his views.[25] Yet it certainly reflects one side of the debate between Judaism and Christianity in the early- and mid-second century, whether the purported setting be wholly fact, embellished incident, or pure fiction.

The clearest parallel between Justin and the enemies of the rabbis has been discussed elsewhere.[26] By means of Gen. 10:24 Justin proceeds to show that a second divine figure, Christ, is responsible for carrying out divine commands on earth:

"The previously quoted Scriptural passages will make this evident to you," I replied. "Here are the words: 'The sun was risen upon the earth, and Lot entered into Segor. And the Lord rained upon Sodom brimstone and fire from the Lord out of Heaven. And He destroyed these cities and all the country round about.'"

---

21 Several scholars have pointed out Justin's relationship to the aggada. See A.H. Goldfahn, *Justinus Martyr und die Agada* (Breslau: Glutsch, n.d.). Friedländer, *Patristische und talmudische Studien* (Wien: A. Hölder, 1878). Büchler has further emphasized the relevance of Justin for the two powers controversy around Sepphoris and Tiberius; see "Minim." Also L. Ginzberg, *Die Haggada bei den Kirchenvaetern* (Amsterdam: Inaugural Dissertation Heidelberg, 1899).
22 *Dial.* 120.
23 *Dial.* 29.
24 *Dial.* 108; *Apol.* 1.31, for example.
25 E.g., Weissäcker, *Jahrbuch für Theol.*, 13 (1867), 63.
26 See Segal, *Two Powers*, 13, 221-23.

Then the fourth of the companions who remained with Trypho spoke up: "It must therefore be admitted that one of the two angels who went down to Sodom, and whom Moses in the Scriptures calls Lord, is different from Him who is also God, and appeared to Abraham."

"Not only because of that quotation," I said, "must we certainly admit that, besides the creator of the universe, another was called Lord by the Holy Spirit. For this was attested to not only by Moses, but also by David, when he said: 'The Lord said to my Lord: Sit Thou at My right hand, until I make Thy enemies Thy footstool,' and in other words: 'Thy throne, O God is forever and ever; the sceptre of Thy kingdom is a sceptre of uprightness. Thou hast loved justice, and hated iniquity; therefore God, Thy God hath anointed Thee with the oil of gladness above Thy fellows.'" (Ps. 45:7-8)[27]

It is a Jew, not Justin, who admits that another divine being, "The Lord," was present at the destruction of Sodom and Gomorrah, and that this divine being was different from God. From our previous discussion, there is no reason to doubt that such heterodox Jews existed as early as Philo. Justin only endeavored to prove that this second divinity is the Christ. It is significant that the angelic figure is accepted by the Jew—only his messianic status is questioned. This is another piece of evidence that Christianity was the first to connect the messiah and the principal angel. In this place he relies primarily on the various descriptions of vindication and enthronement found in the Psalm texts.

Like Philo, Justin calls the *logos* another God (*heteros theos*), distinct in number, if not in essence (*Dial.* 56). The sharply drawn personality of this manifestation (together with the doctrine of the incarnation) is the element which most distinguishes Justin's concept of *logos* from Philo's. But, as Goodenough has persuasively argued, both Justin and Philo should be seen as providing examples of the same Hellenistic Jewish traditions.[28] Like Philo, Justin believes the *logos* is an angel in that it is a power (*dynamis*) radiating from God. Like the angels it has freedom of choice, but unlike the angels, Justin's *logos* has self-direction (*Dial.* 88). Therefore, although Justin implies that the *logos* is the same as an angel, he emphasizes its distinctiveness in ways that never occurred to Philo.

As further evidence that these traditions had a background in Hellenistic Judaism before they were put to Christian use, Goodenough shows that most of the titles applied to the *logos* by Justin are the same as those used by Philo and other Hellenistic Jewish

---

27   *Dial.* 56.
28   E.R. Goodenough, *The Theology of Justin Martyr: An Investigation into the Conceptions of the Earliest Christian Literature and its Hellenistic and Judaistic Influences* (Jena: Frommann, 1923), 147f.

writers: *theos, kyrios, aggelos, dynamis, anatolē, litha, petra, archē, hēmera (phōs), sophia, anēr, anthrōpos, Israēl, Jacob*, etc.[29] As Justin says:

> "So my friends," I said, "I shall show from Scripture that the God has begotten of Himself a certain rational power as a beginning before all other creatures. The Holy Spirit indicates this power by various titles, sometimes the Glory of the Lord, at other times, Son or Wisdom or Angel or God or Lord or Word. He even called himself commander-in-chief when he appeared in human guise to Josue, the son of Nun."[30]

To substantiate the claim of the *logos'* primacy in the divine economy, Justin points to the grammatical plural referring to God in Gen. 1:26 and Gen. 3:22.[31] After this he adduces passages to support the incarnation from the virgin birth to the ascension.[32] Of course, the argument is not well received by his Jewish opponents, even those who admitted the existence of the second power, and Justin is required to emphasize his argument by coming at essentially the same scripture from a variety of different perspectives. At one point he goes into a rather fanciful exegesis to show that the name of God, which the angel in Exod. 23:21 carried, is "Jesus," a motif which cannot be original to the name of God tradition:

> Now from the book of Exodus we know that Moses cryptically indicated that the name of God himself [which He says was not revealed to Abraham or to Jacob] was also Jesus. For it is written: "And the Lord said to Moses, say to this people: Behold, I send my angel before thy face, to keep thee in thy journey, and bring thee into the place that I have prepared for thee. Take notice of him, and obey his voice; do not disobey him, for he will not pardon thee, because My name is in him." Consider well who it was that led your fathers into the promised land, namely he who was at first named Auses [Osee], but later renamed Jesus [Josue]. If you keep this in mind, you will also realize that the name of him who said to Moses, "My name is in him," was Jesus. Indeed he was also called Israel, and he similarly bestowed this name upon Jacob.[33]

While it is clear that Justin is using the "two powers" traditions to discuss Jesus, the traditions could hardly have originated with the identification of Jesus as the angel in Exodus. The attempt to see Jesus (Joshua) as the angel's name is secondary. Rather, Justin is taking over a previous exegetical, possibly mystical tradition, applying the name of his particular saviour, and defending his belief against the other candidates for the office of angelic mediator. The tradition itself, without the Christian colouring, can be seen as early as Philo.

---

29   E.R. Goodenough, *The Theology of Justin Martyr*, 168-72.
30   *Dial*. 61.
31   *Dial*. 62.
32   *Dial*. 63-65.
33   *Dial*. 75. Probably, another form of the traditions evinced in the Prayer of Jacob lies behind this argument.

The Growth of Gnostic Exegesis

Is there anything further in the rabbinic evidence which might help us to understand the relationships between Judaism, gnosticism, and Christianity? The answer, I feel, is "Yes." There are some clues about the relationship between them in the scriptures they use. Gnosticism is an extremely widespread phenomenon in late Hellenism, occurring in many different communities—Jewish, Christian, and pagan—so no history of traditions in any one community can account for the whole development definitively. Nor can any single argument be viewed as absolute in such a complex situation. Nevertheless, one significant aspect of the development of gnosticism in the Jewish and Christian communities is highlighted by the scriptural traditions which we have been tracing, when seen together with the gnostic texts found in the church fathers and those from Nag Hammadi. The change from binitarian to dualistic and gnostic systems seems more closely related to polemical exaggerations between groups than to the earlier sectarian dualisms (like Qumran, for example). To see precisely what I mean by this remark several systems leading to gnosticism will have to be investigated.

The Poimandres is one of the earliest examples of these traditions. C.H. Dodd dates it just prior to the time of Valentinus (130-140 C.E.) but remarks that its exact date cannot yet be fixed.[34] As Dodd shows, the work is an amalgam of the creation story based on the Bible and various conceptions current in Stoic and Platonic thought. At the base of the cosmos there is only a primal God, *Nous* or Mind, who is manifested to the seer as the figure Poimandres. Creation is carried out by the primary manifestation of the highest being, the *logos* or Word. This *logos* is personified as the Son of God in ways similar to those in Philo and the Wisdom of Solomon (18:15-16).[35] It is clear that, whatever else may be of interest in the document, it would be considered "two powers in heaven" by the rabbis. We can see that those powers are complementary.

Among the Greek philosophers, just as among the theosophists who produced the Hermetic Literature, the concept of "second God" appears to have achieved some limited use, partially based on Plato's idea of the demiurge in the Timaeus and partially based on the application of the idea to the *logos* by Philo. Numenius of Apamaea, for instance, though his work survives only in fragments, is known to have been influenced by Jewish scriptures.[36] Origen, in the *Contra Celsum*,

---

34   C.H. Dodd, *The Bible and the Greeks* (London: Hodder and Stoughton, 1935), 209.
35   C.H. Dodd, *The Bible*, 117-19.
36   For the history of scholarship on Numenius, see the new edition of the *Fragments*, edited by Edouard des Places (Paris: Les Belles lettres, 1973). The numbering of the

remarks that Numenius was familiar with the scriptures of the Hebrews, which he endeavored to synthesize with Greek philosophy by means of allegory.[37] Numenius calls the first divinity "The Good" or "Reason or Thought,"[38] even "the Standing God."[39] But because Numenius also distinguishes radically between God and matter, he finds it necessary to assume a "second God" who mediates the chasm while participating both in divinity and matter. With this cosmology, Numenius has appeared to many scholars as a gnostic.[40] However, he can hardly be a radical gnostic, for the soul, while divine in origin, is distributed in sentient beings through the rational agency of the second God.[41] Thus, Numenius' second God is hardly the evil demiurge of the radical gnostics. However, when seen together with the Hermetic Literature[42] and possibly even the Chaldaean Oracles, Numenius' writing suggests that there was an occasional interest in Jewish thought among the pagan mystics and incipient neo-Platonists of the second century.[43] Perhaps some philosophers like Numenius, as successors to Philo, together with Gentile Christians were included among the "nations of the world" identified by the rabbis as believing in "two powers in heaven." This philosophical usage of the term "second God" in the successors of Philo may be the basis of the use of the term in rabbinic literature and the christological controversies of the second and third centuries.

Some of the documents called "gnostic" by church fathers seem to play an intermediary role in the development towards radical dualism. Hippolytus gives us several instances of gnostic writings which have interesting conceptions of a second power in heaven together with the now familiar, concomitant, scriptural passages. In the Naasene Preaching[44] considerable Adam speculation is combined with the idea of a primal creature on the one hand and the saviour on the other. The primal man is the bisexual Adamas. He makes everything but is not identical with anything he makes. Apparently he is the primal helper of

fragments will be according to des Places' system, not according to the numbering of Leemans.

37   Origen, *Contra Celsum*, 4.52.

38   Fr. 16-17.

39   Fr. 15. Notice the affinities with Philo's discussion of God, based on the LXX phrase, "place where God stands." In fact, since the study of K.S. Guthrie, *Numenius of Apamea: The Father of Neo-Platonism* (London: G. Bell and Sons, 1917), some relationship between Philo and Numenius has generally been assumed.

40   See, for example, the study of R. Beutler in *Pauly-Wissowa*, Supplement 7 (1950), cols. 663-78.

41   Fr. 13. In this fragment Numenius uses the metaphor of a planter of the vineyard for God, as is common in Philo and Jewish tradition in general.

42   *Deuteros theos* appears in CH 8:5 (16).

43   For a more detailed study of this question see A.J. Festugière, *La révélation d'hermès Trismégiste*, 4 vols. (Paris: Librairie Le Coffre/J. Gabald, 1949-54), especially vols. 3 and 4.

44   Hipp., *Ref.* 5.6.3-5.11.1.

the highest principle, the pre-existent, also known as the *logos* or as Hermes, the guide of souls. Evil comes not from him, but from another power who creates this material world without the knowledge and consent of Adamas. The object of mankind is to recognize the divine aspect within and, with this knowledge, to seek to return to the purely divine realm through the mediation of the second figure.

In the *Apophasis Megale*, Hippolytus describes a gnostic system ascribed to Simon Magos of Gitta.[45] The highest power of God is again called the *logos*, who is in charge of creation of heaven and earth. He is described as he "that stands, took his stand, and will stand," (*Ref.* 6.12.3) using terms for immutability reminiscent of the LXX and Samaritan traditions to describe the vision of the elders—namely, "the place where God stands," (LXX: Exod. 24:10) which we have seen before in Hellenistic Judaism.[46] The document uses "place of the Lord" to describe a divine presence (*Ref.* 6.17.7). It is obvious that the document, like many other gnostic works, is a theological reworking of the biblical creation story together with angelophany scenes. So far, all stories posit a principal power of God who functions as his complementary (not antagonistic) helper because the highest God cannot enter into materiality.

Among the Samaritans, as J. Fossum has pointed out,[47] there is evidence that the figure of the angel of the Lord developed into a demiurge. In *Memar Margah*, a fourth century Samaritan work, the Glory claims that it contains the "Great Name" and also applies to himself the basic scriptural passages describing the angel of the Lord. He is said to mediate between God and Moses, as Exod. 23:21 allows. In *The Malef*, a considerably later work, which may yet contain very ancient material, the Angel of the Lord is credited with the creation of Adam from the dust of the earth, while the name breathed life into him. Such concepts are strictly forbidden by rabbinic authority but even in his heterodox environment the demiurge has not yet become an evil or ignorant figure.

The mediating figures in the *Book of Baruch*[48] are especially interesting. Since the Good cannot enter the evil world, according to the gnostic Justin, he is confined to his realm of light. In order to carry out his orders in the material world, he employs two other primal powers—the consorts Elohim and Eden, who are lovers. They sometimes appear to have the characteristics of earth and heaven divinities for they create and rule the earth and heaven respectively with their progeny of angels. Elohim and Eden therefore together function as

45 Hipp., *Ref.* 6.9.14-6.18.7.
46 See n. 39 above.
47 See J. Fossum, "The Samaritan Origin of the Concept of the Gnostic Demiurge," paper read at Yale Conference on Gnosticism, 1978.
48 Hipp. *Ref.* 5.26.1-5.27.5.

demiurge. This is a first example of the Hebrew God represented as the demiurge alone, while a higher divinity rules the entire universe. However, Elohim is not yet the ignorant, arrogant God of later gnosticism. In the process of creating the heavens, Elohim recognizes that a luminary, greater than any he created, can be seen at the limits of the heavens (Hipp. *Ref.* 5.26.15). He alone enters this highest abode through a gate and is enthroned next to the Good (Ps. 110:1).[49] Thereupon, he contemplates destroying the imperfect world he has made, but he is dissuaded by the Good. Meanwhile, down below, Eden at first adorns herself to attract her consort but, when she realizes that she is abandoned, sets out to punish the spirit of Elohim in men. Thus, suffering comes into the world through the jealous female consort of Elohim, while he, the principal demiurge, remains an admirable creature. In any event, we can see a logical progression in the concept of the second power in heaven. Now the Hebrew God designates only the principal angel while there is a high God who is his master. Yet the Hebrew God is not yet evil; nor is he exclusively defined as YHWH.

Radical Gnosticism

Some of the more recently found gnostic documents illustrate the next (though not inevitable) step in the development of the "two powers" heresy. It is clear that the Chenoboskion library found at modern day Nag Hammadi contains many different documents with varying characteristics. Some treatises seem hardly gnostic, others hardly Christian. Some show significant and considerable influence by Jewish mystical sectarianism.

In the midst of these gnostic works we suddenly find traditions that associate the name of God with "place" and make the divine name both a manifestation of God and an independent hypostasis which mediates revelation. All of this strongly suggests that some gnostic ideas ultimately go back to Jewish heterodox traditions. The opposing configuration of deities ensures that at least two (perhaps many) independent deities were present. Therefore it seems clear that the rabbis would have considered it heretical. When the powers are complementary—as they seem to be in the apocalyptic literature of the first century, in some of the "gnostic" and much of the Christian literature—the independence of the second power is a moot question. It is often possible that the later traditions in heretical literature are

---

49 See R.A. Bullard, *The Hypostasis of the Archons: The Coptic Text with Translation and Commentary*, with a contribution by Martin Krause (Berlin: De Gruyter, 1970), 134:27-135:4. Also A. Gohlig and P.C. Labib, *Die Koptisch-gnostische Schrift ohne Titel aus Codex II von Nag Hammadi im Koptischen Museum zu AltKairo* (Berlin: De Gruyter, 1962), 152:131-153:16. See also B. Layton, "The Hypostasis of the Archons," *HTR* 67 (1974), 351-425 and 69 (1976), 31-101.

survivals of heterodox, but not necessarily heretical, exegesis brought into a new context.

For instance, in the untitled document from Codex 2, often called *On the Origin of the World*, and in *The Hypostasis of the Archons*, there are long descriptions of the heavenly throne which depend to a great degree on the traditions based on Exodus 13, 20, and 24 and the beginning of Ezekiel. In both documents, as in those described by the church fathers, proto-Merkabah or apocalyptic traditions abound. We see that the chariot is used as a throne surrounded by a glorious palace inhabited by a plethora of angels. The major cherubim have four faces—that of a lion, a bull, an eagle, and a man, as adduced from Ezekiel 1, the most important Merkabah text. Similar chariots are also employed by the seventy-two gods who give man the seventy-two languages of the world.

Sabaoth, in *The Origin of the World*, has many of the characteristics of the second figure in heaven. His name is evidently derived from the Hebrew YHWH SB'WT, Lord of Hosts or Powers, therefore he may be said to carry the name of God. In *The Origin of the World* (152:10) he is said to be "over all the forces *Dynameis* of Chaos." He also shares some of the characteristics given to Jesus in various traditions. Like Christ in the *Sophia Jesu Christi*, he is said to have created the angels.[50] Yet the parallel between the documents is not complete, since Jesus is himself one of the created angels, seated at the right of Sabaoth in *The Origin of the World* (153:25-29), whereas in *The Hypostasis of the Archons*, it is Zoe who sits on the right of Sabaoth. Apparently, only the figure of the primary angel is consistent in the documents, not his name or identity. In cases of this type, it is the mythical structure, not any single version of the story, which carries the full meaning of the story.

In *The Origin of the World* Sabaoth is the son of Ialdabaoth, the demiurge. As in Valentinian thought, Sabaoth is to function as a saviour. He has learned that what his father told him—namely, that his father is Lord of all—is untrue. Upon realizing this, he is taken to the seventh heaven and enthroned. Some of the "two powers" traditions have been applied to the gnostic saviour and the reason is clear. Sabaoth functions as the role model for the ideal believer, who is to move beyond Judaism (and "orthodox" Christianity) to true gnostic belief.

Other parts of these esoteric Jewish traditions have been applied to the demiurge. This development points out a transformation characteristic of gnostic interpretation of these traditions. Throughout *The Origin of the World* we are informed that Ialdabaoth, the demiurge whose name (like Sabaoth) is an obvious pun on YHWH Sabaoth (the

---

50   See Bullard, *Hypostasis*, 110; also SJC 99:18-100:3.

name of the Hebrew God),[51] had exclaimed at his creation: "There is no other God but me"—paraphrasing the same verses in Exodus, Deuteronomy, and Isaiah, which the rabbis had used to defend their God. In the gnostic text, the claim of the demiurge is patently false, because he is ignorant of the higher, good deity above him.

The pattern is far from unique. It occurs many times in the Nag Hammadi corpus. In every case, the ignorant demiurge (often Ialdabaoth) boasts that he is the only God, quoting or paraphrasing Deut. 32:29, Isa. 44:6, or 46:4. In every case the boast is ironic because the reader knows that there is a God higher than he.[52]

From these texts, it is possible to abstract a pattern which is common to all the versions, even though only *The Origin of the World* contains all the elements.

(1) Setting:

creation story, dependent upon a gnostic reading of the Genesis account.

(2) Introduction:

often containing comments on the blindness, arrogance or ignorance of the demiurge—e.g., *Hyp. Arch.* 86:23-30, "their chief is blind, because of his power and his ignorance and arrogance, he said . . . ."[53]

(3) The vain claim:

in words derived from Isaiah 44 to 46—e.g., *Hyp. Arch.* 86:30-31, "It is I who am God; there is none apart from me."[54] *Comment*: "When he said this, he sinned against the Entirety." Other comments, *Ap. John* CG 2

---

51   See Scholem's explanation of this title, in "Jaldabaoth Reconsidered," *Mélanges d'Histoire des Religions offerts à Henri-Charles Puech* (Paris: Presses Universitaines, 1974), 405-21.

52   According to the more recent numbering of the Nag Hammadi corpus the vain claim of the demiurge can be found in clear form also in *Apocryphon of John* (11, 3), 14:18-21, 13:5-13 (with parallels to BG 44:9-17); *The Gospel of the Egyptians* (11, 4), 58:23-59:4 and often elsewhere. My thanks to Anne Maguire and N.A. Dahl for providing further references for the Nag Hammadi section of the 1976 SBL meeting in St. Louis. See N.A. Dahl, "The Arrogant Archon and the Lewd Sophia: Jewish Traditions in Gnostic Revolt," in B. Layton (ed.), *The Rediscovery of Gnosticism*, vol. 2: *Sethian Gnosticism* (Leiden: Brill, 1980), 689-712; also H.M. Schenke, *Der Gott "Mensch" und der Gnosis* (Göttingen: Vandenhoeck und Ruprecht, 1962), 87f. (quoted by N.A. Dahl, *The Arrogant Archon,* 693). Note the similarity to Rabbi Nathan's exegesis.

53   *Ap. John* BG 44:9-13 "He looked at creation that was with him and the multitude of angels . . . and said to them . . ."; see also *Hyp. Arch.* 94:19-21; *Orig. Wld.* 103:8-10; *Ap. John* BG 112:18-19, 135-38; *G. Gos. Eg.,* 58:23-24; Irenaeus, *Haer.* 1.29.4; 1.30.6.

54   *Hyp. Arch.* 94:21f. (95:5); *Orig. Wld.* 103:11-13 (107:30f., 112:28f.); *Ap. John* CG 2 11:20f.; Irenaeus. *Haer.* 1.30.6; *Ap. John* BG 44:14f.: "I am a jealous God; apart from me there is none" (Exod. 20:5; Isa. 46:9, or sim.). Cf. CG 2 13:8f.; *Gos. Eg.* 58:25f.; Irenaeus, *Haer.* 1.29.4.

11:21f.; *G. Egypt.* 58:26-59:1. *Ap. John* BG 44:15ff.: "Already showing the angels with him that another god existed," etc.; cf. CG 2 13:9-13.[55]

(4) Rebuke:

by a voice from above (from Incorruptibility, from the Mother, or sim.).[56]

(5) Disclosure:

combined with the rebuke or as an alternative to it.[57] "The Man exists and the Son of Man."[58] "An enlightened, immortal man (or: an immortal Light-Man) exists before you . . ."

(6) Challenge:

the Archon calls for a revelation.[59] "If any other thing exists before me, let it become visible to me!"[60] "If someone exists before me, let him appear so that we may see his light."

(7) Appearance of an image:

(in the water) and/or of light.[61] "As Incorruptibility looked down into the region of the Waters, her Image appeared in the Waters," etc. Cf. *Orig. Wld.* 103:28-31; 107:18f. (Gen. 1:2b?). *Hyp. Arch.* 94:28-31: "And immediately Sophia stretched forth her finger and introduced Light into Matter." Cf. *Orig. Wld.* 108:2-14; 111:29-31; 112:25f. (Gen. 1:3); *Ap. John* BG 48:1-9; CG 2 14:18-34; *G. Egypt.* 59:4-9 (Gen. 1:2b-3?).

(8) Proposal to create man:

made by the Archon or his Powers (Gen. 1:26). *Hyp. Arch.* 87:23-26; *Orig. Wld.* 112:32-113:4; *Ap. John* CG 2 15:1-4; BG 48:10-14; Irenaeus, *Haer.* 1.30.6.

(9) Formation of man from the earth:

(Gen. 1:27 + 2:7). *Hyp. Arch.* 87:27ff.; *Orig. Wld.* 113:9ff.; *Ap. John* BG 48:14ff.; CG 2 15:5ff.; *G. Egypt.* 59:9; Irenaeus, *Haer.* 1.30.6.

These several points must be seen as a summary for no document reproduces all the items in this order. Rather, it appears that the myth

---

55 E.g., *Hyp. Arch.* 86:31f., 94:22f.
56 E.g., *Hyp. Arch.* 86:32-87:4: "You are mistaken, Samael." Cf. *Hyp. Arch.* 94:24-26; 95:5-7; *Orig. Wld.* 103:15-18; Irenaeus, *Haer.* 1.30.6: "Do not lie, Yaldabaoth."
57 *Ap. John* BG 47:15-18; CG 2 14:13-15.
58 Cf. *Gos. Eg.* 59:1-3; Irenaeus, *Haer.* 1.30.6; *Orig. Wld.* 103:19-28.
59 *Hyp. Arch.* 94:27f.
60 *Orig. Wld.* 107:6-108:2.
61 *Hyp. Arch.* 87:11-16.

of the arrogance of the demiurge was created to make gnostic sense of particular scriptural references, especially those from Genesis. But the gnostic interpretation appears to have been transmitted in elements as a structure or pattern, rather than as a single exegetical or narrative interpretation.

It is also worth noting that while Christian tradition is evident in most places in the documents, there is nothing specifically Christian about this key scene—no speculation about the *logos* or messiah, for instance. It seems rather to depend on Jewish exegesis of Genesis. This points primarily to a Jewish sectarian origin for the polemic as it entered gnostic thought, even if the Jewish context was occasionally affected by Christianity as well.

In fact, there are a number of mythical precedents within biblical literature which help explain the development of the legend. In scripture the king of Babylon (Isa. 14) and the prince of Tyre (Ezek. 28) are both said to have declared themselves "god" and to have been punished for their impudence. It would not have been strange or unusual for Jews to have applied the same exegesis where the sin of arrogant claims of divinity was suspected. Certainly such claims were made by Nebuchadnezzar in Judith (3:8; 6:12); Antiochus Epiphanes in Daniel (11:36f.); Pompey in Ps. Sol. (2:28f.); Caligula in Philo (*Gaium* 22, 74-80, 93-97; 118; 162); Nero in the Sibylline Oracles (5:33-35, 137-54, 214-21) and the Ascension of Isaiah (4:6-8). In 2 Thess. 2:4 the man of lawlessness is said to proclaim himself to be God (see also Rev. 13:1, 5-6) and thus the arrogant claim becomes part of the anti-Christ tradition. Isaiah 14 is also used in the Christian polemic against Simon Magus and in the Jewish polemic against Jesus. Although the arrogant Archon is not satanic, he may yet be a reinterpretation of the biblical precedent used against those who criticized Christians and others who impugned the uniqueness of the single God.

The gnostics made a different use of the traditions. They cast the creator of the world in the role of the arrogant ruler who claims that he is God. The polemic of the gnostics was that the arrogant ruler who falsely claims to be the sole God was the creator himself. The polemic logically is against the Jews in the first instance, but, in the second instance, against those who value the scripture of the Old Testament too highly—namely, "orthodox" Christianity. Therefore, gnostic interpretation also took over the claims of uniqueness for Israel's God, but applied them to a demiurge. Apparently gnostic exegesis split the tradition we find opposed by the rabbis into two parts. The traditions about a second figure were transmuted into the gnostic saviour, while the scripture characteristic of the rabbinic polemic against "two powers" was associated with the evil demiurge who is still the God of Israel, but not the high God.

Polemic or Natural Evolution?

Of course, it is conceivable that "negative value" Judaism developed independently and not in response to orthodox disapproval in Judaism or to Christianity. The books of Genesis, Deuteronomy, Isaiah, and Ezekiel had been available for many centuries. But several considerations make it more probable that the specifically gnostic arguments date from a period considerably later, when several aspects of the rabbinic polemic against "two powers" had already been developed. First of all, even a quick reading of gnostic texts reveals that the scriptural focus of the gnostic mind was on the first few chapters of Genesis rather than on Deuteronomy, Exodus, or Second Isaiah. The rabbis are the first sure witnesses to the use of Deuteronomy passages together with the principal angel passages. Since they brought them in for decidedly polemical purposes, there is little possibility that gnostics could have brought in the same traditions for any purposes other than polemical ones. It makes good sense to see these distorted claims about the ignorance of Israel's God as a polemical answer to the rabbinic polemic against "two powers" which relied heavily on Deuteronomy 32. Our problem is that we are used to seeing polemics carried on in well-argued treatises. The rabbis, however, wrote down their arguments in abbreviated exegetical comments, while the gnostics fashioned a cosmogony to function polemically.

The beginning of the polemic can be seen in the New Testament—even in the Gospel of John. There, the Jews are represented as opposing Christianity to the point of excluding those who confess Jesus as messiah (9:22). But according to the gospel writer, the crime of Jesus in the eyes of Judaism is not just that he considers himself the messiah but that he seeks to make himself equal with God:

For this reason, the Jews sought all the more to kill him—not only was he breaking the sabbath; worse still he was speaking of God as his own father, thus making himself God's equal.[62]

We stone you for no good work but for blasphemy because you, being a man, make yourself a god.[63]

The penalty for this wrong view in the eyes of the Christian community is that the Jews have given up their role as Israel and become children of the devil: "If God were your father, you would love me, for God is the source of my being .... Your father is the devil and you choose to carry out your father's desires."[64]

---

62   John 5:18.
63   John 10:33.
64   John 8:40f.

Because they do not recognize the divinity present in Jesus and because they oppose the Christian message, the "Jews" give up their historic role and become demonic. The Johannine community uses the gentilic "Jew" in many places where the synoptic gospels would have used the name of a particular Jewish sect. This change appears to record the separation between Jews and Christians. Furthermore, the alternative title for Satan in the Gospel of John is the "Lord of this world."

In other words, the Johannine community has projected a dualistic and incipiently gnostic interpretation upon the Jewish community because it feels itself persecuted by it. It is not yet full-blown gnosticism because the Johannine community values the term "Israel," still claims to worship the Hebrew God, and has not turned over to the Lord of the world the sole responsibility for creation. But the reasons for such a move by later groups within Christianity and Judaism should be obvious.

Some striking ramifications of the evidence in the Nag Hammadi library already seem to be clear. The hypothesis that the Jewish sectarian milieu was a crucial ingredient in gnostic origins as postulated by Quispel, Wolfson, and Scholem seems confirmed.[65] For instance, two documents from the library, which give primary importance to Shem or Seth as revealers, suggest an essentially Jewish sectarian setting for many of the gnostic documents by showing Christian influence to be secondary. In the *Apocalypse of Adam*,[66] Seth functions as the prophet to whom *gnōsis* is given after creation, paralleled by Shem after the flood. Adam is quite important in this treatise. He helps in creation and is higher in rank than the God who created him and Eve. The demiurge attempts to stamp out *gnōsis* by causing a deep sleep of forgetfulness to come over Adam but *gnōsis* later triumphs. Adam is emphasized

---

65 When the *Gospel of Truth* was published G. Quispel recognized that theology of the name goes back to Jewish sectarianism. See "Jung Codex and its Significance," in F.L. Cross (ed. and trans.), *The Jung Codex: A Newly Recovered Gnostic Papyrus. Three Studies by H.-Ch. Puech, G. Quispel and W.C. van Unnik* (London: Mowbray, 1955), 72. See Gilles Quispel, "The Origins of the Gnostic Demiurge," in P. Granfield and J. Jungmann (eds.), *Kyriakon: Festschrift für Johannes Quasten*, vol. 1 (Munster: Aschendorff, 1970), 271-76, and H.A. Wolfson "The Pre-existent Angel of the Magharians and Al-Nahawandi," *JQR*, 51 (1960), 89-106, for exceedingly cogent discussions of gnostic roots in Jewish sectarianism. See G. Scholem, *Jewish Gnosticism, Merkabah Mysticism and Talmudic Tradition* (New York: Jewish Theological Seminary of America, 1965); "Über eine Formel in den koptisch-gnostischen Schriften," *ZNW*, 111 (1931), 176. Based on this evidence Gilles Quispel suspects the presence of a related doctrine of a heavenly journey by which the adept's cosmic twin, the self, journeys to behold the angel of the name who is equivalent to "the Face of God" because he is the visible manifestation of God. See "The Birth of the Child," *Gnostic Studies* (Istanbul: Nederlands historisch-archeologisch Instituut, 1974-75), 1:223. If so, there would be a continuity in thought between early heretical mysticism, Jewish Christianity, gnosticism, and Manichaeanism.

66 See Förster, *Gnosis*, 2:13-23.

throughout the text, but he is not the redeemer, only an angelic carrier of the *gnōsis*. Several other figures, including an "illuminator," function as redeemer. Persian themes are present in the birth of the illuminator, which, like that of Mithras, was from a rock. Yet there is no single myth of a redeemer or *anthrōpos*, because Adam and the redeemer remain separate figures. If any Christian material relating the redeemer to Adam is present at all, it is well disguised. We are therefore justified in describing this document as a non-Christian, heterodox, Jewish-gnostic document, though there is no reason to assume it is pre-Christian in origin.

The same evidence seems to be emerging in reports about *The Paraphrase of Shem*.[67] In this case as well, we have evidence for a primarily Jewish sectarian document in the Nag Hammadi library. Almost no Christian influence can be seen. On the other hand, the dependence on the Hebrew Bible is obvious. Not only are Sodom and the Sodomites mentioned in a favourable sense, but the flood and the tower of Babel also play a role. All of these contain primary places from which the doctrine of "two powers" could be derived. In this case, the major character is called Derdekeas and functions primarily as a redeemer. He is also supposed to be the creator of heaven and earth, rather like Poimandres, except that the atmosphere is not anti-Jewish.[68]

Instead of evidence of de-christianization, we have some evidence that the tractate was christianized. Hippolytus seems to use a form of *The Paraphrase of Shem* as his main source for the doctrine of the Sethians.[69] He calls it *The Paraphrase of Seth*, but the document is essentially the same. In Hippolytus' version, however, several christological interpretations have been added.[70] Preliminary study seems to be showing that this document is an example of non-Christian, Jewish sectarian gnostic work which was later christianized. Like the *Poimandres* it makes use of material from the Hebrew Bible but in this

---

67   See Frederik Wisse, "The Redeemer Figure in the Paraphrase of Shem," *NT* 12 (1970), 130-40.

68   Fred Wisse seems to find that the notion of a pre-Christian saviour myth is confirmed in this material, even though the document is not pre-Christian. It seems to me more warranted to say that many of the aspects of what is called "the gnostic salvation myth" are present, but the late date makes it impossible to decide when or how all the themes—helper in creation, Adam, angelic mediation, and redemption—came together.

69   Hipp., *Philosophoumena* 5.19-22.

70   See 5.19, 20. Since Sethians identified Seth with Christ, this indicates a peculiar relationship of Shem and Seth. We must also remember that Shem and Melchizedek are firmly connected with Samaritanism by Pseudo-Eupolemos. Shem and Melchizedek are also equated by the rabbis. In the Sethian documents of the Nag Hammadi corpus, the vain claim of the demiurge appears often. In *The Second Logos of the Great Seth* (7, 2), for instance, the Cosmocrator says to the angels, "I am God," but was scorned. The saviour in this case has the Hebrew theophoric name "Adonaios" and gnostics ridicule orthodox Christians for believing in "two lords, even a multitude." See above for the complete pattern.

case it is radically transformed into a "negative value" Judaism for polemical purposes.

It is now possible to speak of the history of the dualist polemic in Judaism and its repercussions in Christianity and gnosticism. Just as the rabbis were passionately trying to preserve their faith, so too the various "two powers" sectarians were passionately trying to preserve theirs. They refuted the forceful rabbinic charge against binitarianism and dualism, based on Deuteronomy 32, by revaluing the biblical creation to make their God or hero come out on top. The heretics must have reasoned that Israel's God and Christian orthodoxy's God, who claimed to be unique, as recorded in the monotheistic statements of Exodus, Deuteronomy, and Isaiah, was only an ignorant God. He did not know about the gnostic's God, who was going to save only those who recognized him—that is, only the "two powers" heretics who were also "gnostics." The church offered a possible haven from the battle because some varieties of Christianity maintained christologies which were very close to the gnostic idea of the redeemer, and Christianity shared the experience of expulsion from the synagogue for violating the doctrine of monotheism. But both church and synagogue reacted antagonistically to "gnostic" interpretation. Thus we actually have a three-cornered battle. Extreme anti-Jewish gnosticism can be seen to arise in circumstances where groups holding "two powers" traditions run headlong into the polemic against "two powers" and "many powers" which developed in the rabbinic academies, but which were used by church fathers as well. In a real sense then, both Jewish and Christian orthodoxies and heresies were trying to manipulate scripture in order to demonstrate the veracity of their own beliefs and the authority of their own clergy. The rabbis attempted to use highly rationalized methods of exegesis to show that the stories of the heretics were completely faulty. Their method, midrash, was derived from the discussions of the academies and the sermons of the synagogues. The extreme gnostics countered by developing a massively polemical mythology.[71] The church fathers used both methods against both sides.

---

71 The whole issue of polemical mythology deserves more serious study, both phenomenologically within history of religions circles and exegetically among scholars of this particular period. In this case, for instance, Deut. 32:39 occurs as the boast of the demiurge in such a variety of gnostic systems that one cannot escape the conclusion that the claim itself antedates any mythological setting. Probably many artificial myths were created in order to explain how the claim of the demiurge (that he was the only God) was to be treated. For an analogy see A. Kragerud, *Die Hymnen der Pistis Sophia* (Oslo: Universitatsforlaget, 1967), especially 159-220. In that case, the myths about Sophia were created to provide a setting for the Psalms and Odes of Solomon texts which the sect wanted to clarify and interpret. Elaine Pagels reports in "The Demiurge and his Archons—Gnostic Views on the Bishop and Presbyters?" *HTR* 69 (1976), 301f, that a similar battle can be seen between Christian and gnostic bishops.

More recently, Klaus Koschorke[72] has pointed out that the description of the antagonism between the Jewish God and the Christ in the *Testament of Truth* and the *Apocalypse of Peter* parallels the antagonism between the "orthodox" and the "gnostics" in Christianity. The former brings sin into the world and smites with blindness; the latter forgives sin and heals the blind. In radical gnosticism, the symbolism developed in the Jewish-Christian polemic is being put to a new use. This should not be entirely surprising because the issue of the use of the Old Testament (Marcion), and the term *second God*,[73] had been controversial in the formulation of church doctrine as well. The church fathers even made use of the same scriptural passages as the rabbis did when they felt the need. Koschorke's argument generally supports the observation of Elaine Pagels[74] that there is a parallel between the gnostic description of the demonic archons and the gnostic description of earthly "orthodox" bishops. It is difficult to know whether Jews were ever in a position to discipline and persecute the gnostics, as orthodox Christians were. All that can be said for sure is that the church would have agreed with the rabbis in calling gnosticism a kind of dualistic heresy (though the rabbis would also have opposed the church on the same issues).

The transformation of values seen in Nag Hammadi is not limited to the third century, when gnosticism was already full grown. The story of the arrogance of the demiurge was known to the early church fathers. It is reported in Irenaeus,[75] Hippolytus,[76] and Epiphanius,[77] indicating that the process of transvaluing Judaism to create an evil demiurge in contrast to the saving grace of the gnostic redeemer was already underway by the middle of the second century.

Within the Palestinian community, with its many sects, polemics over monotheism were used in a variety of ways. Paul seems to use anti-"two powers" polemic against Jews whom he charged with venerating angels while he himself could have been charged with the identical crime by rabbinic Jews.[78]

Once the debate is reconstructed, we are able to understand some of the historical issues affecting exegesis. By the time of the consolida-

---

72 *Die Polemik der Gnostiker gegen das Kirkliche Christentum* (Leiden: Brill, 1978), esp. 148-51. He also implies that "gnosticism" existed more in the minds of the heresiologists than as a unified social movement. Certainly the role of the bishops in labeling a disparate group of phenomena as a single heresy has got to be adequately appraised.

73 Novation, *De. Trin.* 30; Hipp. *Ref.* 18.11.12; Origen, *Contra Celsum* 5:39, 6:61, 7:57; *De Oratione* SV, 1 *Comm. on John* 2.2, 10.37 (21).

74 Pagels, "Demiurge."

75 *Adv. Haer.* 1.5.2-4 and 1.30.1-6.

76 *Refut.* 6.33 and 7.25.3.

77 *Pan.* 26:2.

78 Gal. 3.

tion of rabbinic authority at Yavneh and the attempt at a new Jewish orthodoxy, mediation traditions were seen as a clear and present danger within rabbinic Judaism. No doubt the rabbis' concern was linked to the political events which immediately preceded. The war had precipitated a terrible crisis of faith. Furthermore Christians and others had taken the fall of Jerusalem as proof of the end of the Jewish dispensation. Such ideas were heinous to the majority of the Jewish community. A new set of standards was necessary to ensure survival. In asserting further control over the synagogue, the rabbis excluded any sectarian who compromised monotheism from participating in the service. This meant that Christians, among others, were excluded from Jewish life. The growing emphasis on strict monotheism characterizes the rabbinic movement and sets it off from the other sects of its time.

The earliest reports about "two powers" in the rabbinic texts were associated with Gentiles. This may further indicate that proto-gnostic interpretations of angelic mediation originated in a thoroughly Hellenized kind of Judaism or among Gentiles attracted to synagogue services. Apparently, along with the Jewish sectarians, Gentiles, who had been drawn to the synagogue to hear the Bible proclaimed, were attracted to Biblical monotheism in a form that distinguished between the supreme God and a divine agent, possibly in a more extreme form than the system that Philo had described. But "two powers" heresy has a clear Jewish sectarian setting as well. All such doctrines, whether in apocalypticism, Christianity, or philosophical speculations, were probably condemned by the rabbis as early as the end of the first century and the beginning of the second. But the Gentiles opposed as Jewish heretics would have continued to hear the Christian message.

The response of the excluded groups varied. Orthodox Christianity claimed both that the legal aspects of the Torah were void and that the Jews stubbornly refused to hear the message of the fulfilment of their own scriptures. A few Christians relied on the teachings of men like Marcion and Cerdo, who argued that the God of salvation was unknown to the Jews. But that was atypical. Others claimed that the God of the official synagogue, in whose name they had been excluded from worship, was not the high God. By his own intransigence he proved he was an ignorant and vain God. For these gnostics, a higher God was envisioned, one who was the author of salvation. These arguments might be phenomenologically similar to Marcion's, but they differed in their use of Jewish scripture. Unlike Marcion, gnostics used familiar Old Testament verses to help prove their contention of the arrogance of the creator and prophesy the coming saviour. Condemned by the standards of strict monotheism, some of the "gnostics" transformed the distinction between the transcendent God and His agent manifestation on earth into a contrast between the high God and the vain demiurge God of the Jews.

The gnostics drew mainly upon the early chapters of Genesis to prove their point. They inherited many ancient traditions congenial to their perspective. But they also created new interpretations: they elaborated cosmogonic myths in order to provide a setting for their claim that Israel's God was ignorant. They also found ways to turn the insults hurled at them into compliments. However, their knowledge and use of other parts of scripture were more limited. The gnostic use of Isaiah and Deuteronomy passages seems to have arisen as a defence against the previous Jewish and Christian use of those scriptures against them.

There is further evidence that some who cherished moderate "two powers" traditions did not adopt anti-Jewish arguments. Jews who had a closer connection to the legal traditions of the community and were not part of the fierce polemic were able to give the traditions a limited form of acceptability in Merkabah mysticism.

Most others, having been linked together with the Christians by the rabbis, found refuge in the church and incorporated Christian elements into their systems. However, Christianity immediately found itself faced with the same problem that the rabbis were facing. Using the same traditions, Christians began to define orthodoxy and heresy along much more complicated lines. Tertullian claimed that Marcionites, who postulated a *second God*, were anti-Christs like Jews. Monarchians and modalists claimed that "orthodoxy," like the beliefs of gnostics and Marcionites, had compromised Christianity's monotheistic centre. Therefore they used "two Gods" as a term of approbation against "orthodox" Christianity, just as the rabbis did.

Obviously such a complex picture presents many possibilities for interaction and my hypothesis, therefore, cannot be *the* single authoritative reconstruction of actual events. But it seems to be a credible account of the complete evidence. Besides a general chronological scheme, a new hypothesis is assumed—namely, *that the radicalization of gnosticism was partly a product of the battle between the rabbis, the Christians, and various other "two powers" sectarians who inhabited the outskirts of Judaism and Christianity.* The battle was recorded as a debate over the meaning of several scriptural passages, among which were all the angelic or theophany texts of the Old Testament, followed closely by the plurals used by or about God in scripture. Of course, it took many sides to make this argument. The rabbis' polemical statements were justified from their perspective by sectarian readiness to dilute strict monotheism in order to support traditions which applied to their ancestors, heroes, and saviours. From the other perspectives, the attempt to establish a "normative" Judaism was seen as exclusivist and caused the radicalization of the sectarian community. Therefore, it is possible to say that gnosticism arose in Judaism by social polarization initiated by the issue of God's primary angel.

One advantage of this new hypothesis for describing the gnostic debate is that it not only accounts for the large quantity of Jewish material in gnosticism and the phenomenological similarity between various proto-gnostic groups but it also accounts for the anti-Jewish bias of extreme gnosticism. Phenomenologically and historically the gnostic demiurge is the second deity of the earlier "two powers" theology. Usually he has appropriated half of the traditions about the second power, yielding the honourable traditions to the gnostic saviour. The agent manifestation of God was therefore identified with the limited God of the Jews while the high God, unknown to Jews or Christians, was reserved only for the gnostics.

This theory, of course, does not address the history of gnostic and anti-gnostic speculation within pagan philosophy. Many of the concepts employed by the heretics were also developed in neo-Platonism, for example. It is better suited for Sethian than Valentinian evidence. But the theory does give a good account of the history of the phenomenon as it existed within its Jewish context. One ramification of this hypothesis lies in the area of New Testament scholarship. The history of traditions seems to show that radical gnosticism superseded rather than preceded Christianity as a target for the rabbinic debate. The rabbinic polemic seems to have been developed around doctrines like Christianity, to be applied later to more virulent dualisms.

This study began with the observation that rabbinic evidence cannot easily be used to solve the problems of the origins of gnosticism. But as well as illustrating the difficulty of studying rabbinic texts, I have tried to show that some valuable information about gnosticism can be gained when rabbinic exegetical issues are placed in their appropriate contexts by comparison with Hellenistic writers like Philo and the church fathers. Hidden within the texts too is the Jewish witness to the rise of Christianity, even though they date from centuries later. They indicate that the nascent Christian faith began to differentiate and define itself somewhere on the evolving continuum from earlier pluralistic Judaism to radical gnosticism. They also suggest that we can identify diverging attitudes towards monotheism and the "two powers" as one important cause of the separation of Christianity from Judaism—as long as we also recognize that in the complex situation of the first two centuries there was divergence both within Judaism and within Christianity on the same issue. Continued close study of rabbinic evidence may reveal more of this epoch-making period for all the religious traditions of the West.

9

Retrospect

Lloyd Gaston

It is fair to say that all who participated in the seminar on anti-Judaism in the Canadian Society of Biblical Studies were changed by the experience in some way. It thus seemed appropriate for one of the participants to reflect in retrospect on where we have been and what questions we wish we had asked along the way. It was only toward the end of our study that we began to develop some clarity about what we meant by anti-Judaism. In many respects Tertullian represents a turning point in the development of Christian doctrine, in which certain tentative second-century developments receive a clear formulation which will dominate all future doctrine, and that is also the case here. Anti-Judaism, then, can be defined as what Tertullian says about Jews.

A second area which became clearer as our study progressed is the complex relationship between exegesis and hermeneutics. Many of us began with the notion that we were engaging primarily in a descriptive task, the purpose of which was to draw attention to the presence or absence of anti-Judaism in the texts we had been assigned. It soon became apparent, however, that there was a considerable gap between our understanding of the text and its traditional interpretation, since we were bringing to it fresh questions. This often led to a questioning also of the more or less conscious assumptions behind our own exegetical work. Work on second century texts was particularly fruitful in this respect, especially when we began to see the beginnings of the Christian exegetical tradition. In retrospect it seems that our work on earlier texts was written at different points on the hermeneutical circle, dealing sometimes with the anti-Judaism of the text itself and sometimes with the anti-Judaism of the traditional interpretation of that text.

It is time now to do what was not possible as a starting point for our seminar: to attempt to define Christian anti-Judaism. To judge by the work of Tertullian, it arises out of an inner-Christian theological debate rather than out of rivalry with a living Judaism. It seems not to be the

163

case that Tertullian looked at contemporary Judaism and found something lacking or that he was motivated by personal animosity toward
specific Jewish persons. D. Efroymson[1] has shown that Tertullian is
most anti-Jewish not in his *adversus Judaeos* writings but in his struggle
to deal with the crisis posed by Marcion. In reacting to his proposals,
Tertullian in particular was able to save the Septuagint as the Old
Testament of the Christian church only by accepting his concept of
antithesis as the key hermeneutical principle. But how could the
church accept the Septuagint as Scripture without following most of its
commandments? Since the law-giving was accepted, it was absolutely
essential to speak of the later abrogation of the law, for Israel as well as
for the church. The law-gospel antithesis is, I believe, the most fundamental root of theological anti-Judaism. The church also felt that it
could establish its own legitimacy in the eyes of the Hellenistic world
only by claiming for itself the respectability and antiquity of ancient
Israel and denying this to Jews. The displacement theory, then, which
says that the church has replaced Israel as the true heir of the Old
Testament is another key element of theological anti-Judaism. The
God of the Old Testament was rescued from Marcion by Tertullian at
the cost of making him anti-Torah and anti-Israel, and then, to preserve the unity of the testaments, Jesus was understood as the emissary
of just this God. The God-question is then also an element in theological anti-Judaism. Finally, Tertullian makes a number of hateful and
untrue statements about Jews on a less theological level, which would
have to be considered in any definition of anti-Judaism.

   To conclude, we can perhaps define anti-Judaism as a by-product
of Christian self-definition in which the church was led to deny to
Judaism certain central characteristics of its own self-understanding.
This would hold whether we speak of texts or their traditional interpretation, of exegesis or of hermeneutics. We look then for statements
which, whatever they affirm for the church, deny to Israel its Torah, its
continuing election, or its God. We look for statements which bear false
witness against the neighbour, speaking slander against Jews and
Judaism. We are alert for and seek to avoid a hermeneutic of antithesis.

The Second Century

In the light of such a definition, it seems clear that all the second-
century figures we studied were more or less guilty of anti-Judaism.

1   David P. Efroymson, *Tertullian's Anti-Judaism and its Role in his Theology* (University
    Microfilms, Temple University Ph.D., 1976), and "The Patristic Connection," in A.T.
    Davies, ed., *Antisemitism and the Foundations of Christianity* (New York: Paulist, 1979),
    98-117.

A. von Harnack[2] lists the following among elements common to all Christians in this period:

As Christianity is the only true religion, and as it is no national religion, but somehow concerns the whole of humanity, or its best part, it follows that it can have nothing in common with the Jewish nation and its contemporary cultus. The Jewish nation in which Jesus Christ appeared, has, for the time at least, no special relation to the God whom Jesus revealed. Whether it had such a relation at an earlier period is doubtful; but certain it is that God has now cast it off, and that all revelations of God, so far as they took place at all before Christ, must have aimed solely at the call of the "new people," and in some way prepared for the revelation of God through his Son.

While the results of our seminar would in general support Harnack's statement, there are assumptions behind it which we have been led to question: 1) that second century Judaism was moribund and obsolescent and that the Greco-Roman world was ripe for the church's plucking; 2) that those Christian writings which survived represent somehow all "Christianity"; and 3) that the superiority of Christianity over Judaism lay in the Messiah-Saviour who had come and that this must have been the subject of debates with the synagogue.

The Respectability of Judaism

There are many indications that despite the political struggles of 38 to 41, 66 to 70, 117, and 135 C.E., Judaism continued to be held in high regard in much of the Greco-Roman world. Even those writers most polemical against Judaism (Cicero, Tacitus, Juvenal, etc.) are aware of its attractiveness to many of their co-religionists. An impartial pagan observer, if someone like Celsus or Galen could be called that, would have said that if Greco-Roman religion were ever to cede to either, the future lay with Judaism and not the church. We should constantly keep before our eyes the picture of the large, self-assured synagogue in the centre of Sardis, compared with some almost invisible house churches there. Second century Christian writers all wrote in the shadow of the synagogue, of whose existence they were very much aware but with whose leaders they did not dare to enter into debate. Barnabas, Justin, and the like knew Judaism well but their writings are addressed not to Jews but to Christians and potentially interested pagans. Further study along these lines should be helpful in understanding the historical situation.

---

2   A. Harnack, *History of Dogma* (London: Williams and Norgate, 1894), 1:148.

The Importance of Christian Judaizers

It is clear from the polemic of such later writers as Chrysostom, Cyril of Alexandria, and Aphraat that many Christians in their communities were very attracted to Judaism and Jewish practices and presumably also to Jewish persons. Our studies have shown that to be the case also in the second century, especially in Asia Minor. Reading patristic works which have survived means hearing only part of the chorus of second century Christianity, and some of the unheard voices may well have been more friendly to Jews and Judaism. On the other hand, much of the anti-Judaism of the writers we examined was occasioned by the phenomenon of Gentile Christian judaizing. In that sense, anti-Jewish polemic was addressed not to Jews at all but to judaizers within the church, and the very existence of the polemic is evidence of the attractiveness of Judaism for many other Christians. Awareness of the importance of Christian judaizers should help historians see the relationship between church and synagogue in a more nuanced form.

Attention paid to the phenomenon of Gentile Christian judaizing might also cast light on the fascinating question of Jewish Christianity. How many of the texts usually cited in this connection really stem from judaizers rather than Jews? Had our seminar continued it would have been good to devote a year to early Syrian Christianity, where this question would have come more to the fore. Quite apart from the vexed problem of sources, the Didascalia and the pseudo-Clementines in their present form are addressed to Gentile Christians, who were presumably also interested in the theology they contain. We hear there, for example, what is almost a kind of two-covenant theology:

For on this account Jesus is concealed from the Jews, who have taken Moses as their teacher, and Moses is hidden from those who have believed Jesus. For, there being one teaching by both, God accepts him who has believed either of these. But believing a teacher is for the sake of doing the things spoken by God.... Neither, therefore, are the Hebrews condemned on account of their ignorance of Jesus, by reason of Him who has concealed Him, if, doing the things commanded by Moses, they do not hate Him whom they do not know. Neither are those from among the Gentiles condemned, who know not Moses on account of Him who hath concealed him, provided that these also, doing the things spoken by Jesus, do not hate him whom they do not know.

(*Homily* 8:6-7)

The Problem of Scripture

Jews and Christians, living side by side in the same cities, read the same Scripture each in their own context. I believe that it was this fact, and not christology as advocated by R. Ruether, which was the main point of contention between Christians and Jews. We hear several times of Christians being reproached by Jews for claiming Scripture for the church but not following its commandments, and it was not easy to answer such reproaches. Scripture (it was not yet called the "Old Testament") was a problem because it contained the law, and we see various attempts to come to grips with the problem in an inner-Christian debate made all the more urgent by the radical proposal of Marcion. Much of early anti-Judaism arose not out of hostility to Jews but in an attempt to solve this internal problem in the face of Marcion on the one hand and judaizers on the other. Thus the *adversus Judaeos* testimonies use Scriptures not to prove Christ to Jews but to convince Christians that Scripture is compatible with faith in Christ. It is my personal conviction that the question of understanding Scripture without the law but with Christ was not only a major problem for the second century but is still largely unresolved down to this day; but that is a topic which transcends this retrospect.

In the light of developments in the second century, climaxing in Tertullian, what would be some of the questions that would have to be addressed if we were to begin our study of the New Testament anew? Anti-Judaism seems to be a by-product of the need of the early Christian community to establish the legitimacy of its own relationship to the God of Israel, apart from Torah. That means that the distinction between Gentile Christianity and Christian Judaism becomes crucial in interpreting the texts. It also means that we need to guard against a Gentile Christian hermeneutic of antithesis when interpreting texts of Christian Judaism.

The Synoptic Tradition

The synoptic gospels are multi-layered. The last generation was more confident than this one of its ability to distinguish on the one hand oral tradition from final redaction and on the other hand authentic sayings of Jesus from the oral traditions of the church. The latter is not particularly germane to our purposes, but the former is exceedingly important. The beginnings of a displacement theory and a hermeneutic of antithesis seem to be concentrated in the final redaction of the synoptic gospels; we can then ask whether we are correctly interpreting the earlier tradition when we continue to use such a hermeneutic. Some specific observations and questions can be noted:

"Opponents"

Is it the function of individual controversy stories to present a unified opposition to Jesus and the early church or is this part of the redaction process? Indeed, is it their intention to present real opponents at all, or are we dealing only with a literary device to highlight the sayings of Jesus? The evangelists seem not to have a clear understanding of specific groupings such as scribes or Pharisees, and the further back one goes in the tradition the more such designations seem to disappear. Jesus and the early church clearly intended to persuade and clearly not all were persuaded, but it is not at all clear that either side thought of the other as an opponent. We should then not impose a hermeneutic of antithesis which would, for example, present many of the parables not as proclamations of the gospel of the Kingdom of God but rather as weapons defending the gospel against opponents. That aspect of the criterion of dissimilarity which calls only those sayings of Jesus authentic which differ from contemporary Judaism surely only supports the anti-Jewish Jesus of Tertullian. Some have even urged a conspiracy theory whereby the gospels have deliberately toned down the radicality of Jesus' teaching, a Jesus based more on modern presuppositions than on the texts themselves. It would then be desirable to study the entire synoptic tradition from the perspective of a hermeneutic of solidarity rather than antithesis, to see whether or not we can dispense with the concept of "opponents" altogether.

"Pharisees"

There is still no clarity about what is to be understood by this designation in a first century context. To use later terminology, are we to imagine those encountered in the gospel as more like followers of the *Haverim* or the *Hachamim*? If we take a very broad definition and think of them as adherents of a full canon of Torah, Prophets, and Writings; advocates of a two-fold Torah; those who worshipped in synagogues; a popular, non-sectarian movement addressed to the whole of Israel; those who believed in the resurrection of the dead and in the atoning value of the death of martyrs — then it is clear where the affinities of Jesus and the early church lay. If we think of Pharisees as those who distanced themselves from Sadducees, Zealots, Essenes, and even *Haverim*, the picture is the same. Also the indifference to the Temple seen in the early church is not without parallels at Qumran, in Samaria, and among the successors to Rabban Yochanan ben Zakkai. If it were possible to write a social and religious history of Second Temple Israel, it would be desirable to see whether the early Christian movement does not indeed belong among the Pharisees, broadly conceived.

Teaching on the Law

In spite of many attempts to claim the opposite, there is nothing in the gospels, aside from a few obviously redactional comments, to indicate any kind of antithesis between Jesus and the Torah. It is impossible to find a single example in the tradition where Jesus broke a commandment of God or urged others to do so. Even oral Torah is not an issue. If we consider the *Halacha* of Jubilees, Qumran, Bet Shammai, and Bet Hillel all to have been legitimate first-century options, *and* if we consider some of Jesus' statements to be halachic in nature, then his rulings always agree with one or another. The major consideration, however, is whether any sayings of Jesus were intended or understood as *Halacha* as opposed to *Aggada*. In any case, I do not believe that questions of law represent a serious matter of contention between Jesus or the early church and their contemporaries, and they should not do so for any hermeneutic of the synoptic tradition.

Jesus as Prophet

The distinctiveness of the teaching of Jesus is to be found in his proclamation of the nearness of the Kingdom of God and the resultant call to repentance. I believe that this same emphasis was continued by the Aramaic-speaking church. The other side of this proclamation is the threat of judgment, addressed to Israel as a whole rather than to individuals. As with all prophecy, the purpose of the promise and the threat is to call to repentance, so that the former comes about and not the latter. This can no more be called anti-Judaism than can the prophecy of a Jeremiah in a comparable situation. Jesus ought to be understood not so much as a preacher to individuals but rather as a prophetic voice addressing the national political situation of the people of Israel. What he intended to found was not a church as a corporation of Jewish and Gentile individuals but the Israel of the end times, to which the Gentiles would attach themselves according to the vision of the prophets. His proclamation of the coming Kingdom of God and the threat of national judgment are to be seen as alternatives, not as predictions for separate times. In Jesus' teaching, the fall of Jerusalem and the end of the world, historical catastrophe and eschatological judgment and salvation, relate to the political situation of the people of Israel and may not be ascribed to different groups or different times. Should not further study be done along these lines?

Early Christian Judaism

There is as yet no consensus about the size and significance of what is usually called Jewish Christianity. We have no documents that come directly from the Jerusalem church, even if something of their thought can be found in Paul, in the synoptic traditions, and in Revelation. To study that first generation from the perspective of later Jewish or judaizing Christian sects seems to beg the question. There is also the temptation of Christian scholars to want to see the seeds of development in the Gentile church already present in the "mother church," even though their theology was probably much more Jewish and much less "Christian" than many would like. We are in need of a convincing study of early Christian Judaism, if one can be written.

The Death of Jesus

The seminar spent considerable time discussing anti-Judaism in the passion narratives; we discussed only in passing the actual circumstances of that death and the significance of the retelling of it in the oral tradition. Was Jesus executed purely as a political rebel against Rome, and mistakenly at that? Was he really seen as a threat by the Temple authorities? Was it simply the common fate of the prophets, but if so, how? Already Mark has difficulty connecting the two halves of his story, and later interpreters should not try to be wiser in understanding Jesus' death as the natural consequence of his teaching, difficult as this may be to accept. In any case no connection can be made with Jesus' supposed opposition to the law or to the Pharisees, even if such existed. Whatever the historical circumstances, the earliest theology presupposes a Pharisaic doctrine of atonement (4 Macc.) and says that Jesus died in our place, for our sins (note that *hyper* does not mean "because of"), as an expression not of the judgment but the love of God (Rom. 5:6). Any anti-Jewish motifs connected with the death of Jesus derive from Gentile Christian redaction or hermeneutic and cannot be justified either by the actual circumstances or the earliest theological reflections on them.

Paul

Whether or not it is appropriate to speak of theological anti-Judaism in Paul depends on a number of prior questions, which can only briefly be indicated here.

Christian Judaism in the Diaspora

Most commentators make assumptions about the shape and size of communities of Christian Jews in the Diaspora, without much explicit discussion. We know that there were other Christian Jews who served as missionaries, either together with Paul (e.g., Barnabas, Junia) or in opposition to him (2 Cor. 11, Phil. 3). But are we to imagine any

Christian Jews present in communities founded by Paul and addressed by his letters? This is very important in dealing with the accusation found in Acts 21:21, that he "teaches all the Jews who are among the Gentiles to forsake Moses, telling them not to circumcise their children or observe the customs." If there were any Christian Jews present in Galatia, for example, they would be clearly told just this, and Paul would be guilty of the charge. On the other hand, the rapid success of the Pauline mission and his ability in many of his letters (e.g., Romans) to presuppose knowledge of things Jewish lead us to question just who the first converts were. Even though there are many problems with the concept and name of "God-fearers," should we conclude that Gentiles who had been attracted to and were knowledgeable about Judaism might have been an important part of the Pauline churches? It would be helpful if we knew much more about diaspora Hellenistic Jews and their relations with their Gentile neighbours.

"Opponents"

Beginning already with Marcion, it has been the pattern to understand Paul in relation to certain opponents. Given the vividness of the polemic in some passages this is no surprise. A number of questions need to be raised however. Is it proper to posit a unified front of opponents who appear in all the letters, or should we think of quite different groups in each situation? Some at least of the opponents were Christian Jews, but were they advocating conversion to Judaism? Should Paul's arguments against them be understood to be directed against Judaism? There is the additional hermeneutical problem that the existence of opponents is often assumed, even in the case of passages which do not specifically mention them, so that whatever Paul says he must be saying in opposition to certain Jewish views which he is then made to deny. Because of the dangers of circular reasoning and of imposing on the text a hermeneutic of antithesis, the issue of "opponents" should be handled very carefully in each specific case.

The Law

Since the question of the law represents the fundamental source of anti-Judaism in the later church, how we answer this question is absolutely crucial. "Do we then overthrow the law by this faith?" (Rom. 3:31). In spite of Paul's *mē genoito*, almost all of Paul's interpreters have replied with a resounding "Yes." Paul's is not only the most thorough and violent attack on the Torah, but it rests, so it seems, on a fundamental misunderstanding of the relation of covenant and commandments.

One possibility would be to assume that Paul speaks consistently about law apart from covenant, law as it relates to Gentiles, and that he is not speaking in general about law as it relates also to Jews. This is a very large topic and it is doubtful if at the present time we would be able to reach consensus. But the discussion must go on.

Rejection of Election

"Has God rejected his people?" (Rom. 11:1). Again, in spite of Paul's firm *mē genoito*, most of his interpreters would answer "Yes," although this is not as significant an issue for the interpretation of Paul as it is for the synoptic gospels. He did acknowledge the Jerusalem church, with its continued adherence to Torah and its avoidance of Gentile mission. Paul's own major theological concern was the legitimation of his Gentile mission and his law-free gospel, and the election of the church. There are some hints (e.g., Rom. 4:11-12, 16-17) that he was able to affirm these concerns without denying the continuing legitimacy of election and Torah for Israel. Here, too, the discussion must continue.

Redaction of the Synoptic Gospels

Once more, a number of prior questions need to be asked before we can bring up the matter of anti-Judaism here (see our earlier discussion of the oral synoptic tradition).

Audience

Only some of us are convinced that the synoptic gospels are all three addressed to Gentile Christians. Even fewer believe that they were also written by Gentile Christians. If we were to consider a trajectory of the church in Antioch, for example, Galatians 2→ "M"→ Matthew→ Ignatius→ Theophilus→ Chrysostom, it is clear that a major shift occurred at some point, but it is difficult to determine where this point was.

The Fate of Christian Judaism

Some have argued that the relative failure of the Christian mission to Jews represented a major crisis for the early church. Was there such a failure? How extensive was Christian Judaism in the land of Israel during the first generation? Did that church survive the war of 66-73 C.E.? Did it have any successors? These questions may be impossible to answer, but it should be acknowledged that scholars unconsciously imagine quite different answers to them.

The Fall of Jerusalem

How significant was this as an event in the history of the *church*, and what theological response did it call forth from Christians? The surprising paucity of references to it in Christian literature of the period we studied, with the exception of the synoptic gospels, makes these difficult questions to answer.

Displacement Theory

Because of the existence of Acts, a displacement theory is very prominent in Luke/Acts, although it can be argued that it is present in Matthew as well, and even in Mark. It all depends on how one answers the questions listed above. By displacement theory we mean a theology which justifies the legitimacy of the Gentile church by presupposing the rejection of the gospel by Jews and the consequent rejection of the Jews by God in favour of the new entity. The problem is similar to the one faced by Paul, but if we were right above, the solution is quite different. Additional factors which might help account for the difference are the need to rationalize the failure of the mission to the Jews through a hardness-of-heart theology (Isa. 6:9-10), and to provide a kind of theodicy in the face of the disaster of 70 C.E. This could also account for much of the shift in the way the passion narrative is told. The law and other factors seem not to be major issues, and, if not, the main contribution of the synoptic gospels to anti-Judaism lies in the creation of the displacement theory.

From Threat to Prediction

Insofar as the synoptic gospels transmit Jesus' prophetic threat and insofar as they are aware of the events of the Roman-Jewish war, there seems to be a subtle shift from conditional warning to fulfilled prophecy. Even here, as long as prophetic language is coupled with a call to repentance, it cannot be called anti-Judaism. But when along with the shift from future to past references of the prophecy there also occurs a shift of audience, so that the words are no longer direct address but information about others, then we do have anti-Judaism. This is much more evident in later hermeneutic than in the gospels themselves.

John

In terms of its later effects on the church, John contains some of the most vicious language about Jews in the New Testament. Nevertheless, if one takes seriously the growing consensus about the Christian Jewish environment of the Fourth Gospel it cannot be called anti-Jewish. It is sectarian, perhaps, even paranoiac, but it does not deny the central self-affirmation of Judaism. The law as such does not seem to be an issue at all but only a setting for christological proclamation. We may find a narrowing of the concept of covenant and election but not its rejection. The central point of contention between John and Judaism lies in the assertion of the Johannine Jesus that "I and the father are one" and in the accusation that "He makes himself equal to God." Alan Segal was able to find some echoes of this in rabbinic polemic against Johannine Christians or their Gnostic successors.

As an aside, we may note that this is the only place where christology enters into our consideration, and even here not directly. That is, it may be false, but it is never anti-Jewish to claim to be the Messiah or Son of God or the like. It *is* anti-Jewish to deny the oneness of God. Whether the developing doctrine of the Trinity falls under this stricture comes under another discussion.

Rest of the New Testament

In much of the rest of the New Testament the relation of the church and Judaism seems not to be of immediate concern. (I avoid in this summary any discussion of Hebrews, because I do not understand it.) It might have been fruitful to devote some time to the book of Revelation. My major regret has to do not with our topic of anti-Judaism but its opposite. We uncovered at least the possibility in Paul of a theology which was able to affirm Gentile Christianity without denying the legitimacy of continuing Judaism. If this is true, and there was no consensus that it is, then it might have been very interesting to follow up this approach by a thorough study of Ephesians. That remains a strong hope for the future.

While this retrospect is not intended to be a review, I would like to express considerable satisfaction at the results of the seminar. Heraclitus said that no one can step into the same river twice, to which a pedant replied that one cannot step into the *same* river once. Any further work any of us does will be different because of what we have done together. It has been a good journey. I believe we have demonstrated once more that an ongoing seminar on a specific topic, even if it is held only annually, is a good way to study. I further believe that our topic was an important one, of great historical interest and considerable contemporary relevance.

Index nominorum

Aland, B.   46n, 47n, 48n, 49n
Aland, K.   77n
Anderson, C.P.   6n
Andresen, C.   67n, 79
Arndt, W.F.   70n
Avisar, O.   122n
Avi-Yonah, M.   122n

Bacher, W.   30n
Baker, J.A.   63n, 66n
Balas, D.L.   46n
Bardy, G.   39n
Barnard, L.W.   18n, 36n, 59n, 66n, 74n
Baron, S.   34n
Barrett, C.K.   36n
Bauer, W.   34n, 35n, 36n, 37n, 43-44, 45n, 70n
Behr, C.A.   69n
Benko, S.   60n
Benoit, P.   2
Berger, Peter L.   65n
Bertram, G.W.   2
Billerbeck, P.   106
Blackman, E.C.   46n, 47n, 48n, 49n, 54
Blank, J.   82, 83n, 85n, 98, 100n, 102
Bloch, J.   104n
Blumenthal, D.   131n
Bonner, C.   84n, 96n, 99n
Braslavi, Joseph   122n
Braun, F.M.   24n
Brown, P.   124n, 126n
Brown, Roger   65n

Buber, M.   125n
Büchler, A.   133n, 143n
Bullard, R.A.   149n
Burch, V.   4
Burroughs, M.   19n

Campenhausen, H. von   33n, 44n, 50n
Chadwick, H.   60n, 64-65n, 65, 66n, 72n
Cohen, J.   77-78
Collins, J.J.   34n
Colson, H.   114n
Conybeare, F.C.   75n, 76n, 77n
Conzelmann, H.   30n, 43n, 70n
Corwin, V.   36n, 37
Cross, F.L.   155n
Cumont, F.   124n, 126n

Dahl, N.A.   136n, 139n, 151n
Daniélou, J.   35, 40, 63n, 66,n, 85
Davies, A.T.   17n, 33n, 46n, 99n, 164n
Davies, S.L.   40n
Davies, W.D.   19n, 106, 125n
De Lange, N.R.M.   18n
De Vuyst, J.   15n
Dibelius, M.   43n
Dodd, C.H.   146

Efroymson, D.P.   33n, 46, 57, 58n, 99n, 164
Eliade, M.   70n
Ellis, E.E.   19n
Epstein, J.   31n
Evans, E.   53n

175

Index locorum

179

SR SUPPLEMENTS

1. **FOOTNOTES TO A THEOLOGY**
   The Karl Barth Colloquium of 1972
   Edited and Introduced by Martin Rumscheidt
   1974 / viii + 151 pp.
2. **MARTIN HEIDEGGER'S PHILOSOPHY OF RELIGION**
   John R. Williams
   1977 / x + 190 pp.
3. **MYSTICS AND SCHOLARS**
   The Calgary Conference on Mysticism 1976
   Edited by Harold Coward and Terence Penelhum
   1977 / viii + 121 pp. / OUT OF PRINT
4. **GOD'S INTENTION FOR MAN**
   Essays in Christian Anthropology
   William O. Fennell
   1977 / xii + 56 pp.
5. **"LANGUAGE" IN INDIAN PHILOSOPHY AND RELIGION**
   Edited and Introduced by Harold G. Coward
   1978 / x + 98 pp.
6. **BEYOND MYSTICISM**
   James R. Horne
   1978 / vi + 158 pp.
7. **THE RELIGIOUS DIMENSION OF SOCRATES' THOUGHT**
   James Beckman
   1979 / xii + 276 pp. / OUT OF PRINT
8. **NATIVE RELIGIOUS TRADITIONS**
   Edited by Earle H. Waugh and K. Dad Prithipaul
   1979 / xii + 244 pp. / OUT OF PRINT
9. **DEVELOPMENTS IN BUDDHIST THOUGHT**
   Canadian Contributions to Buddhist Studies
   Edited by Roy C. Amore
   1979 / iv + 196 pp.
10. **THE BODHISATTVA DOCTRINE IN BUDDHISM**
    Edited and Introduced by Leslie S. Kawamura
    1981 / xxii + 274 pp.
11. **POLITICAL THEOLOGY IN THE CANADIAN CONTEXT**
    Edited by Benjamin G. Smillie
    1982 / xii + 260 pp.
12. **TRUTH AND COMPASSION**
    Essays on Judaism and Religion in Memory of Rabbi Dr. Solomon Frank
    Edited by Howard Joseph, Jack N. Lightstone, and Michael D. Oppenheim
    1983 / vi + 217 pp.
13. **CRAVING AND SALVATION**
    A Study in Buddhist Soteriology
    Bruce Matthews
    1983 / xiv + 138 pp.
14. **THE MORAL MYSTIC**
    James R. Horne
    1983 / x + 134 pp.
15. **IGNATIAN SPIRITUALITY IN A SECULAR AGE**
    Edited by George P. Schner
    1984 / viii + 128 pp.
16. **STUDIES IN THE BOOK OF JOB**
    Edited by Walter E. Aufrecht
    1985 / xii + 76 pp.
17. **CHRIST AND MODERNITY**
    Christian Self-Understanding in a Technological Age
    David J. Hawkin
    1985 / x + 188 pp.

EDITIONS SR

1. **LA LANGUE DE YA'UDI**
   Description et classement de l'ancien parler de Zencircli dans le
   cadre des langues sémitiques du nord-ouest
   Paul-Eugène Dion, O.P.
   1974 / viii + 511 p.
2. **THE CONCEPTION OF PUNISHMENT IN EARLY INDIAN LITERATURE**
   Terence P. Day
   1982 / iv + 328 pp.

Available from / en vente chez :
Wilfrid Laurier University Press
Wilfrid Laurier University
Waterloo, Ontario, Canada   N2L 3C5

**Published for the
Canadian Corporation for Studies in Religion/
Corporation Canadienne des Sciences Religieuses
by Wilfrid Laurier University Press**